▲

TINY GAME HUNTING

TINY GAME HUNTING

ENVIRONMENTALLY HEALTHY WAYS TO TRAP AND KILL THE PESTS IN YOUR HOUSE AND GARDEN

Hilary Dole Klein and Adrian M. Wenner

Illustrations by Courtlandt Johnson

A
BANTAM
TRADE
PAPERBACK

BANTAM BOOKS
New York • Toronto • London • Sydney • Auckland

TINY GAME HUNTING: Environmentally Healthy Ways to
Trap and Kill the Pests in Your House and Garden
A Bantam Book / August 1991

Designed and project supervised
by M'N O Production Services, Inc.

ISBN 0-553-35331-4

Published simultaneously in the United States and Canada

Bantam Books are published by Bantam Books, a division of Bantam Doubleday
Dell Publishing Group, Inc. Its trademark consisting of the words "Bantam Books"
and the portrayal of a rooster, is Registered in U.S. Patent and Trademark Office
and in other countries, Marca Registrada. Bantam Books, 666 Fifth Avenue,
New York, New York 10103.

PRINTED IN THE UNITED STATES OF AMERICA

0 9 8 7 6 5 4 3 2 1

ACKNOWLEDGMENTS

▼▼▼▼▼▼▼▼▼▼▼▼▼▼▼▼▼▼▼▼▼▼▼▼▼▼▼▼

While much of the information in this book is common knowledge, we found ourselves indebted to certain individuals and organizations whose excellent work was invaluable to us in putting it all together in our own minds. Walter Ebeling's *Urban Entomology* and Ralph H. Davidson and William F. Lyon's *Insect Pests of Farm, Garden, and Orchard* are thoroughly informative books about insects and other pests, while Howard Ensign Evans's *Life on a Little Known Planet* is positively inspiring.

We are also indebted to the National Coalition Against the Misuse of Pesticides (NCAMP), the Bio-Integral Resource Center (BIRC), and Robert Rodale for their impressive efforts and successes in making the world a less poisonous place to live.

Finally, we would like to thank the organic growers of the Santa Barbara Farmers Market who prove, week after week and season after season, that growing food without pesticides is entirely feasible and wonderfully delicious.

▼▼▼

CONTENTS

CONTENTS

INTRODUCTION

They creep, they crawl, they fly, they slime. They chew, suck, nibble, and devour...and they never give up.

We plant our gardens lovingly and laboriously, anticipating the pleasure and payoff of the flowers and fresh vegetables we shall soon reap. Then one day we go outside and the garden looks as if Sherman had marched through it. Armies of bugs have chewed the beautiful (and expensive) little green poppy plants, the lovely lettuce is wilted, and the rosebuds are obscured by a teeming mass of frothy white trespassers. It's war.

Or, we go into the kitchen early in the morning to start making breakfast. It takes a few minutes before we suddenly realize that we are sharing our home with hundreds—maybe thousands—of brazen, creepy-crawly ants who are behaving as if the honey jar were their own gift from the gods. It's war.

The dog does nothing but itch and scratch. He has lost most of the hair off the top of his rear, and the last time we dusted him with flea powder, he seemed to be having some kind of a fit. Damn! Now the left ankle is starting to itch. It's war.

Trying to protect our territory from invaders can't help but stir up the primal juices. It's the good guys against the bad and we know which ones we are. We have the moral righteousness of the invaded on our side, while those tiny trespassers deserve all the fury we can heap on them.

Off we go to any number of home improvement centers, nurseries, or hardware stores. We walk up and down the aisles and study the vast array of poisons available to us. Notice the slightly sickening smell that emanates from the shelves. Squint at the labels with their chemical mumbo jumbo and their warnings. Remember that article we just read about the "end of nature." Wish we knew of a better way to take care of this.

THE CASE AGAINST TOXIC CHEMICALS
▼▼▼▼▼▼▼▼▼▼▼▼▼▼▼▼▼▼▼▼▼▼▼▼▼▼▼▼▼

Before we came up with the "magic bullet" of chemical pesticides, people were much more inventive about their pest problems. Then the idea caught on that we could take care of the whole problem with a few squirts or sprays. And we got lazy. We thought if we dusted the dog, we wouldn't have to vacuum; if we put up a no-pest strip we wouldn't have to repair the screen door; if we had the house fumigated we would never again have to look for termites. We opted for the neutron bomb of pesticides and thought we were winning the war.

We read that 1.5 billion pounds of synthetic pesticides are produced in the United States each year (one-quarter of the world's total). The EPA reports that pesticides are now a major threat to groundwater. Although TV commercials make using pesticides look perfectly safe, safety is one of the great fallacies of these chemicals. The EPA says that from 1976 to 1977, 2.5 million people suffered side effects like nausea, dizziness, and headaches from pesticides. These were just the short-term effects. According to a National Academy of Sciences report, *Regulating Pesticides in Food: The Delaney Paradox*, 60 percent of all pesticides are either known or thought to cause cancer. What are we doing to ourselves?

The blind application of pesticides amounts to an admission that insects are smarter than we are. We believe, however, that human beings are cleverer than insects. Practicing chemical warfare against pests can never take the place of the three Os of tiny game hunting: Observe, Outwit, and Outlast.

Doing battle with pests is actually more fun and more satisfying using the tactics of tiny game hunting than spraying with toxic chemicals. You will get great satisfaction from trapping pests without guilt, poisoning them without peril, and hunting them down and keeping them away by understanding their particular habits. We are born hunters; and even in the twentieth century we haven't lost the thrill of the hunt, the excitement of the chase, the exhilaration of the battle of wits, or the triumph of the catch. There is only one hard and fast rule for the tiny game hunter: You don't use any weapon to kill the pests that could possibly kill you, too.

INCREDIBLE INSECTS
▼▼▼▼▼▼▼▼▼▼▼▼▼▼▼▼▼▼▼▼▼▼▼▼▼▼▼▼▼

Insects have been on this planet since before the first cockroach appeared three hundred million years ago. Not only did they precede us by more than two hundred million years, but termites had air-conditioning before we had houses, and wasps could paralyze their prey before we had anesthesia. Though they appear lowly, small, primitive, thoughtless, and short-lived, insects are nevertheless the most successful creatures on earth.

There may be as many as 10 million different species, of which only a million (only!) have been described. To add to the amazing variety and complexity of life-forms they present, most of these insects change their shape during development, from egg to larva to pupa to adult. Howard Ensign Evans once wrote, "The earth has spawned such a diversity of remarkable creatures that I sometimes wonder why we do not all live in a state of perpetual awe and astonishment."

We do not, however, hold bugs in awe. Even though they can outwork us, outlift us, outjump us, and outfly us, we despise more than we respect them. They seem to us to live only to reproduce and to eat or be eaten. They are so utterly different from us, they seem aliens in our world. Insects have no lungs, yet they must have oxygen to live. Some have no ears, though their sensitivity to vibrations is acute. Others have no noses, but can smell incredibly well. They may have ears below their knees, gills under their abdomens, or breathing tubes on their sides. They learn nothing from their parents, but are born knowing everything they need to know. They carry their skeletons on the outside of their bodies, their blood is seldom red, and they walk on myriad legs. Is it any wonder that we have problems with insects? We regard them alternately with loathing and fear, fascination and disgust. We are woefully ignorant about them and most often end up killing the ones we need, while failing to control the pestiferous ones.

The insect population of the earth today weighs in at twelve times that of the human population. Insects even exist in the Antarctic, where temperatures drop to 85 degrees below zero. Collections made from airplanes reveal that a column of air one mile square probably contains twenty-five thousand insects. One acre of a typical English pasture may contain over a billion arthropods (insects, spiders, mites, centipedes, etc.) We make calculations about the vast incomprehensible distances of space, but right here on earth there may be a billion billion insects. Try to write out that number.

Until the middle of the seventeenth century, most people in the Western world believed that insects came into existence through spontaneous generation. They were generally thought to be "bred by corruption" or from the dew on the leaves. Humans often turned for help from the Church, which regularly excommunicated insects for their misdeeds. Yet little progress was made toward controlling pests; even the most noxious ones, like fleas, rats, and lice, were tolerated as an inevitable part of life.

Insects have always been our prime competitors on this planet. They eat our food, our clothing, and our houses. They even feed on us and give us terrible diseases. A state of complacency regarding them has never been in our best interests. However, once we decided to get tough on pests, we really went overboard. We picked methods that harmed us as much as them.

We embarked on an indiscriminate, all-out war against insects. "Better living through chemistry" tried to teach us that all bugs are bad bugs and that the only good bug is a dead bug. But less than 1 percent of all insects are pests. Most are extremely beneficial. Without insects, animals like fish, reptiles, birds, and certain mammals would have nothing to eat and would starve. Furthermore, as entomologist E. O. Wilson pointed out, without the recycling of organic matter that insects carry out, dead vegetation would pile up and dry out all over the world, killing off plants and animals.

It may seem odd to talk about how necessary insects are in a book on tiny game hunting (and trapping and killing and repelling), but part of the problem with our pest control tactics up until now has been that we tried to annihilate them so utterly, we began to take out the birds and the bees and a lot more along with the pests. If we keep in mind what an important role some insects and spiders play, we can be more successful at controlling them.

TINY GAME HUNTING IN THE HOME

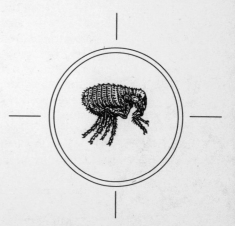

HOUSEHOLD GAME HUNTING

HOME TOXIC HOME

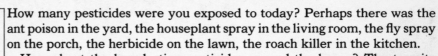

How many pesticides were you exposed to today? Perhaps there was the ant poison in the yard, the houseplant spray in the living room, the fly spray on the porch, the herbicide on the lawn, the roach killer in the kitchen.

How about the long-lasting pesticides around the house? The termite treatment around the foundations, the mothball vapors in the closet, the vapor-emitting pest strip in the basement? And that is just at your own house. The bus you rode today may have just been sprayed or fumigated this morning. The office has a regular extermination contract. The restaurant where you went for lunch may have recently been sprayed, as well as the bank, the doctor's office, the department store, and, of course, the park. Every breath you took today may have had a little whiff of poison in it.

You just can't make the excuse anymore that "it's just a little bit of pesticide." One-third of all pesticides in the United States are used by households. Millions of householders throughout the country spray hundreds and even thousands of times the amount of pesticides on their property, acre for acre, than commercial farmers use.

Many houses today have become traps for long-lasting toxins. Before chlordane was taken off the shelves in 1987, it was used for ants and termites (as well as other pests) in more than thirty million homes. Because it was made to decompose very

How Many Pesticides Were You Exposed to Today?

slowly, it could remain active indoors, protected from the elements, for twenty years. It also accumulates in body fat and is known to make people very sick. Chlordane is also considered to be a carcinogen, as well as a hazardous substance, a hazardous waste, and a priority toxic pollutant (according to the EPA). And yet it is still being shipped to other countries by its manufacturer and will probably return to this country in imported food items.

The one control method that works for all pests is exclusion. Keeping them out of the house is the simplest and most efficient way to deal with them. Screens may be full of fine holes, but they provide a true coat of armor for the home. In hot countries where malaria still rages, many many homes lack screens. Screens should also be placed over chimneys and vents. And since rats and cockroaches live in sewers, city dwellers should make sure that shower and bath drains have strainers.

Houses should be thoroughly inspected for holes and cracks through which insects can enter. Any openings where utility wires and pipes enter the house should be sealed. Because many pests require moisture, all pipes and faucets should be checked for drips. Toilet bowls should be bolted securely to the floor and have no leaks. Condensation of pipes should be prevented with wrapping. "Repair them out!" could be the battle cry of the tiny game hunter.

Always put food away or store in pest-proof containers. Counters should be clean. Regular vacuuming is a major tactic against pests. Make a point to do a thorough "spring-cleaning" at least once a year. Turn the whole house inside out and rout all the critters who have found good hiding places in closets and behind heavy furniture.

Apartment dwellers have to protect themselves on two fronts: from those pests that enter from the great outdoors and from those that wander in from the neighbors. All the occupants of an apartment building should meet and coordinate a sound, safe method of pest control, including how garbage is to be managed and what kind of nontoxic pest treatments can be used. Having each lone apartment dweller fiercely fighting individual battles at different times just makes the pest population move around within the building.

There is no such thing as a permanent solution to our pest problems. Thinking we can get rid of our pests permanently in one fell swoop is like taking a shower and believing we will be clean for the rest of our lives. We need to buckle down to the realization that as long as our pests are going to keep bothering us, we may as well get into the spirit of the battle and hunt them down with savvy, persistence, and impunity.

QUITTING FOR GOOD
AND DISPOSING OF PESTICIDES
▼▼▼▼▼▼▼▼▼▼▼▼▼▼▼▼▼▼▼▼▼▼▼▼▼

Giving up pesticides is a little like giving up cigarettes (only without the pain of withdrawal). One day you think you can't possibly live without them, and the next day you realize how much better everything is now that you no longer depend on them. Soapy water kills ants just as dead as the poison spray that used to go up your nose. The mousetrap kills just as dead as the poison, and it won't kill the dog, either.

When you give up pesticides outdoors, you will have a definite period of higher insect damage. Be prepared to plant more plants, handpick the bugs, and mix a few repellant sprays. The natural predators may take a while to return to your garden. It may take as long as 3 or 4 years for the balance of nature to restore itself and kick in. Remember, the pests always show up before the predators, so don't panic. In the meantime use the tactics described in this book to hunt them down. Improve your soil with lots of organic content and minerals, so the plants are strong enough to withstand insect attack. People who would prefer a garden completely devoid of insects should possibly find something else to do with their time. We have to live with insects; we just don't have to live with the ones that harm us.

The main problem in giving up house and garden insecticides is what to do with the poisons you aren't going to use anymore. Incidentally, if the label says POISON or DANGER, the contents are highly toxic. This is the highest warning given. If the label says WARNING or CAUTION, the contents are toxic, but not as toxic. You would have to swallow more, absorb more, or (more likely) breathe more to get the same effect. If the label says PRECAUTION, it means the government doesn't know if it is hazardous or not. Some people do not even call these chemicals *pesticides*; they call them *biocides* because they kill *all* life.

If you want to know more about any of the pesticides, fungicides, and herbicides you have been storing at your house, you can call the EPA-funded twenty-four hour hotline at (800) 858-7378. Or contact the National Coalition Against the Misuse of Pesticides, 530 Seventh Street SE, Washington, DC 20003, (202) 543-5450.

Do *not* pour any of these products down the drain, or bury them, or flush them down the toilet! Many of these pesticides are highly toxic to fish and other wildlife. Do not toss them in the garbage, either. They must be disposed of according to the laws regulating toxic pollutants. Call your local waste management division or health department and ask if they have a collection program for toxic chemicals. Or look in the yellow pages under environmental groups. Many cities have established certain days and locations where people can bring in their paints, pesticides, motor oil, and other toxic materials. They are then sorted and taken to toxic waste dumps and disposed of, thus preventing (hopefully) their ending up in landfills and groundwater. When you realize the trouble it is just to dispose of these chemicals safely, you begin to understand the problems of using them. And they won't stop being manufactured until we stop purchasing them.

ANTS

Some people say that the cockroach will take over the world. We disagree. If any insect is going to take over, we bet on the lowly ant. After all, the cockroach abandons ship the minute light shines on its activity. But turn on the kitchen light in the middle of the night, and the ants swarming all over the counters don't even pause to glance up.

Although we have no interest in harboring ants in the kitchen, we feel that a great flood of insecticide has been unnecessarily directed at these insects: ants are fairly easy to discourage without poisons. It is also foolish, because in many ways ants are our friends and allies, and we need them.

In China, ants have been used for thousands of years to help control pests in citrus orchards, making them the first insects known to be used for biological control. Here in this country, ants also help control pests that we haven't been very successful controlling on our own. Ants eat the eggs and larvae of fleas and flies (indoors and out). They also go after cockroaches and cone nose bugs. This is noble behavior. Furthermore, ants patrol the perimeters of our houses and keep termites, their mortal enemies, from establishing colonies in our homes. If we let them, that is.

KINDS OF ANTS

Ants

Ants will eat almost any foods, but some species prefer sweets and others go for meat and other greasy stuff. The most common ant seen inside of houses in the lowlands of the Southwest and California is the *Argentine ant*, which nests outdoors. Small and brown, it prefers sweets. This ant eliminates all other species of ants wherever it settles in.

The *pharaoh's ant* is another common household invader, setting up its nests inside walls of houses or apartment and commercial buildings. A small, light yellow insect, it goes for lots of different kinds of food.

The *thief* or *grease ant* resembles the pharaoh's ant. Imagine finding the package of cashews for the party with all the nuts hollowed out by thief ants! They sometimes live in the nests of other ants, stealing their brood. They prefer meaty or greasy foods.

The *pavement ant*, a brown or black hairy ant, nests under stones, in cracks of sidewalks, or at the edges of them, and in foundations. It will eat just about anything.

The worst ant to have in the house is the *carpenter ant*, which lives in wood and can be very destructive by chewing out burrows with its ironlike jaws. Sometimes you can hear the rustling noises of carpenter ants in the walls.

Carpenter ants are easily mistaken for termites, because, like termites, some periodically develop wings and leave the colony in great numbers when forming new colonies. Piles of broken-off wings may be a clue that you have either carpenter ants or termites. If you see the insect itself, which is a half-inch larger than most other ants, you can distinguish it from a termite because this ant has a pinched, wasp waist and elbowed antennae, and its two pairs of wings are of different sizes. Carpenter ants leave slitlike holes in wood that are sometimes visible, as well as frass (fecal pellets) that looks like sawdust.

Unlike termites, carpenter ants leave their nests as they scavenge for food within the house—they especially like sugar. You can trace them back to their nests at this time. Use a boric acid poison (sweet) bait (see formula in *Combating Ants Indoors*), which they will take back to the other ants in the nest. Holes can be drilled around the infestation, and diatomaceous earth, silica aerogel, or boric acid can be blown into them. (See *Termites* for safe ways to control these ants.)

For controlling all other ants, the methods in the next sections are effective.

COMBATING ANTS INDOORS

In the kitchen and bathroom, ants are one of the most common household pests. Ants often get on the move after rain disturbs their nests. Conversely, during the dry season, they also come in the house in search of water. In dry weather, put a few sources of water outside—shallow pans or bowls or a dripping hose—and they may leave you alone. If they don't, and you find that a purposeful, steady stream of them is cruising determinedly inside your house, you can take a number of simple measures without resorting to spraying them with poison, which is needless overkill.

A lot of kitchen-handy products such as window cleaners, furniture polish, and 409-type cleaners will destroy the ants. But we've found that the cheapest, easiest, and most effective method is putting a teaspoon of liquid dish soap into a spray bottle full of water and zapping the ants with it. It kills them off nicely. Later, when you wipe them up (leave them for a while as a dire warning to the other ants), the counter or floors will be cleaner, too.

A solution of blended citrus peels and water (or citrus rind oil, which you can buy from herbal supply stores and health food stores) also kills ants (as well as fleas and garden pests) on contact. It smells good, too.

Before you kill off the invading ants, however, trace the columns back to their point of entry. This is where you have to stop them, and a number of nontoxic products can be used. Boric acid, powdered charcoal, turmeric, black or cayenne pepper (the hotter the better), citrus oil, lemon juice, or a line of chalk all form ant barriers. The barrier doesn't have to be any wider than a quarter of an inch, but it has to make a solid line, because they will find the tiniest pathway. All these barriers, with the exception of lemon juice, remain effective for at least a month. Lemon juice needs to be reapplied daily.

Powdered cleanser containing chlorine bleach makes a terrific ant barrier. They simply will not cross it, although they are marvelously adept at finding alternative routes into your home. Squirting undiluted dish soap into their point of entry also keeps them out. Petroleum jelly smeared over entrance cracks works great because it goes into little crevices and stays there. A silicone caulk will terminate the point of entry permanently.

Sometimes it may seem that nothing can keep ants out of your kitchen. The battle goes on day after day with no final solution in sight. Try moving your barriers, as these wily creatures find routes into your house you never knew existed. But since you are not using toxic poisons, the death count is entirely in your favor. Eventually, they always give up. You may have to place a favorite ant target—like the honey jar or the cat food dish—off-limits by placing it inside a bowl of water. Add a little detergent to the water to make this ant moat even more impenetrable.

Some ants are repelled by cucumber peels or slices, so spread them around the kitchen when you suspect you are under attack. Roaches don't like them either.

Spread coffee grounds around outside near doors and windows where ants are entering. Planting peppermint or tansy outside the door may also deter them. Crushed mint leaves are repellant, as are oil of clove and camphor. Take handfuls of crushed mint and leave them out where you see ants. Pour oil of clove or camphor onto a cloth strip and rub the doorsill with it; for good measure, leave the cloth out, too.

In Germany, forest ants are protected by law because of their vital role in the health of the forests. Germans keep the ants out of their houses by placing lavender blossoms near the doors.

If you feel you have to get rid of the ants, boric acid in the cracks will kill them, as will silica aerogel, diatomaceous earth, and powdered pyrethrins. These are all available over-the-counter, and they are safe to handle; however, they should not be inhaled, and boric acid should not be ingested.

You can also make an ant poison that acts slowly enough for the ants to take back to the nest and pass on. Ants have two stomachs. One of them, the crop, is a kind of communal stomach, so any food taken from your kitchen is shared with the ants back at the nest.

Mix 1 cup water, ⅓ cup sugar, and 1½ teaspoons boric acid. Shake well. Fill small bottles with cotton balls and saturate them with the poison. (*Note:* Label them clearly as poison.) Poke small holes in half the lid so that the ants can get in, but the poison doesn't drip out, and place the bottle on its side. Remember, however, that you may be sacrificing ants that are benefiting your house by eliminating other pests for you.

Ants are lickers, constantly licking something—including each other. Their active salivary glands help them predigest their food, so don't eat anything the ants have swarmed on; it may be contaminated.

Your kitchen is under consideration for attack when you see solitary ants wandering hither and thither, looking for the goodies. This is the time to make your kitchen less hospitable for them. Clean it ferociously. Don't leave dirty dishes around. Rinse off sticky-sweet jars and bottles. Put away leftovers. Wipe the counters down with a cloth soaked in vinegar to make the territory less appealing to the scouts.

ANTS OUTDOORS

If you're trying to have a picnic, and the ants are trying to join you, an easy way to make them stay home or forage elsewhere is to set the legs of the picnic table in pans of water.

And if ants are swarming over your garbage cans, and you're afraid of what the garbage collectors are going to think, a simple way to discourage them is to crush the ones on the ground every time you pass by the cans. Pretty soon they'll give up and go elsewhere. Hopefully, not indoors. Planting tansy and peppermint around the cans will deter ants as well as flies.

If you have ever seen ants swarming over a dead moth on the sidewalk, you have proof of the way that ants clean up dead things in the garden. Spread out over practically the entire world in a vast network, billions and billions of these little creatures go about their business, in and out of nests that range from a few inches under the soil to many feet underground. The earth, in fact, may be just one big, giant anthill, and nature benefits from ants that recycle dead insects and animals to make way for the living.

When ants cause problems in the garden, it is because of their fondness for the honeydew excreted by aphids, mealybugs, and scale.

Look for ants scurrying (do ants ever stroll?) up and down the stalks of plants or trunks of trees. Sometimes the ants are doing good in the tree, like when they eat

Ants on the March

the larvae of the walnut husk fly. To find out if the ants are up to no good, see if there are aphids or scale insects on the plant or tree. Look for black, sooty-looking mold on the honeydew that coats the leaves. If you find it, you need to stop those ants in their tracks.

Sometimes eliminating the aphids yourself—by hosing them off or squirting them with soap spray—discourages the ants, too. And although ants can herd aphids, we can herd the ants. Repellants keep them out of places where you don't want them without eliminating them from places you do.

Paint the trunk of the tree or the stalk of the plant with a band of sticky substance

Ant with Aphid

17

like Stikem Special or Tanglefoot (available in garden centers, hardware stores, and by mail order) to keep the ants away. Grease-banding is another way to keep them from going after the honeydew. Use grease like lard or Crisco. Petroleum jelly will also keep them grounded. Many people paint these substances right on the tree trunk. Others first wrap the trunk with paper or cloth and then smear the barrier on that, but ants can be pretty persistent about getting through the little crevices. (See *Tactics of Tiny Game Hunting* for more information about barriers.)

Bone meal, powdered charcoal, powdered pyrethrum-silica gel dust, or diatomaceous earth, sprinkled around the base of the plant or tree, will keep the ants away.

One person we know puts a little bottle of honey at the base of the plant, causing the ants to lose interest in the aphids. You could also put a fresh, meaty bone down, too.

You might want to get the ants to relocate to another part of the garden where they may not be as bothersome. They are one of the few insects able to pick up and move their whole colony. Spraying the nest repeatedly with water or pouring a liquid solution of blended orange or lemon peels around the top will get them to move. Although you can't guarantee where they will end up, it's kind of fun to herd them around.

Sometimes, especially in very dry weather, the ants get too numerous. Generally, rain keeps down ant populations by flooding the nests and drowning some of the ants. In a drought, however, ants multiply rapidly.

You can attempt to destroy an ant nest by spraying it vigorously with water. When the ants come scurrying out with their eggs, douse them with soapy water or an insecticidal soap (a soap formulated to kill insects) or dust them with diatomaceous earth. Boiling water poured on the nest will also kill them, as will a generous dusting with Epsom salts after stirring up the nest.

For stinging ants, there is even more reason to get rid of the nests. The worst of the stinging ants, the *red imported fire ant*, or southern fire ant, has become one of the major insect pests in the southern states, and it is believed that this awesome little insect will continue to spread to other parts of the country. More dangerous, more aggressive, more destructive, and more prolific than any other ants in this country, the only good thing that can be said about them is that they usually do not enter houses.

Their blister-raising stings are almost as painful as those of bees and sometimes cause severe allergic reactions. They build rock-hard mounds that cause millions of dollars in damage to farm machinery, roads, and airports. And while they eat pests like the boll weevil, they also eat everything else, including birds, lizards, and mice.

In spite of the expensive battle the United States has mounted against these ants, they still thrive. We now know they produce supercolonies containing multiple queens that lay hundreds of eggs every hour. In Texas, where they have been called "the ant from hell," they have become something of a cultural phenomenon, with songs and even beauty contests in their honor.

Even though effective, nontoxic ways to kill these ants are still being tested, for instance, a probe that goes down into the nest and steams the colony to death, there are ways to kill many of them and get them to move their nest. When dealing with fire ants, protect yourself from their stings. Take a pair of rubber boots and smear them around the ankles with a wide band of a sticky substance like that used to band trees. This will stop the ants as they attempt to run up your leg and sting you.

After stirring up the nest with a long pole, pour a generous amount of any of the following substances onto the nest: boiling water, soapy water, diatomaceous earth, boric acid, Epsom salts, pyrethrum insecticide (see *Tactics of Tiny Game Hunting*), or ammonia and water. (A folk remedy in Texas consists of filling up on beer and urinating on the nest.) These treatments work best on cool days when the sun is out because the colony will have moved up near the warmer surface. These dousings may not succeed at first, but if they are repeated frequently, the ants will finally move.

BED BUGS

▼▼▼▼▼▼▼▼▼▼▼▼▼▼▼▼▼▼▼▼▼▼▼▼

Regardless of public opinion, we have not said good-bye to bed bugs. Lusting after our blood, these creatures have the nerve to come crawling into bed with us when we are mostly undressed and entirely unconscious. And yet we joke about it. What's so funny?

One of the worst things about this bug is that each meal lasts from ten to fifteen minutes. (No wonder we thought up vampire legends.) A bed bug's bloodsucking causes no sensation or pain whatsoever, mainly because its proboscis is amazingly fine—hundreds of times smaller than a hypodermic needle. The reaction comes later when inflamed welts appear (some people, however, have no reaction). Intense pain and itching may last for as long as a week. Often bed bug bites have a characteristic pattern—they occur in rows of three on the skin. However painful and annoying, these tormentors have not been known to kill any of us or even to make us sick. Maybe that's the reason we can laugh about them.

Hundreds of years ago, the word *bug* referred to the bed bug alone. The word itself may have had its origins in the Welsh word *bwg* meaning "ghost," thus the word *bugaboo*. One famous entomologist who specialized in bed bugs collected them in hotels, good and bad, across the country. He merely set his alarm for 2 A.M., leapt out of bed, turned on the lights, and collected to his heart's content.

After a blood meal, bed bugs are engorged to a rounded plumpness. The rest of the time they are endowed with very flat, reddish bodies, giving rise to such

Bed Bug

20

nicknames as "mahogany flats," "B flats," or "red coats." Their shape and tiny, one-quarter-inch size allows them to hide in narrow cracks and crevices behind wallpaper and picture frames, in windowsills, plaster cracks, or baseboards. From there they march out at night in quest of a blood meal. They sometimes can be detected by the yellowish to reddish brown excrement they leave around. It looks like specks of dirt, but it is really dried particles of undigested blood.

These wingless crawlers cannot fly, although their ancestors had wings, and they usually shun light. They also have a very distinctive, unpleasant odor—like slightly sickening raspberries—which gives their presence away to the initiated. They will travel far for a meal and have even been known to migrate en masse from a recently vacated dwelling to riper pickings (or suckings) next door. Sometimes they are brought into houses via secondhand furniture and mattresses.

Laying a few eggs a day, a female generates from one hundred to five hundred eggs in her lifetime. These are coated with a sticky cement and adhere to any surface. Even after the bug has hatched, the eggshells remain cemented in place. Newly hatched bed bugs are paler versions of adults, and they require blood feeding before they can reach adulthood.

Like cockroaches, bed bugs are gregarious. They seem to hang out in groups, although they go on feeding expeditions as solo operators. They can last for up to a year without feeding on humans and will take meals from other animals like chickens, birds, mice, rats, rabbits, and guinea pigs.

CONTROL

Over the centuries people came up with numerous remedies for dealing with bed bug problems. The Greek philosopher Democritus advocated hanging a dead stag (a deer) at the foot of the bed. A book from the 1870s, containing advice on killing "vermin," recommended rubbing bedframes with spirits of turpentine and kerosene oil and filling the cracks in floors and walls with hard soap. All very practical advice. But the author went on to recommend putting a quarter of a pound of brimstone (sulphur) on a dish in the middle of the room and lighting it. This treatment, he added, would bleach the paint on the walls. At the turn of the century, an energizing tonic consisted of sorghum juice, black beans, garlic, rum, and seven freshly killed bed bugs. (The thought alone must have acted as a tonic to some.) We have been nothing, if not fearless and rash, when it comes to exterminating our pests.

In his book *202 Household Pests*, Hugo Hartnack complained in the 1930s about a chemical used for bed bugs that was so caustic it took the finish off metal beds. He also described a bed bug trap that consisted of painting a strip of special "glasslike" enamel all around the lower walls of the room, leaving one small opening. The bugs can't get a foothold on the glassy surface, so they come through the opening where a metal container has been set, waiting to trap them.

Although many a parent still says to their child, "Nighty night, don't let the bed bugs bite," bed bugs today are no longer the frequent bedmates they once were. The vacuum cleaner undoubtedly dealt them a big blow, but they are by no means extinct. We may think we are rid of them, like lice—until the next epidemic appears.

If the situation is desperate, an immediate remedy is smearing petroleum jelly all around the legs of the bed so they can't crawl up and get you. Or place each bed leg in a container of water. This will only work if the bed bugs are not already in the bed. Furthermore, a number of victims have described seeing bed bugs walk up the wall, travel across the ceiling, and get in position to drop down on the bed.

The USDA has stated that bed bugs may have become resistant to the more toxic pesticides (lindane and DDT) commonly used against them. Dusting the area with pyrethrum will poison them without poisoning you. Diatomaceous earth can also be applied in cracks with a bulb duster. Use a mask to avoid inhaling the dusts.

As with cockroaches, getting rid of bed bugs involves eliminating all cracks and crevices in a room by caulking, replastering, or painting.

In the 1770s an insect called the *pentatomid bug* was used against bed bugs—one of earliest examples of biological control in America. A few such bugs placed in a room would clear out all the bed bugs within a few weeks. Another insect, the assassin bug (sometimes called the "masked bed bug hunter") was also welcomed in homes for years as a bed bug annihilator, until it was discovered that it bit people when it ran out of bed bugs. Ants, especially pharoah's ants, will also eat bed bugs or their eggs, and spiders make wonderful bed bug predators. This seems only fair, because spiders have traditionally taken the blame for many a bed bug bite. People learned long ago that they got much more sympathy for a spider bite than a bed bug bite; one can easily tell the difference, though. A spider bite is two closely spaced punctures; bed bugs usually leave three in a row.

BEES

▼▼▼▼▼▼▼▼▼▼▼▼▼▼▼▼▼▼▼▼▼▼▼▼▼▼▼▼

Insects can live without people, but can people live without insects? When it comes to bees, we probably can't. You can grow the most beautiful peach trees the world has ever seen, but if you don't have bees, you may never sink your teeth into your own succulent peaches.

Bee populations are declining around the world because of their vulnerability to the excessive use and potency of our herbicides and insecticides. Without bees to pollinate plants we would have little interesting food to eat. In 1970 a pesticide called carbaryl (Sevin) killed off so many bees in Oregon and Washington that two billion of them had to be imported to pollinate the fruit trees. No bees, no fruit.

23

Transporting hives into certain areas (migratory beekeeping) has now become a necessary and standard practice.

Bees have been "farmed" for their honey and "wrangled" for their pollination. No other insect has been used like bees. Bees may also be the most studied of all insects. At the same time, most people want to stay as far away from them as possible. About 1 percent of the population is extremely allergic to bee stings, and many others have strongly uncomfortable localized reactions. The entire human population has a healthy respect for bee venom.

As beneficial to nature as bees are, they can be a real nuisance, especially when a swarming colony gains access to a home through a hole or crack and sets up housekeeping within its walls. In certain instances, bees have been known to fill most of the spaces in the walls of a house, literally creating a house made of honey.

Away from the nest, bees will rarely sting unless they are sat on, stepped on, leaned against, or otherwise placed in threatening situations. Near the hive, however, the guard bees on duty do not hesitate to defend their home.

Certain bee colonies are more irritable than others, and all bees are usually irritable after a rain because pollen and nectar have been washed away. Much attention is being focused on the inevitable northward progress of the "killer" bees, whose threshold of irritability happens to be quite a bit lower than most of the bees we're used to.

CONTROL

One can minimize the chances of getting stung by not wearing perfumes or bright-colored or strikingly patterned clothing. If you do get stung, do not pull out the stinger but scrape at it soon with a fingernail or credit card until you dislodge it. That keeps more poison from being pumped into the skin.

Bee

If you see a swarm of bees landing in a tight cluster on a tree limb or pole on your property, look in the yellow pages and call a beekeeper, who may happily come and take the bees to a good and productive home. It certainly is a lot easier to get rid of them at this point than later.

If you notice a bee or a couple of bees on the outside wall of your house, flying in little bobbles along the wall, they may well be looking for a hole or entranceway, so keep an eye on them. Perhaps you neglected to screen that attic vent, or close up that hole left by the cable company. Oh, dear.

Colonies of bees have invaded one of our houses twice; both times they had to be killed to remove them. The first time, through ignorance and inertia, they had been left alone for several years. By the time we went to get rid of them, the eerie buzzing of their hive could be heard continuously in the walls of the closet of a second-floor bedroom. If left alone, they could have eventually filled up the entire walls of the house with honeycomb.

If bees are entering and exiting from a hole in your house, flying out like a shot, and weaving back and forth on their return, you have a colony in your home. Call a beekeeper first to see if the hive can be taken out alive. If not, call around to find the person who will get rid of them with a nontoxic method. We had a beekeeper who vacuumed out the bees (wearing full bee regalia); he could thereby later take out and use the honey. Afterward he spread diatomaceous earth around to kill any returning to the colony from the field. Ants took on the job of cleaning up the rest of the honey in the walls.

If your problem is one solitary bee in the house, by all means let it out. Open one window and take off the screen. (You do have screens on all your windows, right?) Close all the doors to the room and pull all the curtains shut, except for those at the open window. The bee will fly toward the light and hopefully depart. If this method does not work, you can always vacuum up any bees on the windows. They won't survive long in the bag.

Since one of the tiny game hunter's standard treatments, diatomaceous earth, is lethal to bees, don't dust it on flowers or around places where bees may land in the garden. It is also not a good idea to use *any* spray when trees are flowering. Even pyrethrum and rotenone are toxic to bees, although pyrethrum breaks down much faster (about six hours in temperatures over fifty-five degrees.). If you use pyrethrum, spray at night, after the bees have quit for the day. Ryana is less toxic to bees.

CLOTHES MOTHS AND CARPET BEETLES
▼▼▼▼▼▼▼▼▼▼▼▼▼▼▼▼▼▼▼▼▼▼▼▼▼▼▼

Pests eat our food, our flowers, our houses, and our pets. They even eat us. You'd think the least they could do would be to leave us the clothes on our backs—or in our closets. It just seems so unfair to take out what last year had been a perfectly good wool sweater and discover it is riddled with holes.

Actually, the adult moths are innocent when it comes to ruining clothes, but their larvae eat fur and wool. Adult moths don't even have functional digestive tracts.

If you see a little moth flying around the room, chances are it's either a flour moth (see *Pantry Pests*) or a male clothes moth. The female clothes moth doesn't fly much; she keeps out of sight, and anyway she's too laden down by her burden of 100 to 150 eggs to take to the air. Just barely visible to the naked eye, the eggs, which are laid on fabric, are not attached in any way, so wearing, shaking, or disturbing clothing is a good way to protect them. Be sure to do the shaking outdoors, however.

Clothes moth larvae can take anywhere from a month to four years to develop, depending on temperature and other conditions. Clean wool will not sustain them, because larvae actually need the stains on clothing, including food, sweat, hair oil, and urine to get their vitamins and nutrition or they can't develop properly.

Three species of moths assail clothing: the webbing, the casemaking, and the tapestry, or carpet moth. They all look fairly similar to one another. The *webbing clothes moth* is the most prevalent in our homes today. This moth spins itself a "feeding tube" right on the fabric it's eating, incorporating little bits of the fabric. Besides clothing, it also feeds on carpeting, upholstered furniture, and even piano felts, which is another reason to practice the piano every day.

The *casemaking clothes moth* carries its case with it wherever it goes, like a little sleeping bag, by which it retains moisture. The *tapestry moth* attacks the coarser fabric of tapestries and carpets and can even eat horsehair and horn.

CONTROL

Many people claim that cedar does not repel moths, but it has been used for many centuries. We believe it does, because insects rely to such a great extent on their sense of smell to survive.

The Greeks and Romans used oil of cedarwood on the backs of parchment manuscripts to prevent insects from eating them. The incense cedar tree is itself entirely unaffected by insect pests. Squirrels are known to line their nests with cedar needles, possibly because of their insect repellant qualities.

Sometimes the odor of cedar will weaken over time. This can be remedied by rubbing the wood with oil of cedar or sandpapering it lightly.

Other moth repellants include bay leaves, eucalyptus, tansy, lavender, mint, wormwood, clove, fennel, patchouli, southernwood, rosemary, black pepper, pennyroyal, tung oil, citron, and Irish moss. There's a flavor for everyone here. Even though they may work as repellants, don't think they can take the place of clean clothes in a clean closet.

An article on controlling moths written in the 1950s actually recommended that clothing be saturated with a liquid DDT solution. Another pamphlet from a University extension service recommended painting the closets with chlordane. These treatments are no longer recommended, for obvious reasons, but we are still letting loose in our closets and homes the vapors of mothballs or flakes containing naphthalene or paradichlorobenzene (PDB). Of the two, PDB is by far the most toxic, but both can cause severe health problems in humans. Furthermore, they have to be in a closed and sealed space to work, or the vapors will not build up sufficiently to kill the larvae. Thus many people use them ineffectively. We strongly advise against using these products.

According to the Bio-Integral Resource Center, although camphor is also very poisonous to humans, it does not build up in fatty tissues like naphthalene and PDB. Camphor, which comes from the camphor tree, has been used in the past for medicinal purposes, and it is reputed to have both repellant and insecticidal properties. It can be used just like traditional moth crystals. It also gives off a vigorous smell; clothing should be aired or cleaned after storage with camphor.

Since clothes moths have a definite preference for soiled, worn (handled), or sweat-stained clothing, the very best method of protecting clothing is to clean or launder before storage. Then place it in a sealed container—cardboard that has been securely taped or a heavy plastic bag.

Sunlight is the enemy of the clothes moth. Take clothing out and hang it in the sun, shake it, beat it, or brush it to dislodge any varmints hidden in the folds and seams.

Regular vacuuming will eliminate much of the lint and hair that the larvae live on. Vacuum thoroughly in corners, cracks, crevices, heating and air ducts, and, of course, closets and storage areas.

Clothes moths are often attracted to the carcasses of dead animals. The practice of poisoning rats and mice instead of trapping them may lead to a clothes moth infestation. The moths come along and take care of the fur; then they turn their attention to your clothes.

Ironing clothes will kill any eggs and larvae. They cannot survive high temperatures, and if kept at over 100 degrees for a week they will die. Thus storage during the summer in a stifling hot attic will provide good protection. Placing wrapped items in the freezer for a few days may also kill the larvae.

Certain predatory flies and mites are the enemies of clothes moths, as are many spiders. But the best way to deal with moths is to prevent them from getting started in the first place.

OTHER HOUSE MOTHS

Sometimes moths that are attracted to light get into the house and have a field day around lights and lamps. Although they pose no threat to food or clothing like flour moths (see *Pantry Pests*) and clothes moths do, they can be annoying. To make a simple trap for these night-flying, light-attracted moths, take a night-light, the kind that plugs into a wall socket and uses a fifteen-watt bulb. Plug it into an extension cord and set it on a counter. With little blocks of wood—or even books—build a small enclosure around it. Then place a small glass bowl on top of the blocks so that the night-light shining from below now lights up the bowl. Fill the bowl with water and a little liquid soap or Windex (which seems to attract them). We have caught dozens of moths this way.

Trap for Light-Attracted Moths

CARPET BEETLES

Like clothes moths, carpet beetles eat wool, fur, and feathers. Clothes moths get blamed for a great deal of damage actually done by carpet beetles. When carpet beetles attack clothing or textiles, they leave small round holes instead of long jagged ones like moths.

These beetles are tiny, about one-eighth to one-quarter inch long, and shaped like ladybugs. They can be black with red and white or yellowish markings and they tend to be scaly or hairy. Their larvae are hairy little worms. As with clothes moths, only the larvae do the damage. The larval stage can last from nine months to three years, during which time they will eat dead insects, dust, lint, and hair. They crawl around quite a bit and can even get into food. They also eat holes in carpets, upholstery, and curtains.

The adult beetles will fly and are attracted to light. They can be found sometimes clustered at windows, clamoring to get out. Outdoors, they live on plants and are sometimes brought into the house on cut flowers.

Frequent vacuuming will control carpet beetles, especially if you take the trouble to move heavy furniture and vacuum under it, as this is a favored habitat. Make sure there are no bird, bee, wasp, or rodent nests near the house—all of these can harbor the beetles and the moths.

TRAPS

Two traps from more than fifty years ago can be tried against these pests. Clothes moths are attracted to the smell of fish oil. Impregnate a piece of rough wool with any fish oil (like sardine oil) and set it in the closet. Or try unraveling flypaper onto a piece of cardboard and placing a little fish oil on it—or bits of sardine. See if you can stand the smell yourself.

An old-fashioned trap for carpet beetles is somewhat less smelly. Traps are made out of pieces of wool with bits of cheese placed on them. Put them in an infested room in corners or under furniture. When the beetles have crawled on the traps, dump the bugs into soapy water. Then get out the vacuum and go to work.

COCKROACHES
▼▼▼▼▼▼▼▼▼▼▼▼▼▼▼▼▼▼▼▼▼▼▼▼▼▼▼▼▼

The cockroach has to be the hands-down winner of the award for the most loathed insect on earth. Known as the rat of the insect world, this sneaky night scavenger infiltrates our living quarters. Once behind enemy lines its numbers increase dramatically, and it is extremely difficult to rout.

Even though they don't bite like scorpions and they haven't killed us by the millions the way disease-transmitting fleas and mosquitoes have, they're not totally harmless. Because they sometimes enter dwellings through sewer pipes, having them prancing across your food is definitely a bad idea. They have been suspected of transmitting salmonella, dysentery, poliomyelitis, boils, and typhus. So always, always throw away any food you see a cockroach near. Roaches are also responsible for allergic reactions in humans. Their brittle, discarded skins turn to fine dust and are easily inhaled. It has been estimated that half of the seventeen million Americans who have asthma are allergic to cockroaches.

The Romans named this insect *lucifuga* or "flees the light." Fossilized cockroaches indicate that it has existed for 360 million years, virtually unchanged. It is somewhat discouraging to realize what a successful organism it is. We know they have been annoying humans for many hundreds of years, and they have been called "the exterminator's bread and butter."

The most common cockroach is the ubiquitous *German cockroach*. (The Germans, naturally, call it the Russian cockroach.) This species is the one you are most likely to see in bathrooms, kitchens, and restaurants. It's a real reputation ruiner. One feature that distinguishes this roach—besides the two stripes on the shield that covers its head—is the female's habit of carrying her eggs glued securely into a capsule attached to her own body. She does this about five times in her life; her own offspring are ready to reproduce in about three months. It has been calculated that under optimum conditions, one female cockroach could produce thirty thousand offspring in just one year. Is it any wonder some of us feel overrun by them?

The *oriental cockroach* is one of the largest. A dark, almost black bug, it loves basements, crawl spaces, and dark moist areas like water meter boxes. It also has

German Cockroach

the unfortunate predilection of traveling freely between buildings. People sometimes call it a waterbug or black beetle.

The smallest and palest household cockroach is the *brown-banded cockroach*, so called because of the light tan bands across its wings. These cockroaches like their habitat warm and dry, rather than moist, and are commonly found in other parts of the house besides the kitchen and bathroom. They thrive in temperatures around eighty degrees. This is the one you are likely to see high up on the walls and in the top folds of curtains. They deposit their eggs in clusters on vertical surfaces—behind pictures, on curtains, underneath chairs and tables. They also seek out warm places in electric clocks and televisions—thus their other name, the TV roach. They are particularly disastrous when they get into computers, and people have been known to secure their electrical appliances with rings of roach barriers.

The *American cockroach* is the biggest local cockroach. It can be a massive two inches. The American roach likes warmth and high humidity and will even walk through water, especially in the sewer system.

The *Asian cockroach* is a new arrival on the American scene and promises to be just as unpopular. It hitchhiked into Florida from the Orient some time in the 1980s. It resembles the German cockroach, but unlike other cockroaches this one is a good flier. It lives and breeds in huge populations out of doors. It is attracted to light, so at night people find their houses virtually under siege. These roaches even fly into malls. This is a very prolific bug, and it is expected to spread throughout the country.

Roaches like the warm, slightly humid, protected environments of our homes and the shelter of extremely narrow cracks and crevices. In fact, they need to have both the upper and lower portions of their bodies touching something, which is why they find stacks of newspapers and grocery bags so appealing.

Although poisons can kill a lot of cockroaches initially, they have ultimately

Oriental Cockroach

Brown-Banded Cockroach

33

American Cockroach

proved ineffective. Poisons are virtually useless against the sealed egg cases, unless they are long lasting enough to endure until the eggs hatch or are administered repeatedly. Neither treatment is beneficial to humans, and millions of gallons of cockroach poisons are sprayed around kitchens and bathrooms, places where people spend a great deal of their time.

Dr. Walter Ebeling at the University of California, Los Angeles, showed that cockroaches are repelled by poison and thus avoid spots where it has been placed. Despite their broad tastes in food, they always sample it first with their fine sensory hairs and shun poisons. They are one of the few insect species noted for their learning ability. Roaches have also developed resistance to many pesticides.

True omnivores, their tastes are broad indeed. Besides any leftover food or garbage you care to leave out for them, they will eat wallpaper paste, bookbindings, the glue in grocery bags, soap, dirty clothes, papers, bedbugs, other live and dead insects, and stale beer. Unfortunately, they can also survive three months without any food at all and can go thirty days without water.

CONTROL

A book published in 1885 advised holding up a looking glass in front of a roach. ("He will be so frightened as to leave the premises," the author promised.) We feel this method would be too time-consuming. Furthermore, for each cockroach you see in your home, there's probably at least fifty others lurking in the cracks and crannies.

The best methods of cockroach control are prevention tactics, with special emphasis on sanitation.

Repellants

Bay leaves, cucumbers, garlic, and horse apples are all known to repel cockroaches. Desperate housewives have peeled and slit garlic cloves to release the odor, then put them in drawers, under cabinets, and along baseboards all over the kitchen with some success as long as the odor lasts—about two weeks. Some people, however, have reported that certain roaches are actually attracted to garlic.

Beleaguered chefs in roach-infested kitchens have been known to slice cucumbers and line them up around the perimeter of their work stations to keep the crawlers away. These are not substitutes for cleanliness and dryness, but given the well-known migratory tendencies of cockroaches, you may consider trying these methods to keep them away.

Traps

When the first sticky traps came on the market in the 1960s, they were a welcome relief for many people compared to the poisons they were using. Traps come under a variety of names and usually consist of a small, rectangular cardboard box with sticky bands on the bottom of the inside. The roaches go in and never come out. They are useful for reducing infestations, letting you know where most of the cockroaches are and for proving that you have gotten rid of them, but by themselves these traps will not eliminate all your cockroaches.

Entomologists who maintain live roach cultures keep them in glass jars coated on the upper inside with petroleum jelly. You can make your own trap by painting the outside of a pint jar black or coating it with masking tape. Smear a good two-inch wide band of petroleum jelly on the inside of the jar below the neck. Put dog food, pieces of fruit, or a little potato or bread inside for bait. Place the traps along the wall, with a ramp extending from the floor to the rim of the jar. The insect will crawl in but can't get out. The trap works even better with a few trapped cockroaches inside. It won't work for the flying Asian cockroach, however.

A very old cockroach trap consists of dampening a rag or cloth with beer and placing it on the floor in an out-of-the-way place. The cockroaches are attracted to the beer and will congregate under the cloth. In the morning stomp on the cloth.

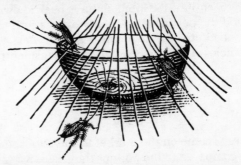

Beer Trap for Cockroaches

Another trap that makes use of their attraction to beer is putting some beer in a bowl and carefully balancing long wooden skewers or straws from a broom around the edge. The roaches will crawl up the sticks to get to the beer, and their weight on the end will tip them into the liquid where they will drown.

This trap has another variation: Use soapy water instead of beer and put bait on an inverted container in the middle of the bowl. Make a ramp with a tongue depressor, using the same teeter-totter principle as the beer trap. Make a hinge by using masking tape attached to the underside of the tongue depressor and the outside of the bowl. The cockroaches go for the bait and get tipped into the soapy water. The hinge on the tongue depressor resets the trap for the next crawly victim.

The most ambitious and impressive trap we have come across is called the Zap-Trap. Manufactured by Bi-Pro Industries, this trap features a triple whammy of pheromone lure, electric voltage, and sticky glue trap. The lure, which combines attractants for six kinds of roaches, draws the roaches to the trap. It reportedly works over a two-thousand-square-foot area. Once the roaches are crawling on the trap, an intermittent jolt of electricity (once every twenty seconds) zaps them, and they fall onto the glue tray and die. It can hold around three thousand roaches. The only disadvantage for a homeowner is its high cost (several hundred dollars), but it might be worthwhile for tenants of an apartment building to own one collectively and move it about in the building. One can also call around to find exterminators who use that trap, along with boric acid.

Predators

Although there is an old Spanish proverb that says "the cockroach is always wrong when arguing with a chicken," it is not advisable to bring a chicken into the house. However, this might be the reason that people used to let chickens move freely in and out of their dwellings.

Other animals that eat cockroaches include scorpions, wasps, toads, and hedgehogs. Some people have had success with keeping a type of tropical lizard called a *gecko*. This is a nocturnal, insect-eating creature that can get as big as a squirrel but also comes in smaller models. They can walk up walls but for the most part usually stay out of sight. They make wonderful conversation pieces. One of them is said to be able to clear an apartment of roaches in a few weeks, leaving you with the problem of what to feed the gecko. Don't buy one if you have a cat, however, as the cat will likely dispatch it.

Boric Acid

Boric acid is the one anti-insect substance that does not repel roaches; neither have they developed resistance to it after decades of use. It is much more effective and less expensive than synthetic pesticides, and it will not harm people or pets unless they eat a great amount of it.

You can get cockroaches to ingest boric acid by mixing it into a bait, or you can simply get them to walk through it by dusting it around their habitat with a bulb duster. It has to be spread properly, that is, dusted evenly over a wide area where they congregate, not dumped in lumps that they will simply detour. The roaches will ingest it because they are constantly and fastidiously grooming themselves. As with any dust, when applying it be sure to wear a mask and goggles. Or ask around for an exterminator that will treat with boric acid. This is one treatment that, if undisturbed, does not have to be reapplied.

Here is a formula for a bait/killer: 1 cup borax (another formulation of boric acid available in the laundry section of grocery stores), ½ cup flour, ¼ cup powdered sugar, ½ cup cornmeal. Keep it away from children and pets, because the borax is poisonous. There is a certain amount of sneaky satisfaction in concocting a bait that will fool the roaches into consuming it. It can be used where the humidity is too high for dusting with boric acid.

Another bait consists of mixing equal parts of cinnamon and boric acid and sprinkling it in out-of-the-way places where you suspect roaches linger.

Boric acid is not a quick-kill method and generally takes from one to two weeks to work. You may even see more roaches for a while as sick ones start appearing. Blow it into cracks and crevices, between walls and under sinks, and along baseboards with a bulb duster. Spread it around under refrigerators and stoves and other appliances. You can even add it to water and mop the floor with it. Dip a sponge into this solution and wipe down the walls and counters.

Boric acid was commonly used as an eyewash and antiseptic, and you can still find the powder in drugstores. But better formulations of boric acid are now available, ones that have been electrically charged to spread better and keep from caking. Others have been colored or bitterly flavored to keep kids from eating it.

Remember, boric acid is a poison to humans if it is eaten, so handle it carefully.

Silica Gel

Another treatment for roaches is dusting an area with silica gel (aluminum silicate). This chemically inert material, a fine dust, scratches the protective waxy outer layer of the cockroach, leading to desiccation and death. It is applied, like boric acid, in such a way that the insect ends up walking through it. Dri-die and Drione are two names of commercial products. Goggles and a mask should be used when it is applied, as with any dust, even though it is nontoxic in the usual sense.

Fix Leaky Pipes

Cockroaches come into your homes looking for two things: food and water. It is imperative to deprive them of both. Check regularly under sinks and around the house for dripping pipes and faucets. Look for pipes with condensation and watch out for leaky toilets. Check for moisture under refrigerators.

Seal Cracks and Crevices

Make sure that all utility pipes and air vents coming into the house are well sealed. A young cockroach can fit into a crevice as small as one-sixteenth of an inch. Use caulk to eliminate every little crack and crevice along baseboards, shelves, sinks, and inside cupboards. Remove or reglue loose wallpaper. Before caulking, however, treat with boric acid.

Check Appliances

Roaches love the warmth and dark hiding possibilities of refrigerators, stoves, hot water heaters, and dryers. Sometimes a house will be infested as a result of buying a used refrigerator inhabited by cockroaches. Watch out for this. Pull appliances out from the wall when possible and vacuum thoroughly. Remember: the minute an overhead light goes on, the roaches are gone. If you are looking for their harborages, do it with the lights off using a flashlight. When you do find evidence of cockroaches, vacuum very well and then wash with a strong soap. Dispose of the vacuum cleaner bag carefully in a tightly closed container—burn it, bury it, or drench it in ammonia.

General Sanitation

Always remember that roaches are odor-driven. They can smell their dinner from quite a distance.

- Keep food in tightly sealed containers.
- Never, never, never leave the dishes undone—especially at night.
- Wipe off counters thoroughly; sweep the kitchen floor.
- After the pet has eaten, wash out its bowl.
- Use a garbage can with a tight lid.
- Vacuum frequently, especially in areas where the family does its snacking.

- Remove stacks of lumber and firewood near the house, as these can make good hiding places.

- Put a few inches of gravel in your water meter box to reduce moisture.

- Thin out ivy and vegetation growing near the house.

- Remove stacks of newspapers, stored magazines, piles of old clothes, cardboard boxes, and used grocery bags. All of these make superior living quarters for roaches.

FLEAS

▼▼▼▼▼▼▼▼▼▼▼▼▼▼▼▼▼▼▼▼▼▼▼▼▼▼▼

With a mouth like a set of blades, a body like a machine, and an appetite for fresh blood, this pest has probably caused more misery than any other. Fleas are so persistent and so annoying that we bomb our houses and dust and shampoo our pets with insecticides, and still the suffering goes on.

Flea

Commercial flea remedies can be as noxious as the fleas themselves. Flea collars merely move the fleas to the rear end of the animal. These collars are particularly pernicious: imagine having to breath those fumes day in and day out. Isn't the flea itself punishment enough? Foggers fill the house with toxic residue. After setting off a flea bomb, many people, aware of the toxicity, leave their houses. The battle of the insecticidal bath or the flea dip is more than many pet owners can face.

And after all that, your pet only has to go into the neighbor's yard, bring back a few of their fleas, and the whole cycle starts all over again. The least you can do is conduct this battle without harming yourself or your pet.

Like a little armor-coated silhouette, the flea is narrow enough to pass between the hairs on its host. Its hard, chew-proof shell, capable of withstanding great pressure, is covered with a series of combs and spiky spines, while its legs are all bristles and hooks. All of these enable it to latch onto its host and hang in there despite all the frantic scratching, licking, and biting of its victim.

People were once just as plagued by fleas as the most infested dog or cat today. We were inflicted with a species called, naturally, the *human flea*, a parasite we shared with a number of animals. These fleas, crawling around one's body and living off one's blood, were once as much a part of daily life as dandruff and daydreams. When we add to this the additional torments of bedbugs and body lice, we can only surmise that life before washing machines and vacuum cleaners was indeed full of itching and scratching.

Better hygiene is responsible for the demise of the human flea. This flea was no match for a hot morning shower, a pass of the vacuum cleaner, or a tumble through the drier.

Flea remedies, of course, were as common as the fleas themselves. The Egyptians used to smear a slave with the milk of asses and make him stand in the room as a human flea trap. In the sixteenth century women wore fur pieces around their necks hoping the fleas would settle in them. In the eighteenth century decorative flea traps were devised—perforated tubes worn on cords around the neck containing sticky tubes or a blood-soaked cloth to trap the fleas.

Fleas were also the objects of entertainment, appearing as "trained" performers in flea circuses. People paid money to watch them pulling miniature carriages or merry-go-rounds and performing amazing acrobatic stunts.

Flea circuses capitalized on the wondrous capabilities of these insect Olympians. Some fleas can jump eight inches straight up in the air and thirteen inches in a horizontal direction—150 times their own length. That feat is comparable to a person jumping over the Statue of Liberty. A flea's incredibly strong back legs contain a rubberlike substance called *resilin* inside the joint. A flea compresses its legs, releases them, and shoots into the air. Stamina is no problem either: An oriental rat flea was once clocked jumping once a second for three days non-stop.

There are around 1,900 known species of fleas, and each one has its own preferred host. In the absence of the favored host, they readily feed on other animals, including humans. The two fleas found most often in our homes are the *dog flea* and the more pervasive *cat flea*. The cat flea is found on both cats and dogs and, alas, goes after humans, too. It can cause severe allergic reactions in all of them and also feeds on the blood of rats, chickens, opossums, and raccoons, among others.

Another flea, the *oriental rat flea*, was the cause of the terrible pandemic plagues that have periodically swept through civilization. Fleas account for more deaths than all the wars ever fought. However, not until the late 1800s, and another outbreak of plague in Asia—one that killed six million people in India—was the rat flea finally proved culpable in spreading this killer organism. When this disease kills the rats carrying it, their infected fleas immediately look for another host and thus move on to humans. As the bacilli multiply in the flea's intestine, they block up its gut, and the flea is unable to digest its food. Desperate for nourishment, the flea attacks its new host, but as it feeds, it spits up blood, thus infecting the host.

Although it can now be cured by antibiotics, the threat of plague is still very much with us. In the United States wild rodents, like ground squirrels and chipmunks, are likely to be carrying the disease, so it is very unwise to have any contact with ground squirrels or chipmunks, and domestic animals should be kept away from them.

A complete understanding of the cycle of the flea will help us to understand why, in the 1900s, this creature fails to disintegrate under the massive doses of insecticide we commonly use against it. Fleas spend only about 20 percent of their life cycle making pets and humans miserable. The rest is spent away from the host somewhere in your rug, floor, furniture, or yard.

Under ideal conditions, fleas can lay up to twenty-five eggs a day—as many as four hundred in a summer and eight hundred in a lifetime. And since fleas can spend anywhere from ten to two hundred days in their larval stage, and from a week to a year in their pupal stage, one pair of adult fleas can produce offspring that could be in your house for as long as two years. You'd better believe this is no little one-time skirmish. Getting rid of fleas is an ongoing process and requires a full-scale war.

When fleas suck blood, their mouths tear open the skin. Then they send an anti-coagulant (the cause of the itch) into the wound and start pumping out the blood. They take more blood than they need; the excess passes right through them. Later their larvae feed on these little dribbles of dried blood. If you're not sure if your pet has fleas, comb the animal over damp, white paper. The flea excrement, or "exhaust," which looks like ground black pepper, will turn red on the paper.

Fleas usually lay their eggs right on the host, but these soon fall off. When they hatch, the larvae—little white hairy worms—find and feed upon the dried fecal blood of the parent fleas (which has also fallen off the host), dirt, and debris. They then spin a cocoon that is soon covered with dust and hard to see.

In a house that has been empty while the owners and pets are away, the fleas remain in waiting. No sense emerging from the cocoon if there isn't going to be a meal available. If already emerged, they also wait—a flea can survive for months without a meal.

Highly sensitive to vibrations and heat, adult fleas rely on these clues as signals to jump for their blood meal. They also have the ability to detect currents of air and probably carbon dioxide, too. So when people reenter a house that has been vacant, the famished fleas arise and attack en masse. In the South, people used to send a sheep into a vacant house ahead of them, to take the edge off the flea bites.

CONTROL

Fleas thrive in warm, humid weather. A rainy summer is flea heaven. Excessive heat, dryness, and cold are fatal to fleas. Flea populations often explode in the late summer and fall. Get ready to step up your offensive during these times.

Central heating, which is a dry heat, helped eliminate human fleas from homes—as did vacuuming. You might consider turning on your heater occasionally during flea season to warm up and dry out the house.

Poisons are a short-term remedy. All they do is build a better flea, causing pesticide manufacturers to make ever-stronger—and more dangerous—products. In their zeal to control the problem, pet owners often overuse these chemicals. Many flea insecticides contain organophosphates and carbamates, which are nerve-paralyzing agents. They can cause convulsions, nausea, and respiratory arrest. And yet veterinarians say that often the poisoned animals they treat *still* have fleas.

Proper flea control means removing fleas from your pet and keeping them off by eliminating them from the house *and* yard. Think of flea control as a full-time job, like feeding the animal, because fleas always come back, especially if your pet leaves the yard.

Clearing Fleas Off Your Pet

A good long, thorough bath will get rid of many fleas by drowning them. But it can't be a splish-splash, okay-you-win-fella type of affair. Also, we're not talking about a bath with poisonous insecticides, which will be absorbed through your skin and your pet's. A simple mild soap will do the job. Safer's insecticidal soaps for pets also safely kill fleas, and so do flea shampoos containing pyrethrum (derived from chrysanthemum flowers) or D-limonene (a by-product of citrus, which disrupts the moisture balance of the insects). These are much less toxic than most other pesticides, though they, too, must be used with caution. We recommend more frequent

45

baths with a milder shampoo. A friend of ours says his dog never gets fleas—he swims in the pool every day.

One of the most important things you can do for flea control is comb your pet regularly with a special fine-tooth flea comb to remove the bloodthirsty guests. (When pets get accustomed to this procedure, they love it.) Once you snag some fleas in the comb, dip them in a glass of water mixed with rubbing alcohol and watch the routed buggers sink to the bottom. Some people like to use soapy water for this task. Petroleum jelly also immobilizes fleas. Do not crush fleas with your fingernails, no matter how tempting—they could be carrying diseases.

If you find you are snagging more fleas than usual, it's time for other measures to control the population. Dust your pet with a small amount of pyrethrum powder (available from veterinarians and pet supply stores), which will temporarily paralyze the fleas. Stand the pet over some newspaper and comb out the immobilized fleas. Gather up the newspaper and burn it.

You can also make use of the insect-killing properties of citrus. Buy products that contain D-limonene (which also kills ticks) or make your own. Cut up 2 lemons and pour 2 cups of boiling water over them, skin and all. Let this stand overnight, then sponge it on the pet; it kills fleas on the spot.

A reader of *Prevention* magazine suggested scoring the skin of an orange to release the citrus oil and rubbing the fruit right onto the animal. Or, you can collect the skins of 3 or 4 oranges and process them in a blender with 3 cups of boiling water. When cool, take a sponge and rub the liquid on your patient pet.

Getting Rid of Fleas in the House

For every flea on your pet, there may be as many as a hundred in its environment. Some people say that the way to keep fleas out of the house is to keep the pets out

Flea Trap

of the house. We think if people really wanted an outdoor pet, they might prefer a sheep or goat.

To trap fleas inside the house, take a wide, shallow pan partly filled with soapy water. Place it on the floor and hang a low-watt light bulb above it. Or use a sturdy, well-anchored, gooseneck lamp (a Tensor lamp works well), and shine it over the water. The fleas will be attracted to the heat of the bulb—that's how they find warm bodies in the first place. When they jump for the heat, they will slip off the bulb and into the pan. The detergent in the water breaks the surface tension, making it impossible for them to jump back out again. In case you're wondering how they could mistake a lamp for a dog, fleas don't have very good eyesight. Too bad. This particular trap has its origins in much older versions that used candles.

Women used to spread a rough cloth on the bed so that the spiky fleas would get caught in the fabric. Flannel is a good fabric for this. This principle can be used to determine where the worst flea infestations really are: Put on a pair of white fuzzy athletic socks, walk around the house or yard, and the fleas will jump on and get caught. (Throw the socks into hot soapy water in the washer.)

Here is another flea trap: Place a heating pad, set on low, on a low cushion on the floor. Cover it with a piece of flannel. The fleas will jump for the warmth and get stuck. If you want to kill them, have some diatomaceous earth or boric acid waiting on the fabric.

Larval-stage fleas feed on dirt, debris, and hair accumulating in floor cracks, in rugs, and under cushions of chairs and couches. Clean thoroughly to remove the sources of their food. That translates to vacuum, vacuum, vacuum. Vacuuming, of course, also gets rid of flea eggs, larvae, pupae, and possibly fleas themselves. So vacuum again. Be sure to get all the cracks and crannies and around the baseboards.

Put salt or pyrethrum in the vacuum cleaner bag, burn it, or seal it in plastic and place it in the hot sun. Some say to freeze it for twenty-four hours, but fleas have been known to revive after freezing.

Some vacuum cleaners have water filters, which are ideal for flea control. Adding soap to the water really kills them off.

Steam cleaning is even better than vacuuming for killing the fleas in rugs and on furniture. One pest control company in California that specializes in nontoxic pest control uses a dry steam machine that heats up to 250 degrees. It then sprays an insect growth regulator for the next generation. Look for exterminators that use methods like these (liquid nitrogen to freeze fleas is another one) and give them your business.

Sometimes vacuuming alone won't get all the larvae, but several nontoxic products can be sprinkled around the house. They won't harm humans, and when the flea eggs hatch, these substances are still there to kill them. One of these is noniodized salt. Sprinkle your rugs thoroughly—6 pounds per 100 square feet. Wait twenty-four hours and vacuum. The only drawback to this method is trying to keep your pets—and yourselves—out of the mess.

Another product that will kill fleas is horticultural diatomaceous earth. Spread it around in a very thin layer on the carpet and floors, under cushions, and onto clean pet bedding. Use a mask and goggles to avoid inhaling the dust. Wait twenty-four hours and vacuum. Its microscopic, razor-sharp edges will shred the waxy coating of the flea, causing dehydration and death. Silica aerogel, sold in some places as

Dri-die, works well also, if you can keep your pet from inhaling it. Both these products can also be used directly on the animal to kill fleas.

Sprinkle borax on the carpets and flooring. Leave it on for a couple of days and then vacuum. This is a good method to use if you do not have pets but have just moved into an infested home. Do not use it around pets, especially cats, who might lick the borax off their paws.

A growth regulating hormone for fleas called *methoprene* is marketed under the name Precor. It prevents juvenile fleas from maturing. It is safe to use, but fleas may eventually build up resistance to it.

If you can get your animal to sleep in the same place all the time, you can control a prime flea habitat. Start using an easily removable cover on the pet's bedding. Every morning gather it up and drop it into a washing machine already filled with soapy water. Presto. Daily death.

Cedar-filled bedding for pets makes a good flea repellant.

Outdoors

Outdoors, especially around where your cat or dog likes to snooze, you can mix diatomaceous earth with water and sprinkle it around with a watering can or spray it with a hose-end sprayer. Using it dry is even better, but if you choose this method, be sure to wear a mask and goggles.

Safer flea soap can also be used to treat outdoor areas. Make sure that your yard is not harboring rodents who will be carrying fleas. If your yard is extremely dry or wet, fleas cannot survive in it.

PREVENTION

This job goes on and on.

Herbal extracts can be very useful as repellants. Use them to keep your pet from picking up fleas in the neighborhood and bringing them home. Eucalyptus, citronella, cedarwood, and pennyroyal are among the best. You can find them in powders, collars, shampoos, and sprays. You can even make your own herbal collar by soaking a piece of string or light rope in oil of pennyroyal or any other repellant and tying it around your pet's neck. Or string together pods from a eucalyptus tree. Remember to apply repellants outdoors so that the horrified fleas don't jump off inside the house, where they'll just bide their time for better conditions—or jump on you.

Spread fresh eucalyptus branches around the house for a day or two to make the place inhospitable to fleas. If you can find them, black walnut leaves are an excellent repellant. Plant a black walnut tree in your yard.

One of the best ways to prevent the misery of fleas is to improve the health of your pet through diet and exercise. Fleas definitely inflict themselves on certain individual animals more frequently than on others—just as they do on humans—and it is suspected that the better the health and condition of your pet's skin, the more resistant your pet will be.

Some pets get fleas on account of the poor condition of their dry, flaky skin, not the other way around. Fleas love this kind of skin because it's already so raw, they hardly have to bite to get at the blood. Exercise is extremely important for animals. This does not mean merely going outside for a bit. A good vigorous twenty-minute walk is what you want.

Many people believe that feeding processed pet food to pets isn't as healthy for an animal as eating a diet of fresh foods. These should include grains, raw and cooked greens, fresh meat and liver, and a teaspoon of safflower oil (for linoleic acid) daily.

Raw, chopped, or powdered garlic is highly recommended both for health reasons and as a repellant. Use one clove per day for a cat and up to three cloves for a dog, depending on its size. Brewer's yeast, kelp, and zinc added to the diet will also cause your pet to develop an odor unacceptable to fleas. One teaspoon of brewer's yeast for a cat and one tablespoon for a dog is sufficient; but build up to this amount gradually, as the yeast may cause gas at first. Some pet stores or veterinarians have vitamins for animals. Brewer's yeast can also be dusted on as a harmless flea powder.

Take heart in your arduous battle with fleas. We humans finally wrested ourselves and our sanity from the human flea. By paying close attention to the entire life cycle of our pets' fleas, with vigilance and perseverance, we can free them, too.

FLIES

▼▼▼▼▼▼▼▼▼▼▼▼▼▼▼▼▼▼▼▼▼▼▼▼▼▼▼▼

Flies have been an irritant to humans for so long, they have entered into our legends. In Western culture, flies came out of Pandora's box. In Japanese legend, a terrible one-eyed goblin that liked to eat humans was destroyed and burned, but its ashes turned into flies—and so the torment continues.

Does the person exist who has never seen a fly? There are around eighty-five thousand species of flies, and we're still counting. They breed so rapidly that it only takes eight hours for certain eggs to hatch, and they adapt to virtually every environment. Fortunately for us, many flies starve to death, while others are eaten by birds, fish, and other insects—another reason for using nontoxic pesticides.

Sometimes we forget that we are at war with the fly and think if we ignore it, it'll simply go away and die soon. "Oh, what's one little fly?" we say, as we see it buzzing around the kitchen. Well, one little fly carries about four million bacteria. It's a walking, flying, stomping, slurping, soup mixture of germs. Hookworm, tapeworms, pinworms, typhoid, cholera, dysentery, diarrhea, hepatitis, salmonella, and dozens of

House Fly

other diseases have been attributed to the house fly. Ingesting fly eggs can be the cause of severe stomach pains.

Common house flies and their close relatives, dung flies, are sometimes known as filth flies. Blue and green bottle flies also go by the name of "flesh flies." The names fit. They buzz around the world looking for garbage, drawn by the odors of putrefaction. They lay their eggs on rotting material—food, excrement, or dead animals—25 to 100 at a time. The eggs hatch into maggots, destined to feed happily on the rot.

Ironically, the age of the automobile was hailed as an end to pollution—the pollution of flies that proliferated in the manure of so many horses. Today, however, we actually have more horses in this country than before the automobile. We also have incredible amounts of dog feces, which provide major life-sustaining material for these insects.

Flies can walk on the ceiling because they have little pads on the bottoms of their feet that excrete a sticky substance. This sticky stuff also picks up bacteria from everything else they land on, so when they crawl over your food (they taste with their feet), they leave little calling cards.

And then there's their table manners—no biting, no chewing. These creatures suck and sponge their food. To do this, they vomit or dribble saliva into it and liquefy it. Their long tongue (proboscis) then unfurls and sucks it up. Of course, they always leave some dribble, and in doing so they spew around even more bacteria. When you see fly specks, the dark ones are excrement; the light spots are regurgitated food and saliva. This information always makes a good conversation starter.

Flies can reproduce ten to twelve month-long generations over the summer. Most die over the winter, but alas, some manage to hibernate as larvae or pupae and emerge in the spring.

Mosquitoes are actually flies, but dragonflies, butterflies, damselflies, fireflies, mayflies, and stoneflies are not. Midges, bots, warbles, and gnats are also flies.

As horrific as the house fly is when it comes to low-life tastes, bad hygiene, and prolific bacteria, many other flies are much more dreadful.

A horse fly can bite through leather, and it takes big bites. The stable fly has a built-in hypodermic by which it draws blood. It bites the ankles of its victims, and socks are no deterrent. The Congo floor maggot sucks the blood of people sleeping on floor mats. Black flies leave an itching blood blister. The tsetse fly, armed with sleeping sickness, kept the Arabs from taking over Africa. Midges crawl right into eyes, noses, and mouths.

The human bot fly lays its eggs on a mosquito or other biting fly. When the mosquito lands on a person, the egg immediately hatches and burrows right under the skin, where it lives and grows for weeks. The screwworm feeds on raw flesh. It lays its eggs on the edges of any open wound it can find—on an animal or person—and, in sufficient numbers, can even kill.

Not all flies are so terrible. Tachinid flies and hover flies feed on the insides of pest insects while in the larval stage. As adults they live on flower nectar. One species of tachinids saved the sugar cane industry from the sugar cane borer. Others are useful against gypsy moths and Japanese beetles. As a group, flies are also second only to bees in the cross-pollination they perform. And their use in biological control has been a tremendous boon to agriculture.

REPELLANTS

Since flies are drawn into the house by going upwind toward odors, it figures that they will avoid certain odors, too. Here are some repellants reputed to keep them out:

Hang sweet clover in net bags around the room, especially over doorways.

Make a potpourri of bay leaves, cloves (whole or powdered), pennyroyal, and eucalyptus leaves, pounding each substance slightly to release the scent. Place it in bags and hang it near doorways or use it in bowls around the room.

Plant sweet basil, tansy, or rue around doorways. Tansy plants or dried tansy can be used indoors as well.

Both fennel and camphor have been used to repel flies. A camphor tree planted near the kitchen is a wise choice. Chinaberry trees are also said to keep flies away.

Mexican marigold is used as a fly repellant. Its leaves are sometimes hung in dog kennels and around stables.

Mint has been used to keep flies away from barns and stables—and houses. People have even taken sprigs of it, crushed it, and then rubbed it on their animals to keep flies from landing on them and tormenting them.

PREDATORS AND PARASITES

Flies were the first insects to develop resistance to DDT in the 1940s. This must have been quite disappointing, because DDT was touted as "the killer of killers," and people truly believed that flies were going to be eradicated within their lifetime. Parents were even told to use DDT-impregnated wallpaper in children's rooms to protect them from flies. When DDT failed, then other, sometimes stronger, sprays were used—and still are used. And the flies are still around.

Spraying pesticides for fly control results in a spectacular quick kill—at first. Then the resistant "superflies" start multiplying and take over. Unfortunately, spraying kills the beneficial fly parasites and also contaminates the air you breathe. Remember, if you can smell it, it has already passed into your lungs.

Do not use vapor-emitting fly "traps." If, as the directions say, they are not to be used around food preparation, babies, or old people, why should they be used around you?

Using pesticides also lets people get sloppy about sanitation, which is by far the most important means of control. Flies can be battled more efficiently and safely with biological controls and trapping.

Around dairies, chicken houses, stables, barns, or wherever large amounts of manure are generated, flies can be successfully contained by introducing fly parasites on a regular basis. These small fly parasites, who are not pests themselves, deposit their eggs right into fly larvae or pupae in the manure, preventing them from ever hatching into annoying, mature flies. Since the parasites need some dry manure, do not clear all manure away at one time. See *Mail Order* for companies that sell these biological fly controls. Many of them also consult with clients about specific problems.

Both ants and wasps prey on flies. Ants eat a considerable amount of fly larvae in your yard, which is one reason that ants should be tolerated to some extent. In one of our yards, for example, ants climb the English walnut tree and help control the walnut husk fly maggots.

Birds, frogs, toads, snakes, and spiders also eat lots of flies. In the house, spiders are the best tiny game hunters of all, so let them do their share of the fly catching. Incidentally, if a spider web becomes especially noticeable (dust makes it visible), it is likely no longer in use and can be removed.

Years ago people actually used to hang a wasp's nest near barns or stables or even inside their houses, because the wasps were preferable to the flies, whom they preyed on quite efficiently. The rule was, don't bother the wasps and they wouldn't bother you. However, some species of wasps cannot tolerate people near their nests, and we suspect this method is risky, unless you know exactly what you are doing.

TRAPS

Trapping flies, like swatting them, is a reliable way to keep down their numbers. In Africa, amazing progress has been made in the eradication of the tsetse fly using baited traps made from plastic bags, a few feet of cloth, and some staples.

Fly traps are effective because flies are so mobile and so inquisitively hungry. A trap with flies in it will attract more flies, because they are drawn to each other.

Some really fine fly traps are on the market. (See *Mail Order.*) Some of them are as simple as glass bottles with special lids that flies can get into but not out of. Others consist of a baited dish beneath a screen cone that fits inside another screen. The inside cone has an opening at the top. Flies try to exit by going up and out the top of the cone—toward the light—but find themselves trapped by the outer screen that is closed at the top.

The screen trap is one that you can easily make yourself with material from a hardware store. Screen material can be "sewn" together with wire or nylon fish line. One person we know tossed his trap into the fire and burned the flies away when it was filled.

A similar version of this trap can be made by cutting the top third off a large plastic water or soft drink bottle and inserting it up into the rest of the bottle so the top becomes a funnel leading up into the bottle. (See trap for pillbugs.) Use clothespins to raise the trap above a bait station. Puncture holes in the top with a needle so that the temperature inside doesn't get too hot.

Pheromone lures are sometimes used as baits. You can make your own baits using a variety of ingredients like beer, buttermilk, or rotting fruit. Or mix 1 part molasses to 3 parts water and add active dry yeast to make a fermented solution. Ammonium carbonate and yeast is another successful mixture, as is a piece of meat or fish in

Bottle Trap

Screen Trap

water. Cornmeal and molasses ferment into a fine bait. Sometimes a mixture of meaty bait and sweet bait will draw more flies. Be sure to keep the bait moist. Experimentation is at the heart of the true spirit of tiny game hunting.

Directions for these traps always say to place them well away from the house. This is not because the baits—and the dead flies—are going to stink, but because the traps will draw flies from far away; you won't want the new arrivals coming near the house.

Traps are more effective if placed in filtered sun. In direct sun, they get too hot and dry out. If you have ants in the yard, the bait must be kept away from them, either by hanging the trap or putting it in a shallow basin of water. We have seen ants swipe flies away from the bait.

If everyone made an effort to acquire and maintain a few of these traps, the entire population of flies would be considerably diminished.

To make an effective fruit fly trap, put a small amount of cut-up, ripe fruit (bananas are ideal) in the bottom of a jar and place a funnel over the top. The flies enter and can't escape. Beer or a mixture of molasses, water, and yeast are also good baits.

A slight drawback to this trap is that once inside the bottle, the tiny little flies don't really understand they have been trapped. They proceed to eat and breed quite happily. So you must eliminate them within the trap. You can end the party by pouring boiling water into the funnel, killing the flies, and starting all over.

Another good and simple way to trap fruit flies is to place a glass containing an inch or so of brandy or sweet liqueur near the infestation. By morning all the flies will be floating in the alcohol.

Take a used plastic bag and put a generous amount of fruit peelings into it. Use this trap indoors or out, wherever flies are numerous. After a while it will draw a

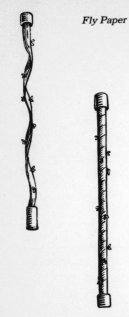

Fly Paper

Sticky Trap

good number of flies onto the fruit. Grab the top, close it off, and twist tie them inside for good.

For fruit flies and other flies, take a glass jar or can and put Stikem Special, Tanglefoot, or flypaper around the inside and then bait it. The trap will do the rest on its own.

You may have thought we had become too modern for the old standby: flypaper. But it has regained some stature. It is most effective when hung near the ceiling. We like the one that has been decorated with little drawings of flies.

To make your own sticky fly trap, smear honey thickly onto yellow paper. Or try using alternate bands of honey and Stikem Special or Tanglefoot.

If you really want to trap flies from scratch, here is an old formula for fly glue. Take 1 cup resin and ½ cup castor oil. Heat them carefully in a double boiler (the mixture is flammable), then stir in 4 tablespoons of honey. Spread on yellow paper plates, or cut brown grocery bags into strips, smear them with the glue, and hang them up where flies are bothersome.

(Resin is available at art supply stores, but don't buy polyester resin. Castor oil can be purchased at a drugstore.)

A note about electric zap traps. Do *not* use these traps outdoors! Flies do not see the ultraviolet light well during the day, and they are not active at night. You will be needlessly, wastefully, zapping beneficial bugs with these traps. They can be useful, however, in an enclosed indoor facility like a commercial food preparation establishment or a barn.

PREVENTION

We highly recommend screens. They work, especially if they are tight fitting and don't have holes.

Fly swatting is a most successful and appropriate way to get rid of flies. For every fly you kill, several hundred (even a thousand) will not be born. Be sure to wash the flyswatter in hot soapy water after you use it. Some people say that a flyswatter made of mesh works best; too much air rushing toward a fly can signal impending doom! We like a flexible one with a wire handle. Others prefer a rolled up newspaper—wide and flat, easily available and conveniently disposable.

In addition to four-thousand-faceted eyes, flies are equipped with ultrasensitive hairs that detect fine currents of air. That's why they seem to take off before they could possibly have known you were coming. Because a fly takes off slightly backward, however, aim just behind it. If you clap your hands over a fly, its takeoff pattern will land it right between your palms. Please wear gloves if you want to test this.

If swatting is not enough of a challenge, try dousing the fly with a squirt of spray starch, hair spray, or rubbing alcohol in a spray bottle. This requires both stealth and a good aim.

If a fly is buzzing around the room and you want to get it, close all the doors and drapes, leaving a slit of light at one window. When you frighten the fly, it will go to that window, and you can swat it there.

Fans deter flies, whose acute sensitivity to air currents makes them uncomfortable in moving air. That's why you see fans in meat markets and restaurants. A fan over or aimed at a doorway will keep flies out.

Do not leave any food uncovered in the kitchen. Wipe counters and sweep the floor after food preparation. Ripe fruit, especially overripe fruit, attracts true fruit flies as well as vinegar flies, which can sometimes enter through screens.

Flies have such amazing senses of smell that some can travel miles upwind toward garbage and detritus. Even fly larvae (maggots), those horrid little worms, can travel fifty feet in a few days to get to the good stuff. Sanitation is the best way to control flies. Don't let your garbage be a breeding area for them. Studies have been conducted on "average" garbage cans, and they have been found to be the source of literally thousands of maggots.

Wash and dry garbage cans thoroughly after they are emptied if they have become wet. Sprinkle the bottoms with dried or insecticidal soap. Making sure that the lids to the cans are as tight and secure as possible amounts to a civic duty. If the lids are cracked, replace them. Ideally, garbage cans should be placed on platforms to allow air to circulate under them and eliminate fly breeding places.

Separate your wet, rottable, organic garbage from the dry garbage and seal it well. The drier garbage is, the less flies will be attracted to it, so first drain it as much as possible. Wrapping it in layers of newspaper and sealing it with tape is a good way to dispose of it without using plastic bags. You can also put garbage in the compost; if you use a hot or a closed container system, flies will not be a problem. Also, cover the top of the organic material with a layer of dirt as quickly as possible before the flies can lay their eggs in it.

If you have to throw away meat, keep it in the freezer until just before garbage day, and then wrap it well in newspaper or put it in empty milk cartons.

Disposable diapers can be fabulous breeding places for flies. Either don't use them or take great care in getting rid of them. Rinse out all cartons, cans, and bottles before throwing them away or recycling them. Flies are especially attracted to beer dregs in containers.

Flies are also crazy for animal droppings. It's their true medium, after all, but it has to be moist. If it's dry, they can't breed in it. If you can't bury or otherwise dispose of the droppings of your pet, cover them with dry sawdust or cat litter.

Don't leave out the dog or cat food. That's like an invitation to a party for flies.

HOUSEPLANT PESTS

▼▼▼▼▼▼▼▼▼▼▼▼▼▼▼▼▼▼▼▼▼▼▼▼▼▼▼▼▼

Houseplant pests often infiltrate our homes by hitchhiking in on new plants. They also sneak in by hopping rides on people wandering in from the garden, hiding out on cut flowers, or blowing in through screens. The pests become a problem because none of their natural predators live inside the house. With nothing to slow them down, the damage can be quick and devastating.

Another reason houseplant pests get out of hand is the too-generous watering and fertilizing that some plants get indoors. This causes a very high nitrogen content, which plant-sucking pests, like mealybugs, aphids, and scale, thrive on.

Many books recommend throwing away plants that are infested. We think most pests can be defeated—and without polluting the house with pesticides. Nevertheless, the presence of pests on a plant may be a sign that the plant is under stress; perhaps it doesn't get the light it needs or is over- or under-watered. So while you're fighting the pests, try improving the plant's environment.

The most common pests of houseplants are aphids, mealybugs, scale, spider mites, thrips, and whiteflies. Aphids cover the tips and buds of plants. Mealybugs look like little tufts of waxy cotton in the crevices between stalks and stems. Scale looks like small bumps on the plant. Spider mites and thrips are very small and need to be identified with a hand lens. Whiteflies are much more visible; when the plant is disturbed a cloud of white insects rises. Less frequent visitors (though their numbers can be great) are ants and cockroaches—if you already have them around the house. (For more detailed information about these insects, look them up alphabetically in the index.)

CONTROL

Cockroaches enjoy houseplants. They may actually be attracted to the water in the plant saucers. And while they're refreshing themselves with all that lovely moisture, they may do some chewing—even quite a bit of chewing—on the leaves. Pine oil cleaners are said to repel cockroaches. Try sprinkling diatomaceous earth around in the plant saucers for a sharp and deadly surprise. See *Cockroaches* for getting rid of them permanently.

Ants will sometimes set up a nest in a houseplant pot (or even in an outdoors pot), where they may disturb the roots of the plant. To get rid of the ants, here is a suggestion from the Bio-Integral Resource Center in Berkeley (see *Mail Order*). Put the potted plant in a big pan or bucket. Set a pot filled with dirt, humus, or compost next to the infested pot and make a bridge between the two pots with a stick. Flood the infested plant with water. The ants will come scurrying out, carrying their pupae, and cross the bridge to the new pot, where they will set up lodgings. Repeat this flooding procedure until all the ants have moved over to the new pot, then take the new pot with the ants outside and dunk it in soapy water or place it some place where the ants won't do any harm.

To keep your cat out of your houseplants, where it seems intent on doing something it ought not to, take a cotton ball and saturate it with lemon oil furniture polish or dampen it with ammonia. Place it on the soil at the base of the plant, and the cat will lose interest.

Do a little indoor companion planting. Plant a single garlic right in the pot with your plant by peeling a garlic clove and placing it, pointed end up, about an inch under the soil between the plant and the edge of the pot. It should help keep pests away. You can also plant chives, which have more delicate tops.

Plants with smooth leaves and stems can be treated successfully by rubbing the stems and both sides of the leaves with a wet cloth, dislodging both pests and their invisible eggs. This technique works especially well for aphids and scale. Or wipe off the leaves with a mild soap and water or vegetable oil and water solution (½ teaspoon to 1 quart water). Not only will this kill or suffocate any insects, but the plants will breathe better and look better if they aren't so dusty.

Use homemade soap spray or an insecticidal soap to squirt attack any pests making inroads on the plants. A double-stick tape wrapped around the stem will keep pests from moving in from nearby plants.

If a houseplant looks mysteriously indisposed, place a pest strip (a strip containing a strong adhesive) near the plant and enclose the whole plant in a large clear plastic bag for a few days. The bug infesting the plant may get stuck on the pest strip so that you can identify it. This won't work for pests like scale and mealybugs, which find a spot on the plant and stick to it. However, putting the plant in a plastic bag is a good method of quarantine and you can keep an eye on it without worrying about the rest of your houseplants.

Taking houseplants outside and giving them a strong squirt of water will rout many pests. If the plant is small enough, simply hold it under the faucet and give it the water treatment. Be sure to spray the bottoms of leaves. We like the idea of setting the plants in the bathtub and using the strong jet of a Water Pik to dislodge the stubborn bugs.

Dips can also be used, but they are not suitable for African violets, cactus, or plants with hairy leaves and stems. If a plant is seriously infested, particularly with aphids or spider mites, the soapy water swirl bath is the treatment of choice. Houseplants have a definite advantage over garden plants in that they can be unceremoniously picked up, turned upside down, and dunked into containers of water, just as

Houseplant Dip

63

long as you secure the soil in the pot first by covering it with plastic, aluminum foil, crumpled newspapers, towels, or whatever.

Use a container large enough to dip the plant into without breaking off its stems—the bathtub, a small garbage pail, or even a large shallow pan like a roasting pan. Fill with warm water and add liquid dish soap at a ratio of 2 tablespoons to 1 gallon of water. Turn the plant upside down and swish it around in the soapy water for several minutes, drowning, killing, and otherwise discouraging the bugs. Then rinse the plant in cold water. Use your fingers to rub the undersides of leaves to displace all holdouts and send them down the drain.

This is particularly effective for thrips, barely visible pests that leave little brown specks of excrement and streaked areas on the leaves. Dips also spell doom for aphids, spider mites, and scale.

A stronger dip can be made by taking a couple of cigarettes (or pouch tobacco), breaking them up, soaking them in water for a few days, and then adding the nicotine liquid to the soapy water.

If spider mites on a houseplant are being really stubborn about departing, try a dip made of 1 tablespoon salt to 1 gallon of warm water.

Another dip for spider mites is to put 2 cups of buttermilk into 1 gallon of water. Dip the plant in this solution and let it remain on the leaves overnight before rinsing it off. (Your plant may think you are crazy.)

A treatment for many pests, including aphids and mealybugs, kills them with hot water. What could be less toxic to the entire household? It requires a hearty houseplant, however, so take care! Instead of putting the plant in soapy water, put it in hot water at a temperature of 120 to 130 degrees. Leave it under water for 5 to 10 minutes. Let the leaves dry thoroughly afterward.

Mealybugs are one of the most common houseplant pests and, if not checked, one of the most destructive. To kill them, take a paintbrush dipped in alcohol (or fingernail polish remover) and swab it onto each one, being careful not to touch the plant. Alcohol kills pests because it penetrates the outer membrane, drying them to death. You can also mix equal parts of water and rubbing alcohol in a spray bottle and spray it on the plant.

Summer oil or light dormant spray is also good for killing pests on houseplants. Test it on a few leaves first. Don't use it on ferns or African violets.

One way to treat pests on African violets or other plants that don't tolerate water baths is to squirt nonaerosol hair spray into a plastic bag big enough for the plant, quickly insert the plant, seal it up with a twist tie, and leave it overnight. This may not qualify as a truly nontoxic treatment.

Another noxious treatment involves putting the infested plant into a plastic bag and blowing cigarette smoke into the opening before sealing it. Victorian greenhouses used to contain smoking cabinets for nicotine treatments.

At the least disturbance, whiteflies take to the wing, making it sometimes hard to zap them with a spray. (See *Whiteflies*). A cheap form of plant rescue consists of constructing a temporary sticky trap right on the plant. Take four light wooden stakes taller than the plant and stick them into the edges of the pot, at a slight angle away from the plant. Then take a roll of flypaper and unravel it around the stakes, so that it forms a band at the top of the plant. Give the plant a little thump now and then to force the flies into the air, and they will come back down and land on the sticky paper.

Pick off scale or mealybugs with a toothpick or pointed knife, or dislodge them with a small sponge or toothbrush.

Pests won't always be visible on newly purchased plants, so the best defense is to establish a quarantine for all new plants. Keep them in an isolated room for several weeks to make sure they are pest free.

If you garden both indoors and out, always do the indoor gardening first. If any bugs happen to get on the gardener, it's far better to take an indoor pest outdoors than vice versa.

If you prefer that others do the dirty work, you can order predators for houseplant pests. For instance, you can get mealybug destroyers for mealybugs, or ladybird beetles for aphids. Tent the plants in fine netting so that the predators stay in place. Use stakes to hold the netting off the plant. It only takes a few predators for an average-size plant, so the rest of those purchased can be released outdoors. When all the pests have been eaten, don't let the predators on the houseplant starve; turn them loose in the garden to carry on the good work.

Spider mites prefer a dry habitat, so mist plants often with a squirt bottle to create an environment they can't stand. If the plants do have mites, use a strong jet of water to dislodge them and their webs. These tiny pests spread very easily, so wash your hands before going to the next plant.

LICE

▼▼▼▼▼▼▼▼▼▼▼▼▼▼▼▼▼▼▼▼▼▼▼▼▼

Among schoolchildren, they spread faster than the flu. To parents, their presence can come as an utter shock. For everyone involved, getting rid of them is a formidable task. There are no shortcuts when it come to hunting down and eradicating lice.

These tiny, bloodsucking parasites are universally despised—except perhaps by monkeys, who eat them. Wherever warm-blooded mammals and birds live on this earth, lice live on them. There are thousands of species worldwide, divided into biting and sucking varieties. We humans have three kinds—head, body, and crab lice. They are all sucking lice and all demeaning, demoralizing, and tormenting. Calling someone a louse is the epitome of contempt.

Lice have been with us right from the beginning. They are thought to be descended from ancient sucking bugs that had wings. Clay tablets dating from 2500 B.C. document a Sumerian doctor prescribing sulphur for use on crab lice. Perhaps the sense of shame we feel about lice comes from the fact that we've battled them so long but are still losing.

Although we can do quite well without lice, they cannot survive without us. Away from the human body, a louse lives only a few days. Like most insects, lice are exquisitely adapted to their manner of getting nourishment—they even have color adaption. Lice on brunettes tend to be darker, while those on blonds quite pale. About one-fifth of an inch long, most of their bodies consist of a big abdomen. They are just thin enough to pass between hairs, and their legs have grasping claws on the ends, which allow them to keep a firm, tenacious hold on their host's hair. With three sharp stylets around their mouths, they drill into the skin and suck out blood. They don't gorge themselves the way fleas and mosquitoes do; rather they feed over and over. A growing louse will feed every one to two hours, making a new puncture and causing new irritation and itch each time. Its anticoagulant saliva causes the itching and burning and, of course, scratching. Scratching in turn can cause more bleeding (which the louse feeds on) and secondary infections.

Climate doesn't matter to lice, because we humans are the perfect temperature for them—except when we die or get a fever. Then lice abandon us.

Traditionally, lice thrive in times of disaster—war, famine, or other catastrophes, when people are forced to live in close quarters without bathing or changing clothes. Because lice are carriers of deadly typhus, as well as trench fever and relapsing fever, their presence during these times has amplified the prevailing misery and mortality.

Nicknamed "cooties" in World War I and "motorized" or "mechanized dandruff" in World War II, lice have always been a fact of military life. In World War II, more than three-fifths of the army toilets had signs posted: "For those with crabs." When Napoleon invaded Russia in 1812, he did so with an army of five hundred thousand men; only three thousand men returned. Most of the soldiers had fallen to typhus.

As members of the same group, body lice and head lice look alike, but their behavior differentiates them from one another. Head lice live on the head, clinging to hair. Body lice have adapted to living in clothing.

Body lice lay their eggs in the folds and seams of clothing, while head lice cement their eggs, or nits, securely onto the host's hair, right near the scalp. No known chemical will safely dissolve their cement, either. The eggs hatch after a week or so, but the empty shell remains on the hair. Technically speaking, nit-picking should really be called eggshell-picking, since by the time many nits are discovered the lice have left the egg. You can tell how long ago an egg was laid by how far up it is on the hair shaft.

A female louse lives only about a month, but she can lay ten eggs a day. Head lice tend to set up housekeeping around the ears or the back of the neck on people with longer hair and at the back crown of the head on short-haired people. The tendency of children these past few decades to wear their hair much longer than the children of the 1950s, for instance, may account for the seemingly greater incidence of lice among children today. Shaving the head or treating it with kerosene used to be a common treatment.

Basic hygiene has a definite effect on body lice. Their presence may truly reflect the state of a person's sanitation, slovenliness, or living conditions, because dirty, continuously worn clothing can harbor populations of lice. Laundering clothes kills

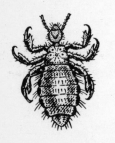

Body Louse

most of them. It's different for head lice, which can often survive a quick shower and actually prefer clean hair.

Crab lice don't help the situation, either, choosing as they do to live "down there." Pubic or crab lice are an entirely different species and somewhat resemble tiny crabs, especially their viselike claws. Crab lice can be spread by sexual contact—in France they are called "the butterfly of love," *papillon d'amour*. Some people also feel that they can be spread by towels, bed sheets, and toilet seats. Victims really suffer embarrassment from them, both because of the urgent need to scratch the parts of the body they inhabit, and because they tend to elevate private moments into public awareness. However, these lice have never been considered responsible for spreading any disease.

We do not recommend use of the widely prescribed treatments for this lice which contain the insecticide lindane. (See *Control*.) Crab lice can be treated fairly easily without using a potentially harmful pesticide. The live ones can be killed by a good long soak in a hot bath. Shaving the body hair of the affected area will get rid of the nits, and no one is likely to notice the absence of hair. Special combs to remove crabs and their eggs are also available. Be sure to launder all clothing and bed linens thoroughly in hot water.

Crab Louse

In this country, head lice are so common among children in certain areas as to be considered practically epidemic. Millions are treated each year for infestations of head lice, and these pests seem to be increasing. Children's school attendance and play habits bring them in close contact with one another. Lice are easily transmitted via hats, brushes, scarfs, collars of jackets, athletic helmets, upholstered furniture, sheets, pillows, bus seats, and other lice "bridges." In vehicles and movie theaters children's heads often come in contact with the seats, which may be another reason why so many more children acquire these lice. Often children bring lice home and spread it to the rest of the family. A school can be reinfested over and over again if just a few families neglect to take care of the problem at home. Taking care of the problem is a lot of work, whether you use a toxic insecticidal shampoo or a less toxic alternative.

Apparently, lice do not make everyone itch. Perhaps evolution is favoring those forms that cause less of an allergic reaction to their saliva. According to a spokesperson from the Hogil Corporation, which manufactures products for the treatment of lice, only about half the population who have lice actually experience burning, itching sensations. People who have no idea they have lice can easily spread them to others.

However, with close observation, lice, especially the nits, can be seen in the hair. Checking for lice is an important procedure, whether you think you have them or not. A magnifying glass helps, but good eyesight often suffices. The nits or eggs look like pieces of oval dandruff right on the hair shaft, but passing the hair between your fingernails will not dislodge them. Once you have found them, don't panic. You can get rid of them, and you don't have to use a toxic insecticide to do so.

CONTROL

Lindane is the insecticide contained in the shampoo most commonly prescribed for the treatment of lice—both head lice and pubic lice. A chlorinated hydrocarbon, its toxicity is equal to or greater than DDT. In laboratory animals it has caused convulsions, seizures, and cancer, and it can affect the central nervous system. It can pass through the placenta and be absorbed through the skin. Because it is applied to the fine skin on the heads of children, especially when pores may have been opened by warm water, its absorption into the bloodstream is all the more possible. Furthermore, in their frantic zeal to get rid of lice, people may unwisely exceed the recommended duration and frequency of applications.

Some lice treatments contain *pyrethrum*, a botanical pesticide made from a particular species of dried chrysanthemum flower. (See *Tactics of Tiny Game Hunting*.) Chemical formulations of pyrethrum are more toxic than the natural ones but they are still less toxic than lindane. However, prolonged skin contact with pyrethrum can cause an allergic reaction in some people.

Although insecticides kill live lice, they do not always kill 100 percent of the eggs. If the eggs are not removed with a special lice comb, the child may be rediagnosed as having lice and thus be retreated, even though the lice themselves are gone.

Some shampoos and soaps containing olive oil or coconut oil may have insecticidal properties. Using these shampoos and then making the effort to go through the hair with a special comb designed to remove lice and nits can be just as effective as using an insecticidal shampoo—and a lot safer.

The Bio-Integral Resource Center in Berkeley describes an efficient, though admittedly time-consuming, method for combing nits and lice out of a child's hair (or anyone else's). They recommend shampooing the hair with a coconut oil or olive oil shampoo, using water as hot as the child can stand. After rinsing, shampoo a second time but do not rinse. Keeping the hair wet, you comb it first to remove snarls. Then, using a metal lice comb, carefully comb out the hair, section by section, working on an inch of scalp at a time. Be sure to start the comb right at the scalp where the newest eggs will be attached.

After each pass of the comb, the nits and lice have to be cleaned off with a tissue and dropped into a bowl of hot soapy water. Finish with a hot water rinse. Then soak the comb in hot soapy ammonia water and clean it with dental floss. (All other brushes and combs in the house should be treated also.) This procedure should be repeated every seven to ten days as long as there is a problem with lice at the school. (See *Mail Order* for sources of combs.)

After treating the child, all sheets and blankets, along with all clothing that has been worn recently, should be washed in hot water and put in the dryer. If this is not possible, seal them in plastic bags for at least two weeks. Or send them to the dry cleaners. Put away in plastic bags any hats or pillows that can't be washed. Vacuum living quarters thoroughly, including rugs, all upholstered furniture (don't miss the backs), pillows, mattresses, car seats, and headrests.

Every member of the family must be checked and treated if necessary. Recheck everyone again after seven to fourteen days and once again after twenty-one to twenty-eight days.

Children need to be taught not to borrow each other's combs and hats and to hang up their coats and jackets on separate hooks from other kids' clothing.

Note: If reading this material has left you scratching your head uncontrollably, don't worry. *Delusory parasitosis* is a genuine condition. People who have it fervently insist that microscopic insects of some sort or other are biting them without mercy. They even develop welts, rashes, and, of course, scabs. The suffering of these people is certainly genuine, but usually no insects can be found. We seem to be as vulnerable to our own feeling about insects as we are to their independent actions.

MOSQUITOES
▼▼▼▼▼▼▼▼▼▼▼▼▼▼▼▼▼▼▼▼▼▼▼▼▼▼▼

First the good news: Only half the mosquito population sucks human blood. The males of the species do quite well on nectar alone. Females, however, need the protein from a good meal of blood to develop and lay their eggs. If they don't get it, the only way they can lay viable eggs is to consume their own wing muscles.

The bad news is very, very bad: The female half of the population has been responsible for some of the most dreaded and deadly diseases known to humankind. Before the twentieth century, one of every two deaths may have been due to diseases transmitted by mosquitoes. In the Spanish-American War, for instance, four hundred men were killed in battle, while five thousand were killed by yellow fever—called yellow jack—carried by mosquitoes.

Although we have succeeded in freeing ourselves from the constant companionship of fleas and body lice, the battle against mosquitoes is far from over. Throughout most of this century, mosquitoes have spread malaria, yellow fever, and encephalitis to millions of people each year. And they continue to cause deaths in the hundreds of thousands.

There are 2,500 kinds of mosquitoes, and they live all over the world. The word *mosquito* comes from the Spanish word, "little fly." Delicate, slender, lightweight members of the fly family, mosquitoes weigh in at $\frac{1}{25,000}$ of an ounce. A mosquito is so light, it can stand on water without getting wet and alight on skin without arousing a tactile response. It may have a light touch, but it's a cruel one.

Mosquitoes

The female mosquito punctures your skin and steals bloblets of blood by using a piercing sucking mouthpart (proboscis) with six stylets: four cut the skin, while the remaining two form a tube that draws up the blood. A duct in the tube secretes saliva as she sucks, thereby increasing the blood flow and keeping it from clotting. Mosquito saliva is what causes an allergic reaction on the skin and the subsequent torments of itching. It also transmits viruses and germs from person to person.

After feeding, the female goes to find water on which to lay her eggs. Different species prefer different bodies of water: tidal marshes, ponds, tree boles or holes, swamps, or irrigation ditches. For some species, any small undisturbed body of

73

water (preferably stagnant) will do—a hoofprint with a little water in it, a pothole, or an old tin can. In fact, old tires do so well that millions of used ones, piled up all over the world, are actually major sources of mosquito breeding grounds.

In the water, eggs hatch in just a few days. The mosquitoes will spend their next two stages of metamorphosis in the water as wrigglers (larvae) and tumblers (pupae), but breathing air. That is why spreading oil on the water suffocates the young.

Of the 150 species in North America, the bite of the *Aedes* is most painful. This is also the mosquito that carries yellow fever and dengue fever. This species holds itself parallel to the surface on which it has landed, holding its butt down.

The *Anopheles*, or "malaria mosquito," which rests with its butt up in the air, often nearly at a ninety-degree angle, transmits this debilitating and even fatal disease.

The *Culex*, our most common house mosquito, transmits encephalitis and dog heartworm. Encephalitis has been increasing alarmingly fast in this country, particularly in Florida, the South, and the Central Valley in California. The *Culex* rests with its body completely parallel to the surface. In addition to humans, *Culex* mosquitoes commonly feed on birds.

Mosquito, Pupa, and Larva

CONTROL

Adult mosquitoes hunt at night, mostly around dusk and at dawn. If you're having a barbecue at this time of the evening, try tossing herbs, like sage and rosemary, on the coals to repel the mosquitoes.

Almost everyone knows the disquieting sound of the whine of a mosquito on the hunt in a bedroom. Like a flea, it is sensitive to the carbon dioxide animals give off. It can also sense the moist warm air around a potential victim and seems to be able to differentiate between chemical blood contents, showing definite preferences for one person over another.

Remember, mosquitoes can breed anywhere! In your house they could be breeding in flower vases, saucers underneath houseplants, or even fishbowls and aquariums.

If you are getting attacked at night, and the thought of going to bed seems like going to the torture chamber, try eating a dinner prepared with plenty of garlic. Rubbing apple cider vinegar on exposed skin is said to deter mosquitoes for a short while. Some people crush fresh parsley and rub it on their skin. One of the great insect repellants, according to the rumor mill, is Avon's Skin-So-Soft. Some people won't travel anywhere without this bath oil.

The most successful repellant in most commercial formulations is a chemical compound nicknamed "Deet." Although we don't question its efficacy, the notion of rubbing something on our skin that also dissolves plastics doesn't seem sensible to us.

Peppermint, vanilla, bay, clove, sassafras, cedar, and eucalyptus have all been used as repellants over the years; pennyroyal and citronella are considered the best ones. One backwoodsman living in the 1880s wrote of his infallible mixture of pine tar, castor oil, and pennyroyal oil, claiming, "I have never known it to fail. A good safe coat of this varnish grows better the longer it is kept on."

To drive mosquitoes out of a room, open a bottle of pennyroyal or oil of citronella. Camping supply stores carry candles that give off the smell of citronella.

Set out your own mosquito trap outdoors by putting water in a bucket or container and adding a good dose of soap. When the mosquito lands to lay her eggs, she won't get out of the water alive.

Many areas of the United States have set up mosquito abatement districts, which will supply people with a mosquito-eating fish, *Gambusia*, for their ponds, ornamental water gardens, and any other possible breeding sites. These tiny fish are only two-and-a-half inches long, but they are tremendous mosquito eaters and are being bred specifically for this purpose in numerous fish hatcheries. In cold climates they need to be restocked annually. You can also get your own goldfish, guppies, or backswimmers (insects) for the garden and put them in a pond or rain barrel. They don't require any special care and are fairly hearty. Minnows also make great mosquito eaters.

As with other major pests that threaten human health, mosquitoes have been the object of a tremendous onslaught of pesticides, beginning with DDT (to which they are now immune). More than eighty million dollars are spent in North America annually to control mosquitoes, often adding toxins to the environment without reducing the mosquito populations. Successful mosquito control means limiting their aquatic breeding areas. Effective biological alternatives now exist, including garlic oil emulsions. (The active ingredient in garlic, allyl sulfide, kills mosquitoes.) One of the most successful biological controls has been a strain of *Bacillus thuringiensis israelensis (B.t.i.)*. It is supposed to give 100 percent control, without harming humans or the environment. It can provide complete killing in twenty-four hours, but since it only lasts for about three days, it needs to be reapplied periodically.

To keep mosquitoes out of the house in the first place, make sure every window of the house has a screen and every screen is in good repair. Screen doors should always open toward the outdoors. Planting tansy or basil near doorways or even around outdoor patios helps create a mosquito barrier. A yellow "bug light" outside a doorway will, in addition to attracting fewer moths, also help keep mosquitoes from coming inside. They do best in darkness or dim light.

If you have a problem with mosquitoes, look for all possible reservoirs of stagnant water, from tin cans to watering cans, from wading pools to gutters. Get rid of them or dump the water. All it takes is one small pint of water to nurture five hundred wrigglers. Fill in holes in trees and stumps. Refill the water in birdbaths every few days. Change your pet's water daily. If you have a rain barrel, make sure it is covered. Many species look for blood no farther than a couple of hundred feet from where they developed.

Encourage mosquito predators in your yard. Praying mantes, birds (purple martins especially), frogs, turtles, lizards, ants, spiders, and dragonflies eat mosquitoes. Bats are superb mosquito eaters. Many reports of bat attacks may really be bats swooping down to expertly pick off a mosquito zeroing in on a person. In the research station on Santa Cruz Island off Santa Barbara, California, a bat makes nightly foraging trips above the bunks of sleeping scientists.

PANTRY PESTS

▼▼▼▼▼▼▼▼▼▼▼▼▼▼▼▼▼▼▼▼▼▼▼▼▼▼▼▼

Nothing is quite as distressing as opening a package of food and discovering that little creatures have claimed it for their own dinner. This can be especially annoying after you have already cooked the rice or cereal, and you open the pot and see the little wormy fragments and insect parts floating to the top.

Pantry Pests

For years, many of our grain products were routinely fumigated with chemicals now banned from use. Currently, one of the most widely used fumigants is methyl bromide, a highly toxic gas. Insecticides are also used on storage bins and added to the stored grains themselves. And then the packages are treated with insect repellants.

Good progress has been made recently in exploring nontoxic pest controls of commercially stored food. Pheromone lure traps—which use the sex attractant chemicals of the insects themselves—are now available for warehouses, stores, and home use, both for detection and control of these pests. Other techniques being used include cooling, using pathogens like *Bacillus thuringiensis* (*B.t.*) to infect the pests with diseases, researching new kinds of packaging that will keep them out, experimenting with insect growth regulators, and even introducing into the stored food bugs that will eat the bugs that eat the food.

There are many, many food storage pests. Here are some of the most common pantry pests that invade our kitchens, pillage our food, and plague our peace of mind. The best methods for controlling these pests are the same for all of them and can be found at the end of the chapter.

Mediterranean and Indian Meal Moths

These two moths are fairly similar in looks and habits. If you have them in your food, you will see them flying around the kitchen at night. Not attracted to light, they are fairly small, light brown moths with a somewhat slower flight pattern than other moths. You can easily kill them by smacking them between your palms. The moths themselves eat hardly at all, but they can lay 300 to 350 eggs, and their hatched larvae—wormy little creatures—eat your food. They'll go for anything dried: soups, nuts, rice, flours, grains, seeds, crackers, candy, chocolate, dried fruit, red peppers, tobacco, and pet food. They dine all over the world.

If you see the moths, look for the food source and get rid of it. You won't always see them, but you can detect them from the silk threads the larvae spin as they eat. These threads cause the food particles to clump or mat together, especially along the sides of the package. You can kill them by freezing the food they have infested, which you can then go ahead and eat. But you might not enjoy it.

Carpet Beetles

Different species of these beetles are black, black and white with a red stripe down the middle, or yellow and white, but all have a white fuzzy spot under the abdomen. They can be brought into the house on cut flowers. Sometimes the mature beetles congregate on windows clamoring to get out. They do the most damage in their hairy, bristly larval stages when they eat carpets, textiles, furs, dried plants, and books, as well as stored food products. Methods for controlling them are similar to those for clothes moths. (For more information about them see *Clothes Moths and Carpet Beetles.*)

Weevils

Weevils are beetles with long snouts that get into grains and seeds. They have a pair of mandibles at the tip of their snout. With these, they eat an opening into the seed, then deposit an egg that hatches into a larva that eats out the inside of the seed, leaving the shell intact.

Flour Beetles

These beetles have been found in the tombs of the pharaohs. Flour beetles eat a wide variety of food—all kinds of grains, crackers, beans, peas, chocolate, spaghetti, dried fruit, nuts. They are tiny—from one-tenth to one-half an inch long. The most common ones are the red flour beetle and the confused flour beetle, so named because we get confused—not the insect—trying to distinguish it from the other beetle. Both are rust red and quite abundant.

The sad thing about them—for us—is that they need absolutely no water. They lay sticky eggs that become covered with flour and adhere to the sides of containers. These hatch into grubs (called bran bugs) that feed, grow, and then crawl to the surface of the food, where they form white pupae.

If you find them in your food, throw it away—they excrete a vile smelling chemical that discolors and contaminates the food.

Mealworms

Mealworm is one of the names for these larval creatures, the young of the flour, darkling, or false wireworm beetle. The adult is shiny black or brown, and the larvae are a yellow to yellowish brown. They live in flour or meal and do well in all kinds of conditions from very very dry to moist. They are most commonly found in areas with poor sanitation, where flour and other grains have fallen to the floor and been ignored.

Pet stores raise mealworms to feed the stock. They are eaten by turtles, toads, fish, and birds. We haven't heard of anyone keeping a turtle in the kitchen to control them, however.

Drugstore Beetles

Sometimes called bread beetles, these insects are colored brown or rust brown. Although they have often been found in stale bread, they were named initially because they infested the dried medicinal plants once sold in drugstores, and they also eat some drugs. In the home, they feed on paprika, hot spices, dried beans, and cereals. They also get into books and leather. In fact, it has been said that these bugs will eat anything except cast iron—including aluminum foil and lead sheathing.

Cigarette Beetles

These beetles are little, reddish brown, and, like the drugstore beetle, covered in fine hair. From the side they look like they have a humpback. Besides tobacco, they feed on just about anything, including dog food, paprika, wool, hair, and even some insecticides. If you have a problem with these beetles, be sure to buy your spices in bottles with screw tops instead of tin cans.

Saw-Toothed Grain Beetles

The midsection, or thorax, of these little brown beetles has sawlike projections protruding on each side. They attack all kinds of food, but especially like grain and grain products, dried fruit, nuts, candies, and powdered milk. The larvae crawl around quite a bit.

Grain Weevil on Grain

81

CONTROL

Repellants

Bay leaves are a well-known repellant for pantry pests. For years people have put them around their shelves or placed a leaf right into the storage container with the flour. Fenugreek and rhizomes (roots) of turmeric have also been used in other countries. Another technique is unwrapping sticks of spearmint gum and putting them on the shelves.

Remember that these are repellants and do not kill the bugs. We think people tend to underestimate the power of a repellant, however. They prefer to go for the big kill instead. Nevertheless, a repellant is often all it takes to keep the bugs away.

The Department of Agriculture's Stored Products Research Laboratory in Savannah, Georgia, has done studies indicating that coriander, dill, cinnamon, lemon peel, and black pepper repel or kill some insects found in stored grains.

Put black pepper into foods you usually pepper anyway—flour you plan to use for gravy or rice, for instance. Black pepper will actually kill the pests. A USDA researcher discovered that a 500 parts per million doseage of black pepper killed 97 percent of the weevils in wheat. It can also be sprinkled on your shelves.

Cold Treatment

Big grain and flour companies, like Arrowhead Mills, which are committed to selling nonfumigated and nonpesticide-treated food, have found that if they store their grains at forty degrees, they can keep the pests out. If you have room in your refrigerator, keep your flour there. To make sure nothing is in the flour when you first bring it home, put it in the freezer. Two to three days should be sufficient, but you never know with these insects; a week or month might be even better.

Heating

You can also treat infested food with heat by putting it in the oven at 135 to 140 degrees for thirty minutes. Spread the product out on cookie sheets to distribute the heat evenly. Use a thermometer to gauge the temperature of the oven: Some ovens are hot enough with just the pilot light. With others, you may need to prop the door open with the stove set at warm to keep it from getting too hot, which destroys some of the nutrients. Set a timer so you don't forget about the oven.

You can drop infested dried fruit into boiling water to kill the bugs. Some people eat it afterward. Somehow this doesn't appeal to us.

Diatomaceous earth, a powder consisting of microscopic, razor-sharp particles, can be used to kill these pests. It is nontoxic to people and is even used in animal feed for internal parasites. It kills insects by lacerating their bodies when they come in contact with it. Grain-storage facilities sometimes add diatomaceous earth at the rate of seven pounds to the ton. We have devised a death trap for these pests by sprinkling an open container of brown rice or unprocessed flour with several teaspoons of diatomaceous earth. When they crawl through it, they die.

Unfortunately, pantry moths are not attracted to light, because they would then be very easy to trap. A number of effective traps are available by mail order. (See *Mail Order*.) These traps contain pheromone lures specifically attractive to different pests along with sticky traps for catching them. You could make one of your own by putting a virgin female moth in a little screened container (a tea ball?) and placing it on a sticky trap. Identifying a female virgin moth may take several years of graduate study first, though.

If you are not sure what kind of pest you have, capture one and put it in a container in the freezer to kill it. Take it to your county agricultural agent or local natural history museum for help in identifying it.

As a general rule, try to keep as little stored food on hand as possible. Look out for the opened box that has been sitting in the back of the cupboard for months.

If you do have an infestation and are serious about getting rid of it, get your stored goods down to an absolute minimum and keep what you do have in the refrigerator. Don't give the pests anything to eat, anything at all. Starving them out will take some time, even several months.

Insects do not like to be disturbed. An old-fashioned way of keeping weevils out of grain was to shift the grain by turning the bags upside down in the storage room. Other storage places make a regular habit of stirring or agitating the grain. When you rummage through your own pantry you can pick up the boxes or containers and give them a good thump.

The cooler and drier the storage area, the fewer the pests. You may not be able to lower the temperature, but you can purchase dehumidifiers like silica gel from hardware stores and keep them where you store your food.

PREVENTION

One of the favorite remedies we have come across for keeping pests out of stored food dates back to classical times. Before filling a storage room with grain, a toad was tied by the leg to the door. There, it apparently stood sentinel against encroaching bugs.

Many pests of stored food can be found in the nests of birds and rodents. Eliminate these from the vicinity of the house. It is not a good idea to let a bird build its nest under the eaves of your house. Its mites and other pests can become your pests, too.

Dead rodents also attract these pests, as well as clothes moths. Remember, beetles and moths have their place in nature, where they recycle dead matter. Rather than poisoning rodents, trap them and dispose of them so that they don't die in places where beetles and moths will come after them.

Inspect all packages carefully before you bring them home from the store. Some of these pests lay their eggs under the flaps of packages, so look for loose seals. Inspect boxes for the tiny holes they have used to gain entry to the food.

When you get the food home, put it immediately into bug resistant containers. Plastic bags and boxes—especially opened ones—are extremely easy for these pests to get into. Transferring the food into other containers will also allow you to inspect it right then and there. Look for clumps that cling to the sides of the package. Some of these pests produce unpleasant odors, so use your nose, too.

Metal cans with very tight fits and screw-top glass jars can be used for storage. However, some of these pests can even crawl around the grooves of screw-top jars to get to the food. We prefer a glass jar with a rubber seal and a metal closure that clamps the lid down tight.

Do not use pesticides! Using poison around your own food supplies is as close as you can get to ingesting these poisons yourself.

Throw away any packages that are infested. But don't just dump them in the kitchen garbage, because these moths and beetles are quite mobile and will go from the garbage back to the shelves. Place the infested food in a sealed plastic bag in the sun to kill them off.

Quarantine the packages you're not sure about. Put them into plastic bags and keep an eye on them for a week or so. Treat them with heat or freezing.

Once you have examined and removed all infested food, do a thorough scrubbing of the area where the food has been stored, as these pests seek out corners and crevices to lay their eggs. Some larvae also crawl away from the food to pupate elsewhere in the cupboards or kitchen. Some of these pests can live very well on the littlest bit of spilled food, and we all know how messy flour can be. Vacuum the shelves thoroughly. Scrub with a strong soap or ammonia-laced solution, or a strong solution of wormwood tea.

The shelves—particularly the cracks—can be dusted with diatomaceous earth or silica aerogel to kill the insects as they crawl around in it. Use a mask and goggles when applying the dust.

RATS AND MICE

▼▼▼▼▼▼▼▼▼▼▼▼▼▼▼▼▼▼▼▼▼▼▼▼▼▼

RATS

Rats have adapted so successfully to a life-style entwined with ours, we can't even call them wild animals. Quintessential freeloaders, they eat our food, give us their diseases, live in our homes, or skulk about the premises. The more we try to beat them back, the more they are with us.

Rats can reproduce at prodigious rates and endure incredible physical challenges. In a year, a rat can have between thirty and eighty offspring, depending on the species—one pair could generate fifteen thousand rats in their life span. A rat can fall fifty feet with no injury (it lands on its feet), climb a pipe only an inch and a half in diameter, squeeze through a hole the size of a quarter, tread water for three days, dig four feet straight underground, and survive an atomic bomb test. Is it any wonder we can't get rid of them?

Rats and mice destroy innumerable tons of food, causing billions of dollars in damage each year. Urinating and defecating in food, they ruin much more than they eat. Although their favorite food is grain, they survive beautifully on anything that we eat, and can even subsist on manure and urine. Rats can also chew through paper, bone, wood, plaster, and metal.

Rats (and mice) chewing through the insulation in wires probably cause most unexplained fires. They also spread diseases, including typhus, salmonella, Lassa fever, tapeworm, hookworm, rat bite fever, LCM virus (a form of meningitis), and the plague, which is still with us. No wonder they have been called the "lapdogs of the devil."

The *Norway rat*, also called the brown rat, wharf rat, sewer rat, or wander rat, is the most pervasive in the United States. A large (seven to ten inches), aggressive specimen, it prefers urban areas, likes water and damp places, and lives at ground level or underground in burrows and sewers.

The *roof rat* (*Rattus rattus*), or black rat, also called the house rat and the "baretail squirrel," is a great climber who lives in dense vegetation, trees, vines, and attics and likes coastal towns and rural areas. This rat infested most ships, because of its ability to climb ropes. It is also the nefarious rat that carried the black death to so many millions of people throughout history.

MICE

Our feelings about mice are so convoluted that it is not unusual to find little pet mice tenderly nurtured in cages in the kids' room, while the parents put out mousetraps in the kitchen.

87

The name *mouse* is said to derive from the Sanskrit word *musha*, which means "to steal." This clearly describes its nighttime forages among our food supplies. Despite its fragile frame, dreadful eyesight, and delicate little legs, this tiny mammal has managed to extend its habitat all over the world, finding homes in the depths of English coal mines as well as the tops of Hawaiian volcanos. As Richard Conniff wrote in *Smithsonian Magazine*, "The Bible says the meek shall inherit the Earth. The house mouse is living proof that they already have."

Their reproductive capabilities are almost explosive. A female starts to bear young at around six to eight weeks and thereafter can have a litter of four to six babies every four weeks. Attentive nurturing of its young (and its harmless little furry size) has made it an object of sentimentality in children's literature—minus the mouse droppings, of course.

Unlike rats, mice can and do live quite independently of man outdoors. Among the many species of this little creature—deer mouse, meadow mouse (vole), Mickey Mouse, and harvest mouse, to name a few—the house mouse is by far the most prevalent.

CONTROL

Many of the methods for dealing with rats and mice are similar. Nevertheless, it is important to determine whether you have a rat or a mouse problem. It is unlikely that you have both. Rats kill mice, and it has even been suggested that placing several rats in cages around the premises will prompt the departure of all mice.

Most people realize they have a problem when they hear sounds of scampering in the ceiling or walls at night. Or they find droppings, gnawed wood, or even dirty smudge marks along the rodents' runways. Or the cats and dogs start acting funny and excited around the house. Finally, there is the best evidence of all: seeing one with your own eyes.

You can tell if your problem is rats or mice principally by the size of their droppings, since those of mice are considerably smaller: ¼″ while rat droppings are from ½″ to ¾″ in size. Also any gnawing or bites taken from fruit or butter will reveal the size of their teeth. If you are still not sure, put a fine sprinkling of flour or talcum on the floor and then analyze the footprints, which can also lead you to the nest site. Rats generally leave tracks that are approximately 3″ wide, while mice leave tracks that are ½″ wide.

No person should ever handle a dead rat or mouse with bare hands. Getting infected by a disease or acquiring the rodent's parasites (fleas, lice, and mites) are very real dangers. Use gloves, along with tongs or two long sticks. Place them in sealed plastic bags to trap the parasites.

Rats have been fed poisons by the ton. Since the 1950s, warfarin has been the chief rodent poison used worldwide. An anticoagulant that causes internal bleeding, it was highly popular because if it were ever ingested by humans or animals, an antidote (vitamin K) could prevent a fatality. However, rats and mice by now have a genetic immunity to it—strains of super rats can survive a dose 100 times stronger than what was once enough to kill one. Currently a poison, Quintox or Rampage, is being used that contains vitamin D_3, which is lethal to rodents because they are unable to process it; it leads to a fatal calcium buildup in their blood. In small doses, it is not toxic to other mammals and is considered even less toxic to humans. It offers the convenience of poisons—until rats and mice become immune to it.

Besides breeding resistant rodents, many poisons and fumigants present definite dangers to people and other animals. They cause rats and mice to die in the walls of buildings, where they attract flies, carpet beetles, and moths. The stench can also be offensive, and the rat's parasites—fleas and mites—can move to people.

Don't rely entirely on a cat to kill all the rodents, although it can be a good deterrent. Dogs have actually been the traditional rat killers—that is how rat terriers got their name. Other predators that should be encouraged are buzzards, ravens, snakes, and owls. In an effort to cut down on poisons (spurred on by the rat's immunity), New York City built nesting boxes in its parks to attract families of barn owls, citing the fact that a family of six owls will consume 15–18 rats per night. Unfortunately, the boxes were vandalized; however, in your own garden, you could certainly try putting one up.

Trapping

After eliminating all food and water sources for rats and mice, trapping is the best way to kill them. It does require time, dexterity, and a certain hunting instinct, but the results are good and visible. Sometimes, one individual in a household shows an aptitude for trapping, with the patience and cunning required to be an excellent tiny game hunter. Cherish this person! Do not let this person move out!

Trapping rats and mice has been a human pastime for ages, and the search for a better mousetrap may never end. Since 1838, four thousand patents for mousetraps have been registered in the United States. Despite competition from traps that guillotine, harpoon, incinerate, and tranquilize, the standard old wooden base snap trap is still considered the most reliable.

Set your traps where you find rodent droppings, as close to the nest as possible. Rodents travel along a system of "runs" along walls because they can't see well, and they mark the path with fairly constant urine dribbles; they usually don't deviate from these routes. For roof rats, the traps may need to be nailed onto tree trunks or vine-covered fence tops, where the rats are known to travel. If you suspect there may be a lot of rodents, set numerous traps all at once, every couple of feet.

Although this costs more, it will be more effective because rodents learn fast and quickly start avoiding traps.

Traps should be set with the baited end closest to the wall. Or a pair of traps should be set parallel to the wall, with the bait facing outward in opposite directions. A box moved close to the wall near the traps will force the rats or mice along your runway of death.

New traps can be left outdoors or buried to get rid of human smells, but coat the metal with oil to prevent rusting before you do this. When setting traps, use heavy rubber gloves to eliminate the human smell. If they are going to be reused, scrub in soapy water then dip in boiling water and rub with a little vegetable oil.

Tiny game hunting experts all seem to have their own favored baits, ranging from walnuts and peanut butter to bread and raw bacon. Gumdrops and dried fruit are said to entice mice. Norway rats like meats such as hot dogs, whereas roof rats prefer fruits and nuts. In tribute to their dexterity, fasten the bait onto the trap with a little fine wire, fish line, or thread. One person we know places the traps in the toaster oven to melt the cheese in place. Placing a piece of cardboard slightly bigger than the width of the trap under the bait holder will cause the trap to be sprung more easily, since it will go off merely by having the rat or mice step on it instead of requiring the rodent to have contact with the bait. Instead of food, a piece of fluffy cotton, string, or twine can be secured to the trap. Desiring it for nesting material, the mouse or rat will try to pull it off. Snap!

Mice are said to be eagerly inquisitive, but rats are suspicious of anything new. Outsmart them. Bait the traps for a few days without setting them so the rodents get used to feeding from them. Once a rat has sprung a trap without getting caught, it will be exceedingly shy of it. Some people bury their traps in pans of sawdust or cornmeal so the rat doesn't even see them.

Other Traps

Glue boards are popular for rodent control because they do not require the dexterity and cunning that spring traps do. Using these boards is criticized because the rodents don't die quickly and "worry" themselves to death. This is not always the case, however. These traps are extremely convenient, and they don't leave you wondering whether you should extricate the animal and reuse them or not—you can't. A bait placed in the middle can make them more attractive. Leave them in one place for at least a week before trying another location, as sometimes the rodents have to get used to them. However, check them several times a day; if you find a live rodent, pick it up with two sticks and drop it in a bucket of soapy water.

You can make your own glue trap by fashioning a four-inch by six-inch tray out of aluminum foil with the edges turned up, and filling it with a layer of a sticky substance like Tanglefoot—at least a quarter of an inch thick. If these glues get dusty, they will not be as effective and will have to be stirred a little. Place them right along the edges of and parallel to the walls. If you get any of the sticky stuff on your hands, cooking oil will remove it.

Live traps, such as Havahart traps, are available commercially. They are non-lethal, simple to use, and much easier on the conscience. Some mail order companies sell traps, including a tin one that holds up to thirty mice. Once a curious mouse enters, others may follow to keep it company. These kinds of traps are essential if the mouse in question happens to be one of your kid's pets. (See *Mail Order*.)

To make your own version of a soft-hearted live trap, take a big stainless steel bowl and smear it generously with butter. Place a little bait in the bottom and then improvise a couple of ramps leading up to the edge—small boards, books, toy tracks. The mouse will go down into the bowl for the food and be unable to escape because

Live Trap for Mice

of the slippery sides. This is an especially good trap for pet mice, hamsters, and gerbils that have escaped from their cages.

On a much larger scale, a rat trap can be made out of a full-sized garbage can. In a dark corner of the garage or garden, where you know or suspect there are rats, place the can with about a foot of soapy water in the bottom. Use laundry detergent and even add a little bleach for good measure. Tape a single layer of paper securely over the top, tight like a drum. Cut a slit in the form of a cross in the paper right in the center. Hang some bait so that it dangles above the slits. Set up a few boards as ramps so the rats can travel to the top of the can. Going for the bait, the rat will think the newspaper is secure but will fall through to a clean death.

In a chapter entitled "The Extermination of Vermin" from *Dick's Encyclopedia of Practical Receipts and Processes*, the author, William Dick, advised placing the bait for several days on the paper without slitting it, "until they (the rats) begin to think they have a right to their daily rations from this source." He also said to place a rock in the barrel with room for only one rat. The first rat that falls in will climb on the rock. When the second one falls in, a fight for the space on the rock will ensue. According to the author, the sound of the battle is guaranteed to draw numerous other rats.

In Southern California, the roof rat seems to be increasing. Numerous fruit trees give it ample food to eat, and many typical ground covers like ivy provide perfect habitats. These ground covers not only give them ideal hiding places, they also provide a habitat for one of the rats' favorite foods: snails. Six ground covers that give rodents neither food to eat nor a comfortable place to live are: carpet bugle or ajuga, cape weed, chamomile (snails hate it), Indian mock strawberry, gazanias, and creeping speedwell. If you have a fruit or avocado tree, remove ripened fruit as soon as possible and clean frequently under those trees.

Most literature on the topic indicates that electronic sound devices for repelling rodents do not work. Furthermore, they may be harmful to other animals or people. However, a person we know uses one in the basement of a Montana house, which is empty for long stretches of time. He is not bothered by mice infestations, possibly because the device is used in a bare, open room and nothing obstructs the "sound" it emits.

PREVENTION

Whenever poisons eliminate great numbers of rats, those remaining immediately begin breeding and quickly restore the population. The limiting factor for rat populations is not death by poison, but rather availability of food, water, and shelter. Therefore, limiting rat populations means limiting their access to these essentials. This means good sanitation and careful control of garbage. It means changing human behavior.

Any opening into a building, including holes for utility cables, basement windows, pipes entering the house, vents, and cracks in the foundation, should be rodent proofed with caulking, hardware cloth, steel wool, or metal barriers. Make sure the bottoms of doors have metal guards. Seal up even the smallest cracks, because mice can enter through holes less than three-quarter inches wide.

In an emergency, a hole can be temporarily stuffed with a rag soaked in a strong mixture of cayenne and water. Rodents are also repelled by the smell of mint (especially peppermint), camphor, and pine tar.

All sources of food should be out of reach. Fruits and vegetables should not be left out on counters, and all stored food should be in rodent-proof metal or glass containers. Counters and floors should be clean and free of crumbs. When you discover you have rats or mice, keep as much food as possible in the refrigerator until they have been eliminated.

Get rid of piles of newspapers and magazines where rats or mice can make nests. Inspect storage closets, attics, and basements regularly. Storage boxes should be put on raised platforms at least twelve to eighteen inches high.

Garbage and pet food should be entirely inaccessible. Ideally, garbage should be stored in metal containers on platforms eighteen inches high. Keep dogs out of the garbage. Even wood should be stored on a raised platform.

SILVERFISH
▼▼▼▼▼▼▼▼▼▼▼▼▼▼▼▼▼▼▼▼▼▼▼▼▼▼▼▼▼

These pearly, primitive, wingless nibblers are thought to be relatives of the oldest six-legged creatures. They belong to the order of bristletails because of the three long filaments at their posterior end, but they get their name, *silverfish*, from their silvery, overlapping scales. These scales rub off easily if you touch them, giving the impression that this insect is greasy.

Silverfish

Tape-Covered Glass Trap
for Silverfish

Silverfish move as if they are swimming. They slither and slide about, hiding between narrow cracks. They usually stay out of sight and do their scavenging at night. They'll eat stored food if they can get it, particularly moist flour, and they love the glue and sizing in books. They will also eat wallpaper paste, the glue off postage stamps, and the coating off glossy paper. Because they nibble on linen, silk, rayon, and dirty or starched clothing, they are also sometimes called fish moths.

Silverfish like damp basements, but can get into all parts of the house. A close relative, not as silvery colored, the firebrat, prefers hotter temperatures and has been known to hang out around heating ducts, furnaces, hot water pipes, or bakeries. They do not, contrary to popular opinion, come up through the drain.

They arouse distaste in people, but they don't smell and they don't bite. They even get into ant and termite nests and eat their young.

Light, cleanliness, and ventilation help eliminate them. Remember—they like high humidity, so don't provide it. If you have silverfish in your bookshelves, take out all the books and vacuum thoroughly. Put out bags of dehumidifying gels (available in hardware stores). Then set out the traps described below. The herb santolina, sometimes called lavender cotton, can also be put among books to deter insects like silverfish.

Using boric acid, silica aerogel, or diatomaceous earth in cracks and crevices will kill them, just as these products kill cockroaches. Stored books may benefit from being placed in a box that has been treated with one of these dusts. Take care not to inhale the dusts when using them—use a mask and goggles.

A bait made up of equal parts of cinnamon and boric acid has been used for silverfish. Do not use it where children could get to it, as it is poisonous if ingested.

A good silverfish trap can be made by taking a glass jar and wrapping the outside with masking tape. Bait the jar with wheat flour and a little sugar. Place it near a wall or corner of the room. A tongue depressor can serve as a ramp to the top of the jar, making it even easier for the insects to get up and into the container. The silverfish climb up, drop off the lip, eat the food, and can't get out. Another trap can be made by spreading a sticky substance (Stikem Special or Tanglefoot) on a piece of heavy paper and baiting it in the middle with a small pile of oatmeal. The silverfish will be trapped on the sticky substance before they get to the food.

Perhaps silverfish, with their fondness for the coating of paper, could be enlisted to recycle the millions of copies of glossy magazines that can't be processed because the coating clogs up the machines. We can just see the field trips with hundreds of schoolchildren taken to watch millions of these little chompers slithering around in giant vats of old magazines.

SPIDERS

▼▼▼▼▼▼▼▼▼▼▼▼▼▼▼▼▼▼▼▼▼▼▼▼▼▼▼

For many people, spiders are the scariest bugs of all. However, they merit our greatest respect and admiration, for spiders are the finest tiny game hunters we know.

There are around forty thousand species of spiders, and virtually all of them are carnivores, their meat of choice being insects. Their entire lives are spent hunting and devouring bugs. They have been called the dominant predators on earth, because they kill more insects than birds do and destroy them more efficiently than insecticides. Someone estimated that the bugs spiders eat in one day outweigh the entire human population.

In China, farmers build little teepees out of straw and thereby aid hibernating spiders which kill the pests in their fields. Gardeners everywhere would do well to cherish the spiders that kill their own pests. Household spiders also make their living by killing lurking insects. Exterminators who create a fear of spiders generate a market for their services. But spiders are the *real* exterminators. They eat flies, bedbugs, gypsy moths, cockroaches, and grasshoppers. Just name a bug you don't like; chances are it's eaten by a spider.

Like the praying mantis, spiders also consume beneficial insects, like bees, and even other spiders; but the good they do far outweighs the bad. The worst enemies of spiders (besides spiders) are humans, another example of how we don't always behave in our own best interests.

Spider silk is stronger than tensile steel of the same diameter and so fine it has been used as cross hairs in optical instruments and gun sights. It has also been used to clot blood in wounds. Attempts have been made over the centuries to harness silk-spinning spiders the way we have silkworms. These attempts were greatly hampered by the need to supply the captive weavers with live insects. Capturing living flies to feed the spiders was just too labor-intensive for spider silk to become a big industry. The spiders didn't like being crowded together either; most of them much prefer to live in solitude.

The old Saxon word for spider was *attercop* or "poison head." Almost all spiders possess venom and paralyze their victims, but few spiders can harm humans, for their jaws don't have the strength to break human skin. Most bites that are blamed on spiders are really inflicted by fleas, mosquitoes, bed bugs, and other insects. Even the dreaded reputation of the tarantula is quite unfounded—its bite is no worse than a bee sting for most people.

Of the three thousand species of spiders in North America, only two cause serious injury to humans: the black widow and the brown recluse. Both bite only defensively, but their venom is quite powerful, depending on how much is injected. The very young and the very old are more vulnerable to their bites. Nevertheless, you stand a much greater chance of getting hit on the freeway in a week than you do getting bit by one of these spiders in a year. If you are bit, try to capture the spider in a jar, don't panic, and get medical attention as soon as possible.

One way to tell if you've been bitten by a spider is to look for two tiny red spots; most insect bites and stings leave only one mark.

If you find a spider in the house, we would recommend leaving it alone to assist in tiny game hunting. Removing it is easy, though; quickly cover it with a glass jar and slip a stiff piece of paper between the jar and the surface. Even then, you will be doing yourself a favor by releasing the spider outdoors instead of killing it.

It is also important to realize that spiders prefer a tranquil, undisturbed existence. Shy and unaggressive, they will run away or try to hide if hassled, and for the most part they just want to be left alone to hunt. Most of them can't even see very well beyond a few inches.

If you are afraid of a spider and would like to have it identified, put a top on the jar and place it in the freezer for a day or two. Or pour rubbing alcohol in the jar to kill it instantly. Then take it to a natural history museum or county extension agent for identification.

If a cobweb in the house is visible and dusty, generally it is no longer being used and can be vacuumed up without destroying the spider. So, being tolerant of spiders doesn't mean you have to put up with old dirty webs all over the house.

BLACK WIDOW SPIDERS

Black widow spiders have probably been responsible for the deaths of millions of innocent spiders (because of arachnophobia). A black widow spider only bites on extreme provocation or if her web, containing an egg sac, is disturbed. She is much more likely to run away and hide than to stand and fight. Nevertheless, her bite can be extremely painful and is not to be taken lightly.

A big shiny black spider, it has been called "the fat lady of the spider world" and

Black Widow and Prey

99

is found all over North America. Its distinguishing feature, a red (or sometimes orange or cream) hourglass mark, is located, quite inconveniently, on the underside of its abdomen. The male of the species doesn't resemble the female and is not nearly as dangerous to humans. The name of this spider comes from attempts by the female to eat the male after mating.

Black widow spiders live in out-of-the-way, undisturbed spots like piles of wood, rubbish, stones, wood stumps, corners of garages, basement windows, and sheds. This spider makes an untidy looking web—then hangs upside down in it waiting for victims. The web is usually low to the ground. Only a small percentage of bites have been fatal.

BROWN RECLUSE SPIDER

A yellow/tan to dark brown spider, the brown recluse is also called the violin spider because of the light violin-shaped mark on the back of its head and body. The first documented bite in this country was in 1957, and the spider used to be almost unheard of. It is now fairly common in the South and Southwest and seems to be spreading. A fairly small spider—three-sixteenths to five-sixteenths of an inch—it has long slender legs. It also has only six eyes, whereas most spiders have eight.

Like the black widow, brown recluses spin a messy web. This spider can be found indoors more frequently than the black widow spider—in attics, boxes, piles of paper, closets, and clothing that has been untouched for a while, especially if left lying on the floor. Like the black widow spider, it only spins webs down low and in undisturbed places. But unlike the black widow, the recluse spider generally hunts away from its nest and will sometimes take temporary shelter in clothing or blankets. People are most likely to be bitten if they put on clothing or shoes that a spider has crawled into. A good precaution is to always shake out these items before putting them on. Outdoors, the spider inhabits rock piles, rubbish, wood, and inner tubes or old tires.

The poison of this spider is necrotic—it destroys the tissue around the bite and can even cause gangrene. The bite becomes very unsightly (gruesome actually), and is slow to heal but rarely fatal.

CONTROL

The fewer insects you have in the house, the fewer spiders will be around for the feast.

- Screening and sealing out insects will keep out spiders, too.

- Trim plants and hedges and prevent them from growing near the building to keep spiders away from the house and reduce the number entering the house.

- Don't let refuse build up in the yard.

- Always wear gloves and a long-sleeved shirt when cleaning out places likely to be infested with these spiders.

- Always shake out clothing and blankets that have not been used for a while.

- Don't allow spiders (or other insects) access to boxes and other storage containers. Seal them well. When going through boxes and stored papers, be especially careful.

- Vacuum frequently around the floor, the baseboards, and inside of closets.

If you go looking for these spiders, search at night with a flashlight, since they are mostly nocturnal hunters.

Any time you find a spider in an unwanted place, you can easily kill it by crushing

it with a stick. But, if you don't want another spider to move in and take its place, change the habitat where you found it or its nest.

When you think a spider has bitten you, take that spider to the doctor for identification, even if you have squashed it. Far too many bites are blamed on the wrong creature.

TERMITES

▼▼▼▼▼▼▼▼▼▼▼▼▼▼▼▼▼▼▼▼▼▼▼▼▼▼▼▼

One of the strange ironies of this planet is that the supreme builders of the insect world are those who eat, ravage, and destroy our own dwellings. Every year termites cause more damage in the United States than fires, storms, and earthquakes combined. Last year, according to the *Los Angeles Times*, termites ate the equivalent of fourteen houses in Los Angeles County. The money that homeowners spend on exterminators and repairs is astronomical—around 750 million dollars in 1986 and probably well over a billion last year.

In the forest, termites recycle dead wood and timber, eliminating trees and debris that would otherwise take hundreds of years to decompose and thereby prevent vital new growth. In tropical climates, they also turn and aerate the soil. Humans have traditionally eliminated forests and trees when they clear the land for agriculture, and they unwittingly substituted their own homes for the termites to live within and upon.

Termites

Thanks to central heating, termites, which are tropical insects, have migrated steadily northward and are now in every state except Alaska. The two major house-damaging species are the subterranean termite and the drywood termite. The subterranean termite is more widespread and causes by far the most damage. The Formosa subterranean termite, long a major pest in Hawaii, and a much more aggressive and formidable termite, is currently making headway in the mainland United States.

The more a homeowner knows about termites and how to detect them, the easier they will be to deal with. A typical colony might have a quarter of a million insects. They are master architects, building nests of wondrous design and symmetry. In Australia, Asia, and Africa they build tall mounds from their underground nests—the equivalent of a person building a skyscraper by hand.

Termites (sometimes called white ants) are often mistaken for ants, particularly carpenter ants, who also make their homes in wood, grow wings, fly off, and establish new colonies. (See *Ants.*) Termites, however, are much more closely related to cockroaches.

If you do see a termite, chances are it will be in its winged stage—the only time one ever leaves its nest. Inside the nest, the termites are much lighter colored, and their wingless, segmented bodies look wormlike. In fact, their name comes from the Latin word *termes*, which means "wood worm."

It is important to know the difference between termites and ants, because different methods are used to deal with them. Basically, a termite has a thick waist, whereas an ant has a pinched or wasp waist. Ant antennae are elbowed while those of termites are not. Termite wings are bigger, too, almost twice as long as their bodies, and their two sets of wings are equal in size. Winged ants have pairs of wings of unequal sizes.

CHARACTERISTICS OF VARIOUS TERMITES

Subterranean Termites

These termites live in huge underground colonies that may number a quarter of a million insects. They have to have regular contact with moisture to survive. That is why they build distinctive tubes in which they travel between soil and wood. In the winged stage, termites are brown to brownish black.

Formosa (Subterranean) Termites

If you don't have anything else to worry about in the middle of the night, worry about these guys. Mostly in Hawaii and the southwestern part of the United States (so far), they are similar to other subterranean termites but are more aggressive; they also eat a wider variety of wood. They do more damage, do it faster, and are also more resistant to pesticides than other termites. A colony can consist of two to three million individuals and can take up more than an acre of land. They have a pale yellow body color, and their soldiers have oval-shaped heads instead of square ones.

Drywood Termites

This species is found predominantly on the West Coast and in the South. They are larger than subterranean termites and live in much smaller colonies. They build their nests right into wood, in locations removed from soil. They do not have high requirements for moisture. Because their colonies are much smaller, they can be moved from area to area in lumber. They eject little fecal pellets through holes that they then plug up. Winged termites are reddish brown.

Dampwood Termites

Similar to drywood termites, except they are found in wet, decaying wood. They are large, up to an inch long, with even bigger wings. They are found up and down the Pacific Coast.

A new colony forms when a number of winged termites, potential kings and queens called *reproductives* or *alates*, exit from the colony and fly away. This is the only time in a termite's life when it will experience light, sight, and flight. These colonizing flights take place in the fall, early spring, or summer (depending on the species), generally just after a rain when the earth is damp and soft. They can also be precipitated by heavy watering or irrigation. In our city, Santa Barbara, termite flights are most common on the first clear day after the first heavy rain of the season.

Any home, even a home that has been recently tented and fumigated for termites, is vulnerable to these random landings of winged immigrants. Fortunately, termites on the wing are highly vulnerable to predators. Birds and dragonflies eat them by the thousands. And once they come down to earth, they are preyed on by ants, frogs, spiders, mantids, lizards, and snakes. When they do come to earth, a male and female pair up, break off their wings, run about in tandem, and burrow under a rock or into a hole in the ground. They then seal themselves in—now mated for life.

The colony will grow very slowly at first. As it develops it will include workers, who take care of the young and provide all the food, and soldiers, who protect the colony. The workers, whose jaws have sawlike edges, do all the damage. They usually tunnel into wood that has been wet and damaged by fungus.

Ironically, termites cannot digest wood. In their guts they harbor colonies of microscopic, one-celled protozoa, which break down the cellulose for them and make it digestible. Because they are born without these protozoa in their intestines, they must acquire them by eating each other's fecal matter. They also eat the skins they shed and their own dead and dying.

Drywood termites occasionally push their fecal pellets out of their nests through "kickout" holes. Little piles or sprinkles of these dark-colored, granular particles are a good indication that termites live with us. Look for them directly above these piles of *frass*.

105

DETECTION

The termites' greatest advantage is that they are hidden from sight. We need to be vigilant around our homes to detect them. Have at least one thorough inspection of the house every year, on your own or by a professional.

The homeowner can be on the lookout for the exodus of winged termites or for signs that they have entered the house. Sometimes they accidentally emerge into a brightly lit room instead of outdoors. Look for masses of their transparent wings, which they tear off before starting to burrow.

Subterranean termites, which cannot survive without moisture, live entirely underground. If you open up a termite nest or burrow and expose it to air, their soft, uncovered bodies will dry up and they will die.

Because they must have moisture at all times, they can't simply crawl out of the earth and climb up the side of a building. Naturally, wood that sits right on the earth is ideal for them. Never, never build so that this condition exists—anywhere. In many cases termites stream up through cracks in the foundations to get to the wood. They can travel though a crack as fine as one-thirty-second of an inch.

Termites frequently build tunnels, called *shelter tubes*, which get them over concrete foundation walls and up through cracks to the wood. They will also build shelter tubes over wood and bypass treated wood. These tubes are made from particles of dirt and wood and a cementlike substance that the termites secrete. They look a little like dribbled sand and are quite distinctive. Sometimes a tube, called a *drop tube*, can be seen suspended from wood, hanging down in midair like a creepy invasion probe.

Keep an eye out for these shelter tubes at all times. If you see one, knock it apart. If it is rebuilt within a few days or a week, you know that termite activity is going on.

If you destroy the shelter tubes and keep them from being rebuilt, the subterranean termites in the house will die, because they have to be able to return to their underground headquarters to replenish their moisture. Destroying the tubes will also give their enemies, the ants, a way to get at the termites.

Another way to check for the presence of subterranean termites in your yard is to drive untreated and weathered wooden stakes into the ground. Pull them up in sixty days to see if they have been attacked by termites.

Inside the house check for wood (especially flooring) with a slight rippling or pebbled look or darkened patches on it. Use an ice pick or screwdriver to tap the wood. if the termites have been at work it will easily give way. Test windowsills and window frames also.

Sometimes the clicking and chewing sounds of termites alert people. Knock on wood and listen for the warning ticking sounds made by soldier termites. A stethoscope comes in handy for this.

Money spent on a professional inspection (provided you are not pressured into using poison treatments) is a good investment for a home owner. A truly complete inspection is a laborious physical feat and requires poking into the farthest recesses of the attic (for drywood termites) and crawling around dirty, dank crawl spaces.

A company called Tadd Dogs takes a visual inspection one step further. Tadd dogs are trained to detect insects that chew cellulose material, including termites, carpenter ants, and powderpost beetles.

Sometimes physical evidence from termites may be old, and yet the house will get treated over and over just because this evidence was never removed. (It happens.) The dogs detect only living insects. Because they are so accurate, the house need only be spot treated at the site of infestation. The argument for tenting and toxic fumigation ("we don't want to miss any") is eliminated.

The Tadd dogs are being used all over the country. They are a little more expensive than an ordinary inspection, but they are also insured for errors. For information about these dogs, call 1-800-354-TADD.

CONTROL

The greatest enemy of the termite is the ant. By being barricaded in wood, termites escape this mortal adversary.

One of the most foolish things a home owner can do is spray a ring of poison or set out a series of poison ant stakes around the house. So, if you see ants crawling up and down the walls of the house and they're not bothering you in the kitchen, leave them alone.

If you suspect a termite colony is in the ground near your house (wood in the woodpile, tree stumps, or fence posts show signs of being eaten), get out a shovel and start digging. You can't totally expose a very large colony, but you can create access to it for ants and other termite enemies. Also any time you find shelter tubes of subterranean termites, break them apart to allow the ants in.

Traditionally, the treatment for subterranean termites has been the use of insecticides injected into the soil around and beneath houses. Chlorinated hydrocarbons, such as the chemical chlordane, were used routinely for termites (and ants) in millions of homes. A known carcinogen, chlordane remains active for twenty-five years. No longer on the market, its use (and overuse) may be one of our all-time great pesticide disasters.

People commonly buy and sell at least one or two homes during their lifetime, and renters move even more frequently; but little information is kept on the pesticide-use history of a dwelling. How are you to know when you move into a house that it has been treated with gallons of chlordane, not once, but over and over again?

When a house is tented and fumigated, the chemical methyl bromide is pumped into the house. Like chlordane, it is one of the most toxic chemicals on the market. Fumigation only kills the termites in the house and does not affect the underground nests. Houses can be reinfested immediately afterward, although evidence that a colony exists then may take a few years to show up. And often after pesticides are used, people do not attend to the important tasks of monitoring and detection.

Some new and nontoxic treatments for termites are now being used by exterminators. Call around to locate these people and give them your business. The more we demand nontoxic treatments, the more operators will begin to use those treatments.

Biological Control

One treatment now available uses nematodes—microscopic parasitic organisms (little worms)—that attack termites by invading them through their body openings. They then kill the termites by releasing bacteria into their system. They are marketed under the name of Spear, and are simply poured into the soil in a water mixture. Termites eat their own dead and also pass their food around, so it doesn't take too many nematode-infected termites to infect a whole colony. The nematodes do need a moist environment, however.

Another biological control that is being tested are bait blocks saturated with insect growth regulators. Some of these regulators turn the workers into soldiers, thus depriving the colony of the right proportion of food providers. Another regulator (methoprene) prevents termite nymphs from maturing into adults that can reproduce. These products can be applied by coating a stake with the chemical and driving it into the ground in the path of the workers, who take the wood back to the colony as food. This method is environmentally safe, but it takes between six months and a year to eradicate a colony.

Cold

A simple idea, based on the fact that there are no termites in the cold climate of Alaska, led to the development of a technique that freezes termites. The Blizzard System uses liquid nitrogen pumped into small holes drilled in the walls of infested areas. This chemical drops the temperature within the wall to twenty degrees below zero. A majority of the earth's atmosphere is composed of nitrogen, so this gas is entirely harmless to humans (unless they breathe it exclusively without oxygen). Although the procedure is expensive, the company that pioneered it in California in 1987, Tallon, has had remarkable success with it.

Heat

An exciting new method for treating insect infestations, heat, was pioneered by Walter Ebeling of the University of California. The principle of heat treatment is that at a temperature of 120 degrees an insect can only live for twenty minutes. Higher temperatures and a longer time is required to kill insects living in wood. The process uses a portable propane heater that blows hot air into a tented house. Spot treatment can also be done by blowing heat onto a section of a wall by means of a flexible duct. For the temperature inside the wood to reach 120 degrees, the temperature in the house must be about 150 degrees, slightly less than a sauna. Some objects in the house must be removed—computer equipment, plants, chocolate, medicine, some plastics. The process costs more than fumigation because it is more labor-intensive, but it is completed in less than a day. Every other bug in the house dies, too.

Electricity

For more than a decade, a company called Etex has manufactured and leased an appliance called the Electro-Gun, which kills drywood termites and powderpost beetles by zapping them with electricity. Despite opposition from the pest control industry, use of the gun has steadily increased. Its only limitation is that it can't be used in any part of the home that the operator can't get to. Because the insects themselves and their tunnels are slightly moist, the arc of electricity goes directly into the burrow and travels along the galleries, killing the termites. The pulsed high-frequency current doesn't damage wood. The operator can easily return and treat places where new termites are discovered, and it is safe to use.

Barriers

Subterranean termites have been successfully prevented from getting to a building by the use of sand barriers, according to the Bio-Integral Resource Center in Berkeley, California. The termites find it impossible to tunnel through the sand because their galleries won't hold up. The sand, however, must consist of particles of a certain size, ranging from 1.6 to 2.5 mm (10- to 16-mesh). This method has already been widely tested in Hawaii, and Honolulu has even incorporated it into its building code.

Incidentally, insecticides work as a barrier when poured into the soil around the foundations of a house. Why not use a nontoxic barrier?

BIRC is a nonprofit organization that provides extensive information on the least toxic ways of dealing with pests. For more information see *Mail Order*.

PREVENTION

• Do not let the exterior paint on wood structures deteriorate. This makes it no contest for termites burrowing in.

- No wood should ever come in contact with the soil. Inspect wooden porches or steps that touch the soil. These provide perfect access for termites.

- Wooden trellises or planter boxes next to the house should not have contact with the soil.

- Remove all wood, firewood, scraps, stumps, building material, and unfinished building projects away from the house. Get rid of it as soon as possible. Firewood should be stacked on a poured concrete foundation. If you find termites in this wood, burn it, or soak it in soapy water or water laced with ammonia.

- Crawl spaces and areas under buildings should have adequate ventilation to keep them dry.

- Shrubbery should be cut back from around the outside of the house to keep vents open.

- Cracks in concrete or masonry should be patched and repaired. They provide good access for termites.

- Check areas where pieces of wood join together or abut—corners of houses and walls or up under eaves. These are good entry places for insects, particularly if they have shrunk or split.

Drywood termites often enter attic areas through vents, then crawl around on the floor until they choose a spot to burrow into. Have silica aerogel dust or boric acid blown onto floorboards in the attic and into spaces between walls. These dusts can be applied during new construction, but you can also drill holes into walls to have it blown in. These dusts will kill termites if they crawl over it, but they are better for prevention than for treatment. They also are effective against cockroaches. See *Tactics of Tiny Game Hunting* for more information about these products.

You are more likely to have termites (and wood-destroying fungi) if you provide them with lots of moisture within the house. Are there leaky pipes or a leaky roof? Is there condensation anywhere? Is there a leaking shower pan or moisture around the base of the toilet?

Be vigilant against any moisture opportunities for these wood chompers and eliminate them. Keep gutters clean. Make sure downspouts direct water away from the structure. The soil line around the house should slant downward so that water runs away from the house. Make sure sprinklers are not dampening the sides of the house as they water.

TICKS, CHIGGERS, AND MITES
▼▼▼▼▼▼▼▼▼▼▼▼▼▼▼▼▼▼▼▼▼▼▼▼▼▼

Ticks, mites, and chiggers are all related to spiders (Arachnida), and it's perfectly all right to have arachnophobia about these disgusting pests. Atrocious little creatures, the ones we know best attach themselves to our bodies and feed off us, leaving calling cards that range from the agonies of itching to serious illnesses and even death.

TICKS

Most ticks like a long, slow feed of our blood. Although frequently painless and unnoticed, their bite can cause reactions from severe pain to paralysis. Ticks are also vectors of dozens of quite serious and debilitating animal and human diseases. In the first century A.D., Pliny the Elder called them "the foulest and nastiest crea-

113

tures that be." In this country, they are considered more dangerous than fleas and mosquitoes. Because they get their start in the great outdoors and only attack humans who venture into their territory, controlling them is a seemingly impossible task.

Few animals on earth are immune to the bite of the eight hundred species of these bloodsuckers. They feed on birds, as well as mammals, and will even live on reptiles. Because they have a variety of hosts, they pass diseases between these hosts. They themselves have very few predators. After a female has had a good blood meal, she drops off her host and lays thousands of eggs. Ticks also pass any disease they are carrying to their eggs, so the next generation of ticks are ready-made disease carriers.

Ticks hatch in the spring or summer and attach themselves at first to birds or very small mammals, like rodents and squirrels. Not until they have reached the nymph or adult stage do they climb up onto tall grass or bushes and wait for larger hosts, like deer and humans, to pass by. After climbing up the vegetation they hang on with their back legs and wave their forelegs in the air like little radar monsters. They can't jump or fly; when a host walks by they drop or grab onto it.

Once a tick gets on a human being it wanders around, taking its time to find a suitable spot to feed. A tick can move with a very light touch and often causes no sensation at all when it bites. This is why looking for and spotting ticks is one of our main defenses. Once it selects its site, the tick grabs on with a set of curved teeth and also begins to secrete a cementlike substance to help it stick. It goes into the skin, head first, like an ostrich going into sand, and feeds very slowly, often taking several days to finish, sometimes swelling to the size of a pea or a small grape. Once imbedded, a tick is very hard to dislodge and will readily leave its mouthparts in the skin if pulled away. This can cause an infection for the person, but the tick gets away scot-free and regenerates the mouthparts it lost.

Ticks can be classified as either *hard* or *soft*. Hard ticks have a "shield" on the back and are more common than soft ticks. Since they feed longer, they tend to be found more often. The following give diseases to people.

Lone star tick: Named because of the white mark on its back, this reddish brown tick is found in the southeastern United States. It feeds on both deer and on humans. A large tick, it transmits tularemia (rabbit fever) and Rocky Mountain spotted fever.

American dog tick: Most common in the East, it can also be found in other parts of the country. This is a large tick, between one-quarter and one-half inch long, and brown with silvery gray markings on its back. Although it prefers dogs, it will also feed on humans. It carries Rocky Mountain spotted fever, as well as tularemia, and causes tick paralysis.

Dog Tick

Rocky Mountain wood tick: Also called the Rocky Mountain spotted fever tick, this creature resembles the dog tick. Found west of the Rocky Mountains, it transmits the disease it is named after, as well as tularemia, Colorado tick fever, and tick paralysis.

Deer tick: This tick is named because its primary host in the East is the white-tailed deer. In the Midwest, however, it is called the bear tick. This tick is famous for transmitting Lyme disease. It is extremely small: As a nymph it looks like the period at the end of a sentence. When it first matures, it is little larger than a poppy seed. Most people don't even know they've been bitten by it.

Deer Tick

Western black-legged tick: Found in the West, this is the cousin of the deer tick, which it resembles, even in size. It also transmits Lyme disease. It is reddish brown, with black legs.

Diseases Transmitted by Ticks

For many years, Rocky Mountain spotted fever was the worst disease given to people by ticks. If untreated, this illness has a high mortality rate—around 20 percent. Other common diseases spread by ticks include relapsing fever, tularemia, and tick paralysis. Tick paralysis mostly affects animals and children who have been bitten around the back of the neck.

In the past decade, Lyme disease has become the most serious disease carried by ticks. First identified in the Northeast, Lyme disease (or Lyme arthritis) is now carried by ticks in forty-six states. One of the reasons it has spread is that these ticks normally feed on several kinds of birds. An early symptom of the disease is a target-like (or bull's-eye) red rash expanding from the bite locus. This is followed by flu symptoms and aching muscles. If untreated, it escalates to symptoms that mimic meningitis and rheumatoid arthritis. It can also cause permanent damage to the joints, heart, and nervous system of its victims. Some say that had it not been for AIDS, Lyme disease would have been called the plague of the nineties.

Control

The season for ticks is early summer to early fall, so be prepared for careful and constant vigilance during this time. Don't be passive when it comes to ticks. Also, in certain areas of the Pacific Coast, ticks can be active during the winter.

Animals are prime hosts of ticks and should be examined daily for infestation. Check your pets while they are still outdoors, so they don't carry ticks into the house. Some ticks brought in by animals will breed indoors. Look especially carefully around the head and neck and between the toes of your animal. A flea comb can be used to remove ticks on dogs and cats. Lint cleaners, made of a roller with sticky masking tape (available from hardware and large drugstores) can be used to remove ticks from cats. Animals can also be treated with nontoxic tick shampoos similar to the ones discussed in the section on fleas.

To find out if an outdoor area is infested with ticks, tie a large piece of white flannel to a string and drag it around on the ground. Turn it over and you will be able to see the ticks that have jumped on. If you see a lot of them, leave the area. Another way to check for ticks is to place a block of dry ice onto a cloth spread on the ground. You can put the dry ice into a colander with a lid or into a box with holes drilled in it. Ticks—like fleas and mosquitoes—are drawn to carbon dioxide, which dry ice gives off, and they will travel over the cloth where you can pick them off.

If you know for sure that a place is heavily infested, you can take several measures. You can treat it by spraying with insecticidal soap or diatomaceous earth. This would only be practical near the house, of course. Treating large areas with toxic insecticides, as has been done in the past, has probably done more harm than good.

When you are outdoors in an infested area, try to avoid walking in tall grass, brush, or shrubbery. Avoid narrow paths commonly traveled by animals—that is where ticks hang out.

Wear suitable clothing. Ticks are more visible if you wear light colors. Long pants and long sleeves are recommended, and pants should be tucked into socks or boots. Some people wrap masking tape around the bottoms of their pant legs, as this is one of the most common entry points for these marauders. Check for ticks on your clothing every thirty minutes.

Even though products containing Deet have been found to effectively repel ticks, they have also been known to cause allergic reactions and even seizures. They should not be sprayed on bare skin. If you use it, only apply it to clothing before you put it on. Products containing permethrin (a chemical form of pyrethrum) repel ticks when applied to clothing.

On returning to the house after walking in an infested area, remove all clothing and put it immediately into the washing machine. If you have picked up a tick, it may be wandering around on your body, still searching for a feeding site. Do a thorough tick check of your entire body, especially the groin and armpit area. Get a friend to look in places where you can't see, or use a mirror. Take a hot shower, then check again. These frequent inspections are important, because diseases carried by ticks usually require that the tick be attached for eight hours or more before the infection begins to take place.

If you have ticks in your region, examine your children every day, especially the back of the neck and under the hair.

Keep long grass and weeds cut short around your property. Eliminate underbrush around trees. Remove leaf litter and prune trees so that sunlight can dry the soil. Ticks thrive better in a humid environment.

Reduce the rodent population so that ticks have less to feed on. Some people set out permethrin-soaked cotton (a product called Damminix) in little containers around their property. Small mammals collect it as nesting material, and it later kills the ticks. Pretty clever.

Since the presence of deer—especially in the Northeast—has been associated with disease-carrying ticks, exclude them from your property. (See *Animals*.)

Consider planting molasses grass around the circumference of your property. The tiny, sticky hairs on this plant are believed to trap the ticks and keep them from climbing up it. Fewer ticks are also said to be found where sage, pyrethrum, and lavender grow as ground covers.

Removing Ticks

It used to be recommended that the tick be twisted or unscrewed off the body. This is no longer advised. To best remove a tick, take a pair of blunt, curved tweezers or forceps, grasp the tick very close to the skin, and pull it firmly and steadily out. When you remove a tick, do not crush it with your hand or touch it with your bare skin. Drop it into alcohol or soapy water, otherwise it can release toxins. If you use your fingers to remove it, cover your skin with plastic or tissue to avoid infection. Another method recommended by some is to put a little petroleum jelly, rubbing alcohol, or fingernail polish on the body of the tick. It will release its grip, but it will take its own sweet time—at least thirty minutes—so be patient. Clean the bite area with rubbing alcohol or another antiseptic and wash your hands with soap and water.

CHIGGERS

Like ticks, the modus operandi of chiggers is that of waiting on grass and brush for likely victims to pass by. Next to chiggers, which look like tiny red specks, ticks seem gigantic. But small as they are, chiggers are actually considered to be mid-sized mites.

Chiggers are found in the midwestern, southern, and southeastern areas of the United States. They are also known as jiggers, red bugs, and hot weather bugs because they flourish in the summertime. People can pick them up from grass, weeds, brambles, and even their gardens.

If bloodsucking sounds like a bad way to make a living, chiggers have even worse habits. Once they get on your skin, they inject an enzyme that literally causes cells to disintegrate. Then they suck and slurp up the juice. It can cause unbelievable itching, but the reaction usually comes long after the mites are gone.

119

After feeding, they don't stick around but drop off, burrow into the ground, and molt.

The adult chiggers are harmless but the bright red, blind baby chiggers attack anything that gives off carbon dioxide—people as well as numerous other mammals, rodents, reptiles, frogs and toads, and even turtles. They usually jump on people around their feet and make their way up the body until they get to an obstruction like the tops of socks or a belt, and then they start to feed.

If you have chiggers in your area, cutting down high grass and brambles may help. Also wear tight fitting clothing. The best treatment for chiggers is taking a hot soapy bath as soon as you come in from outdoors. This will kill them before they have time to do a lot of damage.

Some people recommend dusting areas known to be infested with chiggers with sulfur. You can also dust your clothing with it, using a duster, but wear a mask and goggles when applying the dust. Once the dust settles, you can go back in.

SCABIES AND OTHER MITES

Ranging in size from nearly invisible to half an inch, mites inhabit land, water, and air. Of the thirty thousand known species of mites (there may be a million), a full half of them live as parasites on other animals. One mite lives exclusively in the ear of a moth. Humans are hosts to a number of mites besides chiggers. (Ticks are not mites, but they belong to the same order.) One of these, the hair follicle mite, swims around in the oily sea that surrounds facial hairs. Some even live in eyelids. Whether these mites are harmful or beneficial has never been established. We can only be grateful that they are invisible, because, like lice, they look like little monsters.

House dust mites are probably the most numerous mites who live off us. A favorite habitat is the hollows in mattresses, where they wait for skin bits (or bites) to float through the sheets. These mites are thought to be the cause of many allergies and asthmatic attacks, and they are one more reason to get out the vacuum cleaner frequently.

Itch mites or *scabies* are a particularly virulent type of people-invading mites. Also called seven-year itch or mange, scabies can spread with great ease from person to person. You can get them from shaking hands or from clothing and sheets that have been infested. Because it takes from six weeks to several months to develop a sensitivity to scabies the first time you get them, you can be spreading them unknowingly for quite a while.

The larvae of scabies mites travel freely over the skin looking for a spot to settle in. They don't start burrowing until they are adults, however. When they do burrow, they choose the most delicate, sensitive skin, like that found between fingers, at the bends of elbows and knees, or around private parts. Females live for several months eating and laying eggs under the skin. The tunnels they make, as they proceed to nibble along, look like whitish hairs on the skin, and the mites can actually be removed with a needle. Under a magnifying glass they look something like a hairy turtle. If you suspect you have mites, you can diagnose them by digging them out with a sterile needle or sharp blade, but you might prefer that your doctor do this for you.

Infested people usually don't realize they have mites until they become sensitized to them. Then they develop a rash and unbearable, excruciating itching. Because cortisone ointments are now readily available, many cases of scabies go undiagnosed.

Control

Those who have scabies should avoid any physical contact with others. Part of the treatment consists of frequent hot baths or showers—which will kill scabies crawling on the surface of the skin. Changing and washing linens every day and washing all clothing in hot water is also advised. Scabies mites only live a few days away from people, so any items that cannot be washed can be sealed in plastic for a week.

Traditional treatments for scabies involve using soaps containing the insecticide lindane. We do not recommend using these. (See *Lice*.) A less toxic insecticide (or miticide) available from drugstores is sulfur, and various preparations containing this powder can be purchased.

TINY GAME HUNTING IN THE GARDEN

INTRODUCTION

We have actually bred armies of superbugs that our poisons can't kill. In 1938 there were seven insect pests known to be resistant to at least one chemical. Now there are 450. Furthermore, there are about 30 species that no "approved" chemical can kill. Most of the "bad bugs" were around long before chemical pesticides. And after all these years of spraying (CAUTION!), dusting (WARNING!) and soaking (DANGER!), the same bugs are still coming around to see what's growing and get as much as they can. The general failure of chemical pesticides to eradicate these insects is a good reason to give them up, given the inherent danger they present.

Just because we've given up "spraying," however, doesn't mean we've given up the battle. It just means we're using a more varied and inventive approach, one that is easier on us and our other allies in the garden. We are still at war with the bad bugs, but we're no longer killing all our fellow hunters in the field.

Think of it as a game. The bad bugs may be crop connoisseurs, but you're smarter than they are. And you don't have to get rid of them entirely. Total annihilation is not even advised. All you have to do is make sure that the level of damage they inflict is within a tolerable range. If they get a plant or two, plant two more. Some say that a plant cannot be considered lost to the insects until more than a quarter has been eaten.

Superbug

124

Another reason you don't have to obliterate every single one of the bad bugs is that the natural predators have to eat. If they don't have anything to prey upon, they go away, and they won't be there when the next inevitable pest invasion arrives.

Regular inspection tours of the garden are essential for the tiny game hunter. Know when the enemy is starting to advance and become familiar with the signs of encroachment. When you spot an infestation in your yard, study the situation carefully. Is that green worm on your rosebuds really a threat to the perfect flower you hoped to get, or is it a hover fly larva hunting down the rose aphids alighting from the sky? If you mistakenly spray your friend (the green worm, the hover fly larva), more aphids will land and reproduce ever more rapidly.

If you know your insects and all the options available, you can be on the front line of defense. Put away the "bug bombs" and try some of the different control techniques we suggest. Above all, experiment! The various remedies provided here have been culled from both scientific and nonscientific sources and may not work every time. (Use of trade names does not necessarily mean we endorse that product.) Scientists have no corner on the market on how experiments should be conducted; lay people sometimes come up with much better experiments and results. If you have a pest in your strawberry patch, apply one treatment to one part, another treatment to another part, and leave one alone. Check them every few days. Observe carefully and take notes. That's how Thomas Jefferson worked, and he had a remarkable orchard and garden.

THE HEALTHY GARDEN

Bullies attack weaklings; insect pests do much the same. Some biologists believe that distressed plants release chemicals that are picked up by insects searching for food. Insects may even be performing a beneficial function in the garden by getting rid of ailing or feeble plants, thereby allowing the healthy ones to flourish. We should observe insects and let them reveal to us which plants need better care.

Strong, healthy plants, on the other hand, resist bugs and can survive surprisingly well even when insects are feeding. Using chemical nitrogen fertilizers makes plants grow fast, but it does not give them the strength or range of nutrients they need to resist insect attacks. In fact, nitrogen feeding actually attracts some insects. The best way to get healthy, vigorous plants is to provide them with good soil. As the saying goes, "Feed the soil, not the plant."

Good soil consists of four things: organic matter (humus) from plants and animals, inorganic matter from rock and mineral particles, air, and water. A soil rich in humus is full of beneficial bacteria and fungi; chemically treated soil is lifeless. Organic matter is the magic ingredient, loosening heavy soil and binding sandy soil, making it easier for water and air to move through it. Vegetables grown in soil containing good, rich humus have been found to contain 400 percent more minerals than those grown with chemical fertilizers.

The healthy garden is one in which the gardener gives back to the soil that which has been taken out. The best way to return nutrients to the soil is to add organic matter through compost, mulch, organic fertilizers, and cover crops.

COMPOST

▼▼▼▼▼▼▼▼▼▼▼▼▼▼▼▼▼▼▼▼▼▼▼▼▼▼▼▼▼

Composting might be considered both a science and an art. Like cooking, it has expert practitioners and elaborate recipes. But it can also be done quite casually, and it's virtually impossible to ruin. However you go about it, compost is probably the most important thing you can do for a healthy garden.

Composting is a means of speeding up nature's process of changing once-living material into a soft, crumbly soil conditioner called "black gold." Composting requires raw organic material, nitrogen, air, and moisture, along with some bacteria to start the breaking-down process.

Raw organic material: This can be leaves, prunings, garden cleanup, spent vegetables and flowers, weeds, seaweed, kitchen scraps, coffee grounds, eggshells, cornstalks, shredded paper and newspapers (no colored inks), sawdust, or pine needles. You also need some good soil or compost containing the bacteria to get it started.

Nitrogen: You can get this from fresh or dried manure (from any animals except pets), blood meal, cocoa shells, feathers, seafood scraps, grass clippings, guano, and hair.

127

*Wooden and Cinderblock
Compost Bins*

Air: In *aerobic* composting, the oxygen-consuming bacteria need air as they break down organic material. They heat up the compost quite a bit as they "cook" (metabolize wastes). Air is incorporated by turning the compost pile every day (if you have the energy) or every week.

Anaerobic, or airless composting, can be done by leaving the pile alone and forgetting it for a year or so, or by putting it into plastic bags with about two quarts of water, sealing them, and leaving them in the sun. This process is smelly (if the bag is opened), and takes about a month, but it's a good way to get dry leaves to compost, and it rots weed seeds into infertility. If the bag contents are later spread out in the sun, the smell goes away fairly quickly.

Moisture: If the compost pile is too dry, the process slows down. Ideally, compost should feel like a slightly damp sponge.

Limestone, phosphate rock, greensand, granite dust, and wood ashes can also be added in small amounts to provide the soil with minerals.

Compost piles are as individual as their creators. They can be in an out-of-the-way corner in the garden where leaves and clippings are piled in a heap, or in a sleek, mail order compost bin. Bins can be made from concrete blocks, chicken wire, slatted wooden shipping pallets, or snow fencing. Many people have a series of bins: one for filling, one for aging, and one for emptying around the garden. The process can take from two weeks to three years, depending on moisture, heat, frequency of turning, and how finely shredded the raw material happened to be. The location should be sunny, level, and open to the ground to permit earthworms and microorganisms to enter from below. Once compost gets going, the second team of decomposers—worms, insects, and lower animals—gets in on the action and goes to work.

Although they can be a pest elsewhere in the garden, pillbugs and sowbugs break down compost very rapidly. Collect them in traps around the yard and add them to the compost pile. They tend to stay there as long as you keep adding food. (See *Sowbugs and Pillbugs*.)

EARTHWORMS
▼▼▼▼▼▼▼▼▼▼▼▼▼▼▼▼▼▼▼▼▼▼▼▼▼▼

Called the "intestines of the soil," earthworms perform the invaluable task of literally eating their way through the earth, digesting organic matter and minerals, and transforming it into richer, more usable soil. These underground tillers or soil factories, as they have been called, also break up and aerate the soil. Soils without them are hard and difficult to work. Earthworms also attract birds, who then eat insects. Charles Darwin concluded that no other animal had played so important a part in the history of the world.

By all means, order earthworms and disperse them in the garden so they can go to work. However, be sure to add organic matter to the soil so they have something to work with, or they will go elsewhere. Earthworms cannot tolerate chemical fertilizers and are killed by pesticides like slug and snail poison.

MULCH
▼▼▼▼▼▼▼▼▼▼▼▼▼▼▼▼▼▼▼▼▼▼▼▼▼▼

Mulch consists of a layer of organic matter spread around the plants right on top of the soil. There's nothing like a good mulch to keep down the weeds, hold moisture

129

in the ground, regulate the temperature, create a favorable habitat for earthworms, and add organic matter to the soil. Mulching also cuts down on a lot of gardening chores, as Ruth Stout described in *Gardening Without Work*. What could be more appealing than never having to dig, plow, spade, hoe, cultivate, weed, water, or irrigate? You, too, can "garden from a couch" if you mulch.

Although Stout used salt hay at least eight inches deep or garden leaves covered with hay as mulch, any number of materials can be used: compost, bark, wood chips, alfalfa hay, buckwheat hulls, cocoa shells, coffee grounds, corncobs, grass clippings, evergreen branches, hops, peanut hulls, peat moss, pine needles, sawdust, wood chips and shavings, ground cork, ground seashells, and newspapers. Seaweed also makes a great mulch; furthermore, little animals, like mice, dislike it.

We like writer Barbara Coyner's idea of keeping gerbils to turn paper into mulch. She claims that, in addition to scrap paper, these industrious animals will shred toilet paper rolls, boxes, and cardboard into confetti mulch.

ORGANIC FERTILIZERS
▼▼▼▼▼▼▼▼▼▼▼▼▼▼▼▼▼▼▼▼▼▼▼▼▼

A number of organic fertilizers are available, and most contain a much wider spectrum of nutrients than petroleum-derived chemical fertilizers. Some organic fertilizers consist of soybean meal, hoof and horn meal, bone meal, and worm castings (earthworm manure).

Fish fertilizers and seaweed meal or kelp are a few of the best. Seaweed has been used for hundreds of years by farmers. It contains hormones, fifty-five trace minerals, and soil conditioners. Many people believe that seaweed gives plants insect resistant properties. Its taste may repel them, and it also makes the leaves stronger, healthier, and thicker. Apply as a liquid spray on foliage or pour it on the ground. Seaweed meal can also be worked into the soil.

To make instant blender fertilizer, throw all your kitchen scraps into a container by the sink. Stale bread, leftover cereal, vegetable parings, eggshells, leftover salad—anything that would go down the garbage disposal, except grease and meat scraps. In the morning, throw it into a blender and fill with water. Liquefy it, then take it out and pour it around your plants. You may want to buy a used blender and keep it just for this purpose.

COVER CROPS
▼▼▼▼▼▼▼▼▼▼▼▼▼▼▼▼▼▼▼▼▼▼▼▼▼▼▼

Sometimes called green manure composting, cover crops are an inexpensive way to add a great deal of nitrogen to the soil while improving its structure and adding organic matter. Seed an area with plants like vetches, clovers, legumes, beans, peas, barley, buckwheat, or rye. After they have matured, turn or dig them into the soil and wait a month or six weeks for them to decompose.

COMPANION PLANTING
▼▼▼▼▼▼▼▼▼▼▼▼▼▼▼▼▼▼▼▼▼▼▼▼▼▼▼

If you plant certain species together, they help each other thrive and they repel insects. This also adds to the variety of plants—which is the way Nature's gardens thrive. The more interplanting you have in the garden, the less chance a particular pest population can get out of control. Many pests are fairly specific about what

131

they will eat and will voluntarily starve rather than eat a different plant. The exception, of course, is an insect nightmare like grasshoppers.

The champion insect repellant plants are members of the onion family, including garlic. You probably can't plant too many of these, and they are particularly good as borders. Other "protector" plants include tansy, coriander, wormwood, rue, thyme, sage, and members of the mint family. Flowers include nasturtium, marigold, petunias, geranium, and chrysanthemum. Just for good measure, throw in a few hot red pepper plants. More than one plant is generally needed to have much effect against insects, so be liberal.

We also strongly recommend rotating plants every year to remove them from the sphere of influence of pests living in the soil. Buying resistant varieties will also save a great deal of time in the trenches.

TACTICS OF TINY GAME HUNTING

Gardening means war, but we have only ourselves to blame. We plant the most delicate of seedlings, and then are amazed when they tantalize the taste buds of hungry slugs. We try to grow the sweetest, best-tasting corn and expect the raccoons to ignore it. We lovingly nurture spectacular roses and are horrified when aphids find them attractive, too.

Although the delirious days of DDT, the wonder poison, ended in the 1960s, its spirit lived on; DDT was superseded by more and more poisons, all promising the perfect kill. However, the quick-fix days of bomb the house and nuke the yard to get rid of everything that scurries, crawls, climbs, digs, or flies may be coming to an end.

In the new battle plan, we enlist Nature on our side, using her own soldiers for our cause. After all, no one understands aphids better than the ladybug whose life centers on eating as many of them as possible. And no one makes a better hunter than the beetles and spiders who devote their entire lives to trapping and capturing insects. Simply by understanding who is on our side and who isn't puts us well on the road to success.

In addition to creating the healthiest, most resistant garden and taking the time to learn a little bit about our specific adversaries, here are the tactics that we favor.

HANDPICKING

▼▼▼▼▼▼▼▼▼▼▼▼▼▼▼▼▼▼▼▼▼▼▼▼▼▼▼

The first line of defense. You can't find a much older method of pest control. Bugs just never seem to develop resistance to it, either.

Gardeners used to like to put the bugs they handpicked into kerosene—we're not sure why, unless people have always had an urge to mix their insects with strong, foul concoctions. A jar with soapy water or water laced with rubbing alcohol will do just fine. Or simply smear the inside of the jar generously with dish soap or petroleum jelly so the bugs can't exit.

This chore should immediately come to mind—before taking out the garbage or doing the dishes—whenever any young person wants to earn money. Pay them by the bug, and make sure they can tell the good ones from the bad.

Handpicking in the early morning, when the bugs are still too cold and lethargic to move quickly, can bring rewarding results. Be sure you know exactly what you are picking, however. If in doubt, put the insect in question in a glass jar and place it in the freezer until it expires. Then take it to the local natural history museum or agricultural extension agent. Or consult an insect guidebook with good illustrations.

Some of the worst garden assailants are the tiniest, and a magnifying glass can be an invaluable tool. First, look to see if any predators are at work. If they are, give them a good word or two and go back to headquarters.

Sometimes a lighted magnifying glass makes identifying the trespassers easier, especially in the shade. To make a handy device for checking out what's going on

Magnifying Mirror on Spatula

underneath the leaves (scenes of major assaults in the garden), glue a magnifying mirror onto the flat end of a spatula, then hold it under the leaves. One gardener we know had heard that birds have eyesight equivalent to seeing through binoculars. Now he imitates birds and looks for his bugs through binoculars.

Many people say that the asparagus beetle can't be handpicked because it drops to the ground as soon as it sees you coming. The trick is to place the "picking" container under the beetle first, so that when you move your hand toward the insect, it drops right into the can. Practice makes perfect.

Shaking insects out of hiding is another way to pick them off by the dozens. For small plants, use an old, preferably white, umbrella. Slip it under the plant, then give the plant a couple of shakes or whack it with a stick. When trees are infested, place white sheets under the branches and shake them. You'd be amazed at what the poor tree was putting up with.

WATERWORKS
▼▼▼▼▼▼▼▼▼▼▼▼▼▼▼▼▼▼▼▼▼▼▼▼▼▼▼▼▼

If bugs are assaulting the plants, assault the bugs with the power of water. Give them a liquid eviction notice by turning a strong stream of water from the hose on them. This is especially good for insects that are too small to see or handpick effectively, like aphids, thrips, and spider mites. Water can totally rout a good number of them, and these insects will be unable to get back on the plants to resume their feasting. It can even kill some of them outright. Block any attempts to return to the plant by spraying the ground nearby with soapy water.

Water warfare is fun to do—it may even be therapeutic—and it can't hurt you in a million years. A good, adjustable hose attachment from a hardware store is all it takes. Don't forget to get the undersides of the leaves; that's where most of them will be cowering in fear.

This method is not guaranteed to get all the pests all the time, but it's definitely one of the first things to try. You'll enjoy it, and the plants will, too—and the pests should hate it.

KELP

▼▼▼▼▼▼▼▼▼▼▼▼▼▼▼▼▼▼▼▼▼▼▼▼▼▼▼

A magic bullet in the garden, kelp is an important and undervalued defensive weapon. Composted into the soil, it reportedly adds nutrients like trace elements, plant enzymes, and growth hormones that are difficult to find from other sources. As a mulch, it helps retain moisture while gradually adding nutrients to the soil. Spraying kelp on plants as a foliar fertilizer (a fertilizer absorbed through the leaves) strengthens the leaves, making them more resistant to pests. Kelp provides the plants with the means to develop their own arsenal against pests.

TRAPS

▼▼▼▼▼▼▼▼▼▼▼▼▼▼▼▼▼▼▼▼▼▼▼▼▼▼▼

Traps confound pests and delight tiny game hunters. They bring out the cleverness of the trapper and exploit the greed of the trapee. Traps can be used for flies, moths, yellow jackets, aphids, beetles, slugs and snails, and many more pests. They are a recycler's fantasy, since they can be made from old jars, milk bottles, cans, plastic bags, boards, whatever. Baits can be whipped up from kitchen products such as molasses, fruit, eggs, honey, beer, fish, and meat scraps. Fermenting liquids made from yeast and sugars or fruit also make good baits. Sticky glue products or pans of soapy water become death traps when cleverly manipulated. All it takes is a little imagination and some knowledge about the habits of the pests. For instance, when fruit trees are just starting to bloom, coat pieces of white paper with a sticky substance and hang them in the trees. Later, when the fruit begins to set, use red or orange sticky coated balls and hang them up. You've fooled the fruit tree pests another time.

Homemade traps can be augmented by commercial traps that use chemical attractants (pheromones) for specific pests. These are easily available through a number of mail order sources. You can also contact your local farm advisory or university extension service to ask if pheromones are manufactured for the particular insect you want to trap.

Because many pests are attracted to the color chrome yellow, effective sticky traps can be made from yellow-painted cans hung on stakes around the garden. Coat the cans with a sticky substance like Stikem Special, Tanglefoot, petroleum jelly, or a 50/50 combination of motor oil and STP. The insects will land on the can and get stuck. Instead of coating the can itself with the sticky substance, you can cover the can with a clear plastic bag and put the sticky substance right on the plastic. When the bags are full of bugs, discard them and get fresh sticky-coated bags.

A more ornamental version of this trap can be made by cutting heavy yellow paper into flower shapes, coating them with a sticky material, and "planting" them around the garden.

Some traps work on the principle that many insects are attracted to light. Farmers have even rigged up low-level lights around their duck pens so that the ducks can enjoy the repast of insects drawn to the light. Light traps can be as simple as a light bulb strung up over a pan of soapy water, or they can incorporate fans or black

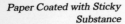

*Paper Coated with Sticky
Substance*

lights and cost money. One that we have tried uses a lighted flashlight placed upright in an empty bucket. On top of the bucket is a large glass bowl or glass pan (larger than the bucket or set on a pane of glass) filled with soapy water. Zeroing in on the light, the moths encounter a soapy demise. Use rechargeable batteries or rig up a light bulb on an extension cord.

Always monitor the traps to make sure they are not catching beneficial insects. Electronic zap traps catch all kinds—good and bad—and for that reason we do not recommend their use outdoors.

BARRIERS

▼▼▼▼▼▼▼▼▼▼▼▼▼▼▼▼▼▼▼▼▼▼▼▼▼▼

Barriers are an undervalued weapon in the battle against pests. They run the gamut, from surrounding the garden with copper stripping to keep out snails to encircling each plant with its own little paper collar to keep out cutworms.

Barriers around tree trunks can be highly effective because many pests in trees

138

either get there by crawling up the trunk or eventually crawl down it. An old method of collecting moths and beetles on tree trunks was called "sugaring." It consisted of mixing stale beer, brown sugar, and crushed bananas in a thick consistency and smearing it on the tree trunk. More recently, tree trunks have been wrapped in cloth or plastic and smeared with grease or a sticky material like Stikem Special or Tanglefoot. Because some insects, like ants, are adept at getting through tiny crevices, the tree is first wrapped in cotton batting. Make sure that the cloth or plastic wrap can grow with the tree or plan to replace it periodically. Sometimes these sticky barriers will be even more effective if placed right on the trunk, but a test should be made on the tree first—some materials damage the bark. Barriers are especially useful in keeping ants away from certain pests, like aphids and scale, which they protect from their natural predators.

Row covers are placed over plants to keep insects away. They are generally used when the plants are first set out in the spring and can be made of old screens bent in half and sealed at the ends. There are also new light fabrics on the market made of spunbonded polyester or polyethylene that let in water, air, and sunshine, while keeping out pernicious flying insects that attempt to lay their eggs on the plants. The entire plant should be covered and the edges of the fabric buried in dirt. The fabric can be set over the plants with enough slack to allow the plants to grow under it.

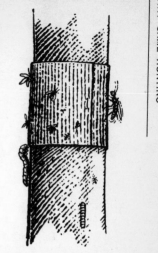

Sticky Barriers around Tree Trunks

SOAPS

▼▼▼▼▼▼▼▼▼▼▼▼▼▼▼▼▼▼▼▼▼▼▼▼▼▼▼

Soaps were once a common weapon for combating insects, both in the home and outdoors, and lately soaps have really come into their own on the shelves of the

139

nurseries. We like them because we've never managed to spray anything in our lives without spraying ourselves. Soap sprays, made from fatty acids, will not hurt us—as long as we don't get them in our eyes.

Insects' outer membranes are very sensitive to these sprays, which seem to make it impossible for them to breathe. Wasps on guard at their nest tumble helplessly to the ground when hit with a soap spray! The soaps also may act to destroy the insects' nervous systems. (No one really understands exactly how they work, however.) We do know that they must be sprayed right onto the insects to kill them. Remember, most insects are found on the undersides of leaves.

Soaps are biodegradable and largely harmless to honeybees, ladybugs, and parasitic wasps who visit the plant later. They are particularly effective on aphids, earwigs, psyllids, sawflies, leaf miners, spider mites, thrips, scale, and whiteflies. Insects may develop resistance to them, however, so use them sparingly.

If you are going to order and release beneficial insects, it is sometimes recommended that you use a soap spray a couple times in the week *before* you disperse the good bugs. That way the predators go farther. On the other hand, if the ladybugs arrive and they've nothing to eat, they're certainly not going to stick around.

Because soaps break down rapidly, they have to be used repeatedly—every few days in some cases. The label will give instructions. Use them when the plants are in morning or afternoon shade. Some soaps should be rinsed off the plant about an hour after using.

Most nurseries carry insecticidal soaps under the brand name Safer. You can buy them concentrated or ready to spray. Commercial soaps have one advantage—they have been formulated to harm plants as little as possible. Homemade soap solutions may burn the plant leaves if the mixture ends up too strong.

We like to use a soap spray made by putting 2 tablespoons of liquid dish soap, like Ivory, into a gallon of water. Some gardeners use soap flakes, Fels Naptha,

Murphy's Oil Soap, Dr. Bronner's liquid soap (made from olive oil and coconut oils), or Basic H, a brand of soap with a vegetable oil base. The same quality that makes soaps effective at cutting grease allows them to cut down wax-coated pests.

Soap can be mixed into other sprays to make them stick to the plants better and to add an extra whammy.

One grower we know mixes Safer soap with fish emulsion and kelp to provide protection, nutrition, and some repellance for his plants. To one gallon of water he adds 2 tablespoons fish emulsion, 2 tablespoons powdered kelp, and 2 tablespoons soap.

Here are a few other double-duty soap sprays:

▲ Lime/Soap Spray

1-2 tablespoons agricultural lime
1 tablespoon soap
2 quarts water

Mix and spray. This is good for aphids and caterpillars, especially the tomato hornworm.

▲ Alcohol/Soap Spray

Soap can also be mixed with rubbing alcohol for extra knock-em-dead action.

1 quart water
2 cups rubbing alcohol
2 teaspoons liquid dish soap

Test the spray on the leaves first to make sure it won't harm them. The alcohol will evaporate quite quickly. Use this spray on scale, mealybugs, whiteflies, and aphids.

HORTICULTURAL OILS

▼▼▼▼▼▼▼▼▼▼▼▼▼▼▼▼▼▼▼▼▼▼▼▼▼▼

Horticultural oils were used successfully for hundreds of years. They went out of common practice when the new chemicals took their place. But not only were the older methods safer, they were effective, too. These oils work particularly well on mealy bugs, aphids, scale, mites, whiteflies, psyllids, and eggs of other pests like leaf rollers and fruit tree moths. They work by suffocating the insect or egg. And you get to destroy the insect *before* it has a chance to do any damage. Insects have not developed resistance to them because they do not survive them, and they do absolutely no harm to people or the environment.

Horticultural oils come in two forms—summer oils and winter oils, so named for the appropriate time of year to use them.

Winter or dormant oils are heavier, slower to evaporate, and meant to be used on dormant trees before the new growth appears in the spring. These oils kill those insects that have been overwintering on the tree.

Summer or superior oils are lighter; they evaporate more readily and thus will not damage the leaves of plants by clogging them. Like dormant oils, they smother pests and their eggs, but they can be used all year round.

Be sure the plant or tree is well watered before you spray. A plant under moisture stress can't take these oils. Don't use the oils if the weather is going to be hotter than ninety degrees, and don't use them on plants that are sensitive. The label on the oil should tell you which plants are suitable for treatment.

▲ Super Oil Spray

You can make a fine spray by mixing an oil with rubbing alcohol. Alcohol kills an insect instantly on contact, whereas oil sticks around and takes care of any eggs.

2 quarts water
2 cups isopropyl alcohol
1 teaspoon horticultural oil (like Volck oil)

Test the spray first on a few branches to make sure the alcohol isn't too strong for the leaves. Use it on the plants daily until the pests are gone.

DUSTS

▼▼▼▼▼▼▼▼▼▼▼▼▼▼▼▼▼▼▼▼▼▼▼▼▼

If you have ever seen an animal giving itself a dust bath, it is probably using the dust as a form of insect control. Dusts are some of the most useful (and underrated) products that can be enlisted in the war against insects, both because of their durable insecticidal properties and their general harmlessness to people. The one precaution that must be followed when using a dust is to wear goggles and a mask, as the dusts can be irritating to eyes and lungs.

Dusts

Here are five of the most common dusts:

DIATOMACEOUS EARTH

Diatomaceous earth is a mined mineral product that consists of remains from fossilized one-celled diatoms that lived thirty million years ago. It kills insects mechanically, not chemically, because its sharp, silica edges puncture their soft, waxy covering. Death is by dehydration. This product is considered safe for humans and is even added to animal feed to control intestinal parasites and worms. It is also used on stored food to deter pests. Birds that eat insects killed by diatomaceous earth are not affected. It can kill individual bees but won't contaminate the hive. Furthermore, it won't kill earthworms.

Diatomaceous earth makes an excellent barrier in gardens, where it deters caterpillars, slugs and snails, borers, leafhoppers, and thrips, among others. In addition to being used as a dust, diatomaceous earth can be applied to plants as a spray. Mix it in water and use it against aphids and spider mites. When the water evaporates, a thin coating of the dust will remain on the leaves. Try not to spray it on blossoms where bees will be landing.

Some people sprinkle diatomaceous earth on manure around barns and stables to keep down the fly population.

Note: Do not use diatomaceous earth that is treated for swimming pool filters. Only use horticultural grade diatomaceous earth. When using it always wear a mask and goggles.

SILICA AEROGEL

The particles in silica aerogel can absorb hundreds of times their weight in moisture. When an insect comes in contact with it, this product absorbs the moisture from the outer surface of the insect's body. Thus the insect dehydrates and dies.

Two commercial products that contain mostly silica aerogel are Dri-die and Drione.

BORIC ACID

Boric acid is similar to other products, like borax, also formulated from boron. Boric acid is one of the most effective and safest ways to kill cockroaches and can also be used for ants, crickets, silverfish, termites, and caterpillars. It was once a common household item, used as eyewash. You can now buy better formulations for use as an insecticide. Remember, it is poisonous to people if ingested.

SULFUR

One of the oldest known pesticides in the world, sulfur is another old-time gardening remedy that has gained new respect. Its use actually goes back thousands of years when the Egyptians fumigated their granaries with it. Homer even wrote about it in the *Iliad*.

Although growers use it for certain plant diseases (mildew, scab, rust, leaf blight, and fruit rot), sulfur is also excellent for controlling mites and chiggers. Additionally, it plays a vital role in plant nutrition and can be used to lower the pH of soil that is too alkaline.

Use sulfur when the temperature is over seventy and under ninety degrees, eighty being ideal. Do not use it within a month or two of spraying horticultural oils.

You can now get it in a powder form for dusting, a wettable powder for spraying, and a liquid spray. If used as a dust, be sure to wear protective clothing, goggles, and a face mask, because it can be quite irritating to mucous membranes.

LIME

This chemical is the name for a compound (calcium carbonate) that comes from limestone, marble, or chalk. Often used to change the pH of the soil to make it more alkaline, it also acts as a good pest repellant or pesticide. Another formulation is called quicklime, or hydrated lime. All draw water out of the insects on contact and thus dehydrate and kill them.

BIOLOGICAL CONTROLS

▼▼▼▼▼▼▼▼▼▼▼▼▼▼▼▼▼▼▼▼▼▼▼▼▼▼▼▼▼

As the saying goes, "My enemy's enemy is my friend." Biological control means using the natural enemies of the pests to fight them. Biological control includes the use of microbes (bacteria, viruses, fungi, protozoa, and nematodes); parasites and parasitoids (parasitic wasps and flies); and predators (beneficial insects or animals). Nature itself keeps organisms in balance in this very way. Without nature's biological controls, insects would take over the earth. Biologist Paul DeBach called biological control, "intellectually satisfying, biologically intriguing, and ecologically rational." More and more, farmers and citizens are turning to biological control, which offers a true alternative to pesticides.

BACTERIAL CONTROLS

Biological control includes the use of disease-causing bacteria to kill the pest. In other words: germ warfare.

Bacillus thuringiensis (B.t.)

Probably the most widely used bacterial insecticide, *Bacillus thuringiensis*, or *B.t.*, occurs naturally. First discovered in 1901 as a silkworm pathogen, it has been widely manufactured since the 1960s and can be purchased under such names as Biotrol, Dipel, or Thuricide. Pathogens like *B.t.* and others are quite selective, so even though they infect hundreds of garden pests, they won't harm plants, animals, humans, or most beneficial insects.

B.t. works very effectively against caterpillars, including armyworms, cabbageworms, cabbage loopers, tent caterpillars, gypsy moths, leaf rollers, and hornworms as well as about two hundred other pests. Since these are some of our most destructive pests, it is only fitting that *B.t.* gives them a deadly flu, paralyzing their digestive systems so they stop eating and die. And a little nibble of a leaf treated with *B.t.* is enough to get a lethal dose.

B.t. only works as a stomach poison, so it has to be eaten. The caterpillars must be in the leaf-chewing stage—not the moth or butterfly stage.

Another formulation of *B.t.*, *B.t.i*, has been found to be successful against mosquito larvae, one of the major pest problems of the world.

Milky Spore Disease

Milky spore is the common name for *Bacillus popilliae*, a naturally occurring bacterium that wipes out the grubs of Japanese beetles, rose chafers, and May/June beetles, among others. The grubs ingest the spores as they move through the soil. This disease causes their normally clear blood to turn milky, thus the name. As they sicken and die, they release millions more spores. Although it can take a few years to get established in a lawn, the treatment is self-perpetuating and can last for fifteen to twenty years. The trick is to get all your neighbors to use it, too, so that their beetles don't come wandering onto your grass.

GROWTH REGULATORS AND PHEROMONES

Another example of biological control involves using the insects' own hormones and sex attractant chemicals to maim, trap, confuse, and otherwise stymie them. For instance, a juvenile hormone for fleas, *methoprene*, has been isolated and is now being used successfully to keep these insects from ever attaining their fertile maturity. Ask around for exterminators who use this Peter Pan treatment instead of more toxic insecticides.

Scents secreted by insects as sex attractants are called *pheromones*. The reason insects know when to arrive at the cabbage patch at just the right moment is because they can pick up odors with their powerful sense of smell when they are in the neighbor's yard and even farther downwind. Many insects that live in isolation—and don't see well enough to case the joint visually for possible mates—are highly dependent on their pheromones to find each other so they can reproduce.

Pheromones can be quite effective when used in traps to catch otherwise elusive and cagey critters. Or they can be sprayed or used without traps to confound and confuse mates trying to find one another. They are also providing scientists with challenging problems: One scientist, Dr. Robert Yamamoto, spent nine months "milking" ten thousand virgin female cockroaches to get 1/2,500 of an ounce of their sex attractant so that it could be synthesized in the lab. Good work, Doctor.

PARASITES, PARASITOIDS, AND PREDATORS

Parasites, parasitoids, and predators are the living troops under the wise command of the tiny game hunter. Not that we issue commands—they merely follow the dictates of their own life forces, which decree that others must die so they can live. Parasites and parasitoids generally attack only one specific victim. For instance, one tiny wasp, a parasitoid, only goes after the alfalfa seed weevil.

Predators are insects or animals that get their nourishment from devouring other creatures. Simple cogs in the food chain, they take on a superior status when they eat the insects we call pests. Most predators eat many, many insects in the course of their life span, and their appetites can be amazing. Toads can eat three thousand insects a month. Predators also attack a great number of species. Some are so broad and nonspecific in their tastes that they even eat their own kind. Our favorite image of the insect predator comes from a description in *Fabre's Book of Insects*—a praying mantis that captured a wasp which had itself just captured a honey bee. Even as the wasp was being crunched and devoured by the mantis, it continued to lick the honey from the bee it had captured.

See *Good Bugs* for examples of the best commercially available predators for the garden, and for guidelines on how to identify, appreciate, and protect these insects who work so hard, so unwittingly, and so selfishly for us all.

Aphidius Wasp Parasitizes
Only Aphids

BOTANICALS

▼▼▼▼▼▼▼▼▼▼▼▼▼▼▼▼▼▼▼▼▼▼▼▼▼▼

Plants have evolved chemical defenses against insects for millions of years. In fact, pesticides made from plants having insecticidal properties were commonly used before chemical insecticides usurped their place in the gardener's arsenal. A classic botanical is made from tobacco.

Just because they are made from plants, however, doesn't mean they are safe.

We actually consider these botanical pesticides to be last resort. Some are harmful to fish and other aquatic life, and so they should never be used around bodies of water. Furthermore, some are also harmful to honey bees. So if you do use one, spray in the evening after the honey bees have departed. They are not always considered safe for humans, either, and have to be used with care. A good rule of thumb is to hold off on these unless more than 25 percent of the plant's leaves have been damaged.

On the brighter side, they do work. They break down easily in the environment, and are not stored in living tissues. Although some poison fish, they don't pose a danger to future generations of humans and wildlife.

Be familiar with the names of these botanicals so that you can buy them instead of the much more dangerous pesticides. Often there is nothing on the label to differentiate them. If you do purchase a botanical, make sure it hasn't been mixed with other chemical pesticides. Sometimes they are.

NEEM

The neem (margosa) tree is an evergreen tropical plant known for its insecticidal properties. It grows in Asia, Malaysia, the African tropics, Florida, and southern California. We advise anyone living where this tree grows to plant one immediately! Termites won't eat the wood. The insecticides produced from the extracts of the tree are known to repel or disrupt the development of at least 150 insects, including leaf miners, grasshoppers, Japanese beetles, Mexican bean beetles, aphids, gypsy moths, and thrips. Because it is both a repellant and an insecticide, insects stand a lesser chance of developing resistance to it, and it doesn't seem to harm beneficial insects. The fruit produces an oil traditionally used as folk medicine in Asia for hundreds of years. In this country look for it under the name Margosan-O.

ROTENONE

A stomach poison for insects, rotenone is made from extracts of tropical plants—mainly derris and cube—and has been used for centuries in Asia and South America. It can be dusted (wearing a mask and goggles) or sprayed to control beetles, caterpillars, weevils, borers, and others. It kills a wide range of pests, but it is also toxic to fish, frogs, toads, and bees. Of all the botanicals it is probably the most toxic to humans, so think of it as a last resort. Care must be taken to apply it after dusk when bees are no longer active. It breaks down in the environment after three to seven days and may not be as effective if mixed with alkaline water.

SABADILLA

An organic pesticide made from a South American lily, sabadilla has been used since the sixteenth century. This same plant has also been used for years to lower blood pressure, so people on blood pressure medication should avoid it. It is a contact killer and is toxic to bees and fish—do not apply it where runoff may occur. When applying it as a dust, use a mask and goggles and avoid skin contact. It works well on hard-to-kill insects, especially when applied directly onto the bug. In sunshine it breaks down in about two days.

PYRETHRUM

Pyrethrum comes from the dried flowers of a daisy plant, *Chrysanthemum cinerariifolium*, which grows in Kenya. The plant was once called the insect flower or insect plant and is thought to have been used hundreds of years ago by the Per-

151

sians against body lice. This is one of the safest of all botanical insecticides, because it breaks down very quickly. Nor have insects developed a resistance to it. It can be used as a contact and stomach poison as well as a repellant against flies, roaches, termites, aphids, fleas, thrips, leafhoppers, whiteflies, and some kinds of beetles. At the same time, it is so safe for people that it used to be dispensed by doctors for intestinal worms. However, bees and ladybugs are killed along with the pests, so take care when using it.

Pyrethrum has a fast knockdown effect, which is good when you think the bugs have had enough and you want them to stop eating immediately. Sometimes, however, the bugs are only paralyzed, and they manage to recover.

Pyrethrum is often combined with synthetic pesticides because of its quick action. Do not buy any of these products.

You can make pyrethrum by growing your own chrysanthemums—but only the species *cinerariifolium*. Gather the flower heads and dry them in an oven set at the lowest temperature or in the sun spread out on newspapers. Grind the dried flowers in a coffee grinder. Add water to this powder to make a paste. Add ⅓ cup paste to 1 quart water, then strain it into a spray bottle.

This plant has been known to cause an allergic reaction in some people—the same people who get hay fever may be sensitive to pyrethrum.

RYANA

Made from the roots of a South American plant, this botanical was discovered in the early 1940s and has proved good for control of coddling moths in apple, pear, and quince trees. Sometimes it doesn't really kill the pests but puts them into a kind of nonfeeding stupor.

NICOTINE

Nicotine is an old, old botanical spray. It can be purchased as a dust, or a spray can be made from the tobacco plant (especially the stems) or even from plug tobacco, cigars, or strong cigarettes. Regardless of what cigarette companies say, nicotine is highly toxic; even though it breaks down fairly quickly, it is one of the most toxic insecticides mentioned in this book, and we strongly recommend doing without it. The nicotine sulfate form is less toxic. Nicotine can also be used as a pesticide in its smoke form. (See *Houseplants*.) Although most insects—except the tobacco hornworm—avoid eating this plant, it is never mentioned as a repellant plant for the garden. Perhaps most gardeners disapprove of it.

REPELLANTS
▼▼▼▼▼▼▼▼▼▼▼▼▼▼▼▼▼▼▼▼▼▼▼▼▼▼▼▼

The following formulas are for sprays referred to in the individual "bad bug" sections. Some of these sprays are so repellant they kill the insects.

Many plants have their own brand of chemicals that combat or resist insect attack, and some of our sprays use those properties. Adding dish soap or a little vegetable oil (1 teaspoon to a quart of liquid) to the spray makes it stick to the plant better. Soap will also coat the bodies of the insects and kill them even faster.

Some of these repellants are made from plants like garlic and onion that we use to flavor our own food. It's hard to believe that insects find them that awful. Others, like quassia spray have an intense bitterness and make more sense to us. A different kind of repellant is made by adding 2 tablespoons of artificial vanilla to a quart of

Onion

water and spraying it around the stems of squash and cucumber plants. It masks the innate bitter smell of the plant that attracts the insects in the first place.

Note: Repellants need to be reapplied after a good rain or overhead watering.

Don't worry too much about using the exact ingredients for these sprays. As with cooking, adjust them to suit you. Many require straining, which can be done well through old panty hose or coffee filter paper. Dish soap is best.

▲ Bug Juice

There is some controversy about this concoction—probably because it is so inherently disgusting. It certainly gives you something to do with all the insects you handpick or vacuum off your plants.

For this spray, use an old blender that has been *permanently* retired from the kitchen. Fill it about halfway with bugs (about 2 cups) and add enough water to cover well. Grind them and strain. Dilute this essence of dead bug concentrate with water at a ratio of 1 to 10. You can freeze the unused concentrate, but don't let anybody mistake it for soup stock.

Some people say it only takes a few bugs to make an effective spray—less than a handful. Don't pick a bug that has been obviously parasitized, but if you see one that is diseased, by all means use it. *Bacillus thuringiensis* (*B.t.*), the widely used insecticide that infects its victims with a deadly bacteria, was originally concocted from infected caterpillars.

When you have a serious infestation of a particular insect, try taking a few of those bugs from the plants they are eating, then grind them up and make a spray to rout the rest of them. Some people have made a spray from ground-up slugs and water, but even for avid tiny game hunters like us this is tough to do.

Bug Juice

The following sprays can be used on any kind of plant that needs rescuing from a pest attack.

▲ Buttermilk Spray

1 cup flour
4 tablespoons buttermilk
1 gallon water

Make a paste of the flour and a little water before adding the rest of the liquid. If the infestation is small, paint the mixture on the leaves instead of spraying. This is good for spider mites, so be sure to get it underneath the leaves.

▲ Mish-Mash Spray

A good, general repellant spray with a little something distasteful for everyone. This is especially good for cabbage loopers, imported cabbageworms, and other caterpillars.

1 cup spearmint leaves
1 cup onion tops
½ cup hot red peppers
1 small horseradish plant—roots and leaves
1 quart water plus some for processing
¼ cup liquid soap

Grind these in a blender or food processor with enough water to liquefy. Add the 1 quart of water and the liquid dish soap. This is the base, and it should be refriger-

155

ated. When you want to use it, add ½ cup to 1 quart water and strain into a spray bottle.

▲ Tomato Leaf Spray

Tomato leaves have insecticidal properties, which can be explained by the fact that they are related to the tobacco plant.

**2 cups tomato leaves and stems
1 quart water**

Chop plant parts coarsely and process in a blender with 2 cups water. Let the mess stand overnight. Strain and add 2 more cups water, then spray on your plants. Excellent for aphids.

▲ Hot Pepper Spray

New York transit officials once tried using hot pepper on turnstiles to keep teenagers from sucking out the tokens. We use it to keep chewing insects like tomato hornworms and other caterpillars from enjoying our plants. It is also good for cucumber beetles.

**½ cup hot peppers
2 quarts water
1 tablespoon liquid soap**

Mix the peppers and 2 cups of the water in a blender. Let stand overnight, then strain and add the rest of the water and the soap.

This can also be made with ¼ cup of dried red pepper, the hotter the better. It's

Hot Peppers

better to dissolve the ground pepper in boiling water first; then let it cool before spraying.

Another way to make use of red pepper's incendiary properties is to dampen plants with a mist of water (or wait for a dew) and sprinkle the plants directly with powdered hot red pepper. It will not harm the plants.

This treatment is good for caterpillars, cabbageworms, and ants, among others.

▲ Garlic Spray

Garlic has wonderful repellant qualities, as anyone who has been around someone with a penchant for eating raw garlic on toast knows. Besides planting garlic—a lovely plant—around the garden, you can use it as a seed dressing to keep birds and rodents away. Dampen the seeds before planting and sprinkle with garlic powder. Try this on bulbs, which mice sometimes like to nibble on. Garlic powder can be substituted for fresh garlic in these recipes.

More than a repellant, garlic also works as an insecticide and has been proven to kill large numbers of mosquitoes, aphids, and onion flies when used as an emulsion with oil.

3 whole garlic bulbs (not cloves)
3 tablespoons mineral or olive oil
3 cups warm water
1 tablespoon liquid soap

Separate the cloves of garlic, but you needn't bother to peel them. Chop in a food processor. Put them in a jar with the oil and let stand for 24 hours. Add water and liquid soap. Store in the refrigerator in a glass jar. When ready to use, strain and

157

dilute with water (½ cup concentrate to 1 quart water). Spray on plants to kill or repel cutworms, wireworms, slugs, and whiteflies.

▲ Onion Juice Spray

3 onions
4 cups water

Take onions and cover them with water in a blender or food processor. Grind as fine as possible, strain, and spray. Good for aphids, mites, flea beetles, sowbugs, and pillbugs.

▲ Hot Pepper/Onion/Garlic Spray

This spray operates under the assumption that if one is good, three ought to be better.

2 hot peppers
1 onion
6 cloves garlic
4 cups water
1 teaspoon liquid soap

Making Hot Pepper Spray

Grind these all in a blender or food processor with the water. Let stand for 24 hours, then strain and add liquid soap. Spray on plants. You can substitute 2 teaspoons hot red pepper (cayenne pepper may not be hot enough) for the fresh hot peppers.

▲ Garlic/Pepper Spray

1 garlic bulb (not clove)
1 tablespoon hot red pepper
1 quart water

Take garlic bulb and chop well. Add hot red pepper and water. Let steep for 1 hour. Strain and spray. Good for aphids and spider mites.

▲ Glue Spray

This will really stick it to them. Use ordinary liquid paper glue or rabbit's skin glue (from an art supply store).

3 or 4 cups warm water
1 tablespoon glue

Mix and spray on plants to make the leaves inedible and to coat insects' bodies and suffocate them. Use it against scale and mites. As the glue dries, it flakes off the plant and the dead insects tag along. Some people use a spray-on adhesive—this works but is detrimental to the ozone layer!

▲ Quassia Spray

Quassia may be one of the safest of all botanical sprays. It harms soft-bodied pests like caterpillars and aphids but won't hurt bees and ladybugs.

1 pound quassia chips (available from mail order sources and some garden supply centers)

159

1 gallon water

Take quassia chips and cover with water. Let soak overnight. Strain. Dilute with water at a ratio of 1 to 10, adding a little dish soap to the spray water.

▲ **Wormwood Spray**

This is like making a tea, and the method can be used with any plants you want to make a repellant spray from.

2 cups wormwood leaves
2 cups boiling water
2 quarts water

Cover wormwood leaves with the boiling water. Let steep for 1 hour. Strain and add to 2 quarts of water. Spray at once. Wormwood is very, very bitter, and insects like flea beetles and cabbageworms don't like the taste of it.

Other plants to make a tea spray from:

Rhubarb leaves: Note: Poisonous if eaten because they contain high concentrations of oxalic acid. That is why people eat the stems and not the leaves of this plant. But no point letting the leaves go to waste.
Coriander: Good for aphids.
Chinaberry leaves: This tree is well known for its insecticidal properties.
Tansy: A strong tasting herb once used as a salt substitute. (It is not recommended for eating because it is mildly poisonous.) Ants, Japanese beetles, flies, striped cucumber beetles, and squash bugs dislike it.

Other plants and herbs include elderberry leaves, eucalyptus, pennyroyal (for ants), cedarwood, sassafras (for aphids), rose geranium, lavender, bay laurel, fever-few (sometimes confused with pyrethrum), mint (for aphids and ants), and onion skins.

▲ Limonoid Spray

According to *Science News*, limonoids have been found to deter agricultural pests such as the fall armyworm and the cotton bollworm. If you make orange juice or, even better, grapefruit juice, save the peels and all the seeds. Chop them up and pour boiling water over them to release the limonoids. Blend the mixture in a food processor, let stand overnight, then strain, dilute, and spray on plants. It has good repellant properties and will keep certain pests, especially caterpillars and beetle larvae, from eating the plants.

▲ Essential Oils

In *Gardening Without Poisons*, Beatrice Trum Hunter wrote of the insect-killing properties of essential oils, like oil of lemon grass, mint, coriander, geranium, laven-der, and sage. Mix these oils with water and use in place of botanical tea sprays.

WILD TINY GAME HUNTERS

Inviting wildlife into the garden by creating a welcome habitat has become something of a vogue. We have long recognized movement in the garden as a source of beauty and created it with fountains. But movement also comes from a hummingbird darting into sight, a bee crawling over a flower, the hop of a frog. Make your garden more beautiful with living things. And the wildlife you welcome will also become your allies as tiny game hunters.

These predators are not usually attracted to perfectly manicured gardens. They do better where the grass is a little longer and there is plenty of native vegetation, a small rock or woodpile to hide in, a pond to hunt around, a few dead branches for nests, and a working compost heap in which to forage for bugs. They also need a good variety of plants, trees, and shrubs. These should take up at least half of any given yard in relation to the lawn area. Consider planting "islands" of native shrubs, tall grasses, and small trees right in the middle of the lawn. And don't use any chemicals on the grass. These are deadly to birds and other wildlife.

Here are some of the wild tiny game hunters that you will want to welcome:

LIZARDS

▼▼▼▼▼▼▼▼▼▼▼▼▼▼▼▼▼▼▼▼▼▼▼▼▼

Lizards love insects, just love them. The only trouble is, cats love lizards, and cat owners permit all too many cats to roam around. Cats eat birds, too, so their presence can be a deterrent in a garden that would accommodate wildlife. We know of one gardener who conditioned the neighborhood cats to stay out of his yard by luring them into metal traps baited with tuna fish and then turning the hose on them.

Lizards have a few advantages over snakes—they don't frighten people, and they don't eat toads. If you live in a temperate climate, you can buy certain kinds of lizards, like chameleons, from pet stores and release them in the yard. Get a pair of them; they may reproduce.

Other lizards can be caught in the wild with the use of an insect net, then put into bags and brought home. Approach them very slowly and cautiously so as not to frighten them.

SNAKES

▼▼▼▼▼▼▼▼▼▼▼▼▼▼▼▼▼▼▼▼▼▼▼▼

We do not admit to any great love of snakes, but because they are so useful and eat so many rats, mice, and insect pests, we have to put them in the hall of fame of tiny game hunters. There are more than two hundred species in North America. Only four kinds (rattlesnakes, copperheads, water moccasins, and coral snakes) are potentially harmful to humans. All snakes, including the poisonous ones, are constantly at work for us cutting down pest populations. It's a pity so many snakes are killed on sight out of fear and ignorance.

163

Bull snakes and gopher snakes eat gophers and do an adequate job of controlling them in the wild. When housing goes up in an area, however, snakes tend to disappear, leaving the gophers free rein. Garter snakes are a great ally in the garden because they feed so readily on slugs. However, they also eat earthworms and frogs. King snakes are especially useful, because in addition to feeding on rodents, they also kill poisonous snakes.

TOADS

▼▼▼▼▼▼▼▼▼▼▼▼▼▼▼▼▼▼▼▼▼▼▼▼▼▼▼▼

Like snakes, spiders, and bats, toads have been vilified and associated with witchcraft and evil in ways they don't deserve. Toads eat hundreds of insects every night. One toad will eat ten to fifteen thousand bugs in a season. As Ruth Shaw Ernst wrote in *The Naturalist's Garden*: "If there is a toad on your property, cherish it. There is nothing a toad relishes more for breakfast, lunch, or dinner than a slug, unless it is a caterpillar, cutworm, or other horrid grub."

Like snakes, toads and frogs only eat insects that move. Sometimes a toad and its prey will play a waiting game of eerie stillness. As soon as the quarry moves, the toad's tongue darts out so fast you can hardly see the insect disappear. Toads eat mosquitoes and termites as well as standard garden pests.

Toads can be mistaken for frogs, which also consume insects. Basically, frogs have much longer hind legs and jump around energetically, while toads seem more lethargic. In fact, toads are so slow, they can be quite vulnerable around a power mower. Frogs have smoother skins than their bump-covered cousins, and they look wetter. They also need to live closer to water.

People often import toads into their garden for tiny game hunting chores—cer-

Toad

tainly more frequently than they bring in snakes. For one thing, toads are fairly easy to catch in the wild near ponds. When you bring one home, it may have to be kept in a cage or an upside-down crate for a while until it loses its homing instinct. Try to capture a young one, as it will be more likely to settle in. While it's in its cage, provide it with plenty of live insects either handpicked from the garden or purchased from a pet store.

Toads do best if they have access to a shallow pool with a sandy bottom. If you can't provide one, make sure they have a shallow pan of water or a ground level birdbath in a shady place. Toads and frogs don't drink water but absorb it through their skin. They also need moisture to breathe. If you want the toad to breed, it will need a small pond.

Provide your toad-in-residence with shady moist havens around the yard. An overturned clay pot sunk into the ground makes a nice toad house. Chip a hole in the clay for a doorway. Or dig out a special toad hole for your new friend a few inches deep and covered with a board or encased with rocks. Put sandy soil in the bottom to make the little creature comfy. A small piece of concrete drainpipe can be used for the entranceway.

Rigging up a low-watt light or a footpath light and having it on for several hours after dark will attract insects for the toad's delight. Place it near low vegetation to give the toad a place to lie in ambush. Some toads have inhabited gardens for dozens of years.

BIRDS

▼▼▼▼▼▼▼▼▼▼▼▼▼▼▼▼▼▼▼▼▼▼▼▼▼▼▼▼▼

Before the turn of the century, farmers firmly believed that birds were eating their crops and could not be persuaded that many were only eating insects. As a result, many beneficial birds were shot almost to extinction by the late 1800s. In fact, the passenger pigeon and the Eskimo curlew were totally exterminated.

Today it is common knowledge that birds are among the most important predators of insects. Swallows have been observed eating hundreds of leafhoppers in a day, and a house wren will feed a hundred bugs to its young in one afternoon. Without birds, our insect infestations would be greatly magnified. Therefore, it makes sense to try to welcome as many birds as possible onto your property (unless they are crows, which feed on baby songbirds).

Birds can be greatly encouraged to visit a garden by providing them with water, food, and shelter. A shallow birdbath can be placed out in the open where the birds can't be ambushed by the local cats. Be sure to find one with a rough surface; the smooth ones don't permit a good footing. Birds are attracted by a fine spray of water or dripping water, so prop a slowly dripping hose over the birdbath. Or make a small hole in a bucket, fill it with water, and hang it over a galvanized pan or a metal garbage can lid set on bricks. The sound will attract birds from far away.

Another way to welcome birds is to provide them with a dust bath. Birds probably

Birdbath

keep down their own vermin (mites and lice) by frequenting dust baths—they also enjoy them. Dig out a spot about three feet square and six inches deep and line it with bricks or stones. Fill it with a mixture of equal parts sand, loam, and sifted ash. Put it where you can enjoy watching them frolic, which is quite a treat.

The purple martin is one of the best insect eaters. The best way to attract them is to build a martin house—or martin condos. Some people build a whole row of them. Put up a variety of houses and nesting boxes. Many books contain plans for making birdhouses. You can also find them in mail order sources.

Some birds do best if they build their own nests, so provide them with materials like hair, string, yarn (four to eight inches long), feathers, or cotton rags. Tack them to bird feeders or place them in a box and hang it from a tree. Don't put out bright-colored material, as the nests are best if camouflaged.

Feeding birds will also bring more of them into the area. But, once you start to feed them, consider it a commitment, because the birds will come to depend on you. A bird feeder can be as simple as a wooden tray with sides, nailed onto a post. Like the birdbath, it should be out in the open so the birds can see approaching predators. Nail sheet metal onto the post to make an upside-down funnel to keep cats or squirrels from climbing up.

In addition to commercial birdseed, birds like black oil sunflower seeds, peanuts in the shell, cracked corn, thistle seed, dried fruit, bread crumbs, peanut butter mixed with cornmeal, and millet. The more kinds of food, the greater the variety of birds you're going to see.

Hang up a suet feeder in a fruit tree to attract woodpeckers, who will eat the caterpillars. Many birds like suet, which is fat from meat and available from butchers or the supermarket. Suet can be put into net bags or melted and poured into a coconut shell and hung in the tree.

Sometimes birds wear out their welcome when they won't leave your cherry tree alone. They may be eating cherries, however, because they are thirsty. Giving them water may be a solution. Spraying your cherries with a mild solution of saltwater will also deter them.

If you want to keep birds away from your sweet berries, provide them with tart berry bushes, which they actually prefer. They love chokecherries, dogwood, elderberries, gooseberries, hackberries, huckleberries, barberries, mulberries, and shadbush.

One method used in the eighteenth century to keep birds out of the kitchen garden was to rig a big bell on a pole and attach a cord that came all the way into the house. Then, whoever happened to pass by would give the rope a yank to ring the bell and startle off the birds.

If you think the birds are taking an unfair share of your corn, give them the benefit of the doubt. They may be after the corn earworms instead. Put paper cups on the ears just in case. When the corn is tempting them, be sure the bird feeders are full. You can also soak unpopped popcorn overnight and throw it on the ground around the corn for the birds.

Netting thrown over trees and strawberries will keep birds out. Timing is important: Put the netting on before the fruit is ripe so the birds don't have a chance to discover what they are missing. Because it is so hard to cover certain trees with netting, some people simply use heavy strong black thread, tossing a spool back and forth over the branches until a good amount of thread crisscrosses the tree. Birds dislike getting entangled in it.

Other items that can be hung in trees to repel birds include sliced onions, empty milk cartons, inflatable plastic owls or snakes, pinwheels, thin strips of black plastic stapled to paper plates, and crumpled balls of aluminum foil. Alternate these materials, as the birds become accustomed to them fairly quickly.

In the past, people would hang a stuffed hawk in a tree or put out potatoes with feathers stuck in them. We know one fellow who hangs a dead crow up in a tree and keeps other crows at bay.

To keep birds out of the strawberry patch, cut up an old garden hose into two- or three-foot lengths and place these around the plants. The idea is to fool the birds into thinking the hose is a snake. Plastic snakes or old cassette tape can be strewn around the plants, too.

To keep birds out of certain sections of the garden, create a maze of stakes and connect them with string. Tie or fasten strips of cloth or aluminum foil streamers to the string. The foil crackling in the breeze is both a visual and an audible deterrent.

Don't forget, birds will eat ten times as many insects as they will other types of food, so sharing some fruit with them may be a good price to pay for their presence.

Planting specifically for birds is one thing that homeowners can do to counteract the frightening and very real loss of their habitat, caused by never-ending development. Large acreage farming has also led to the loss of vital fencerows and woodlots for birds. Here are some of the plantings especially favored by birds:

Shrubs and small trees: Bayberry, cottoneaster, juniper, hawthorn, yews, mountain ash, and verbena.

Vines: Bittersweet, greenbrier, honeysuckle, Virginia creeper, and wild grape.

Trees: Alder, American elm, ash, birch, cedar, crab apple, hawthorn, juniper, maple, Norway spruce, oak, persimmon, pine, red cedar, and white spruce.

Flowers: Aster, bachelor's button, black-eyed Susan, California poppy, calendula, chrysanthemum, columbine, cosmos, marigold, pink, statice, and sunflower.

BATS

▼▼▼▼▼▼▼▼▼▼▼▼▼▼▼▼▼▼▼▼▼▼▼▼▼▼

If birds were considered pests in the fields, bats were thought to be the devil incarnate and as such have been treated far worse. And for much longer, too. We are only just beginning to reverse our long-standing prejudices against these odd and marvelous little mammals, the only ones that fly. Bats are the most important predators of night-flying insects. A good-sized colony of about 250,000 can eat two to four tons of insects each night. Besides being among the best tiny game hunters we know, bats pollinate vital plants and disperse seeds, mostly in tropical forests. Frankly, we need bats.

When birds go to sleep, the bats come out—and remember, this is when mosquitoes get on the move. One bat may eat up to 4,000 mosquitoes in a night—that's a lot of prevented mosquito bites! When habitats for bats were deliberately created in San Antonio, Texas, in 1917, the bats practically eliminated malarial mosquitoes from the area.

Bat with Prey

170

Because they breed very slowly and tend to congregate in large numbers, bats have been extremely vulnerable. With great folly, they have been shot, poisoned, burned, and dynamited by the millions. Pesticides have taken as great a toll on bats as prejudice, and DDT and other insecticides have exterminated untold numbers.

Fortunately, an organization called **Bat Conservation International** has done a great deal to educate people about the true value of bats. Many believe that bats pose a great menace because of rabies and, although some are infected and no bat should ever be touched with bare hands, dogs with rabies create far more problems for humans than bats do.

Bats sometimes set up housekeeping in the attics of homes for the warmth and shelter provided there. They should not be tolerated, however, because of problems with odors, roaches, and mites. Nevertheless, it is not true that the only way to get bats out of a house is to burn the house down. Furthermore, using pesticides to get rid of them only risks poisoning the residents.

Bats can be effectively excluded by figuring out which holes they are entering and exiting from. Then bird netting can be tacked over the hole. The netting should be larger than the hole and left open at the bottom. That way the bats can leave, but they can't get back inside. Do this when there is no danger of baby bats being stuck inside the dwelling to die. The young are generally left in the roost from late May to July at night while the adults go hunting. Once all the bats have been excluded, seal up the holes.

If you find a bat in a room of the house, don't panic. They are one of the most gentle animals on earth. Keeping the bat in sight at all times, close all the doors to other rooms, and open as many windows and doors to the outside as possible. The bat may leave when it detects the currents of fresh air. You can trap it by putting a can or box over it and sliding cardboard underneath. Do not touch it unless you are wearing heavy gloves.

Bat House

171

Many people have begun to put up bat houses to attract these animals to their neighborhood. This has been done with great success in Europe for many decades. It is a way to make up for the loss of bat habitats through urbanization. You can order a bat house from Bat Conservation International (BCI). (See *Mail Order*.) It is specifically designed to meet the bats' need to roost in tight crevices. BCI also sells inexpensive plans for making your own bat house.

People have had the greatest success when houses are placed near bodies of water, on tree trunks between ten and twenty-five feet high, and facing east or southeast. Some people have reported that after putting up a house, the bats were literally lined up on the tree waiting to get in. Others have found that it can take as long as a year or two for the house to be occupied. But the reward of having the bats hunting for tiny game, night after night, certainly makes it worthwhile to welcome and protect them.

GOOD BUGS

The average square yard in a typical garden contains more than a thousand insects. They can't all be gluttonous garden destroyers, or we'd have only plain bare dirt. Actually, less than 1 percent of all insects are considered pests, and virtually all have predators and parasites of their own to contend with. Insects have always done a much better job of controlling other insects by eating them than we have done with poison. At any rate, get to know your bugs—and stop killing the wrong ones.

The idea of deliberately manipulating insects for pest control is not a new one. In 1800, Charles Darwin's grandfather, Erasmus Darwin, suggested deliberately breeding lacewings and ladybirds to control aphids. At the time, people didn't take him up on it, but today the idea has become a reality. Suppliers of beneficial bugs are doing business all over the country. Take advantage of them. Not only will they send you the right insect for the job, many of them also give advice on the best way to manage particular problems. (See *Mail Order* for list of suppliers.)

When ordering and using beneficial insects, do not use any residual pesticides (such as malathion or kelthane) for at least a month before the "good guys" are brought in. The predatory bugs seem to be much more vulnerable to pesticides than the pests. While waiting for the garden to detox, use insecticidal soaps or homemade sprays.

There are several ways to make a garden more attractive to desirable insects. Many of these predators feed on nectar and honeydew while in the adult stage, so plant flowers among the vegetables to give them something to eat. Flowering plants that beneficial insects seem to enjoy include daisies, sunflowers, black-eyed Susan, oleander, and yarrow. Jerusalem artichoke, strawflower, and evening primrose also give encouragement and good harborage, as do plants like wild carrot, parsnip, anise, and angelica. Damselflies like the shelter of a nice nasturtium blossom. Parasitic wasps, who have the tiniest of tongues, need the smaller blossoms of herbs and flowers like wild Queen Anne's lace, coriander, dill, fennel, lovage, and parsley.

When your bugs arrive, follow the directions for their release. They generally prefer a garden with high moisture or some access to water droplets. A two thousand-square-foot garden should have at least four or five permanent sources of moisture. Pans filled with water will do. Change them daily, of course, to keep the mosquito wrigglers out.

A solution of honey and water can be sprayed on plants to supplement the predators' craving for sweets. Commercial preparations of nectar-type food, such as Bio-Control Honeydew and Wheast, are available from mail order sources.

GREEN LACEWINGS

▼▼▼▼▼▼▼▼▼▼▼▼▼▼▼▼▼▼▼▼▼▼▼▼▼▼

This glorious insect with its golden eyes and long diaphanous wings looks incredibly fragile but is one of the most practical and effective of the beneficial insects. A much-admired insect, it looks like an exotic pet for a fairy kingdom.

Some adult lacewings feed on insects, but most feed on honeydew. Their larvae, however, have voracious appetites and eat aphids with such gusto they are called aphid lions. (The larvae of the brown lacewing are called aphid wolves.) They also devour other soft-bodied insects like red spider mites (another favorite), mealybugs, thrips, and scale and the eggs of many worms.

Like ladybug larvae, lacewing larvae resemble little alligators with pincers. They use these hollow mandibles to impale their prey and suck out its juices. Some of them then toss the carcass remains onto their backs.

So greedy are lacewings, they have a tendency to cannibalism. The female lays each egg on the end of a fine, hairlike strand, thereby separating them at birth and preventing this unfortunate occurrence.

When you order lacewings, they will arrive as eggs packed in a feeding material such as rice hulls, in case they should hatch. They are so tiny you may need a magnifying glass to see them; a thimble would hold thousands. If you detect any movement at all, the eggs are hatching, so disperse them right away or they might eat each other up. If you can't release them immediately (and it's not a good idea to do so if rain is imminent), they can be refrigerated for a few days to delay their hatching.

Sprinkle the eggs on foliage around the garden on a warm day wherever pests are present. The lacewings can travel up to a hundred feet in search of food. They may be better at finding potential pest problems than you are.

To hold them in the garden, make sure the adult lacewings are supplied with nectar, honeydew, or pollen. Otherwise they will up and leave without even thanking you for paying the postage.

Lacewing Eggs

Lacewing Eating Aphid

175

LADYBUGS

▼▼▼▼▼▼▼▼▼▼▼▼▼▼▼▼▼▼▼▼▼▼▼▼▼▼▼▼

Convergent Ladybird

Vedalia

Two-Stabbed Lady Beetle

Two-Spotted Lady Beetle

We all know about ladybirds, ladybugs, or lady beetles (which is what they really are). By now we all know they are supposed to fly away home so they can eat up all our aphids for us, instead of dawdling about on our hands and fingers letting us count their spots. (Incidentally, some species will bite humans—but not hard enough to do damage.)

There are around four hundred species in North America, of which the *convergent lady beetle* is one of our most important predators. They love to eat aphids but also devour scale insects, leafhoppers, thrips, eggs, and the larvae of harmful insects, including many moths. Another ladybug, the *Vedalia* beetle, achieved fame when it was imported from Australia in the late 1880s and successfully saved the California citrus industry from devastation by the cottony cushion scale. After a disastrous wipeout by DDT in the 1940s, the insect is back at work in the orchards today.

Their orange eggs, which are laid under leaves and can be seen standing on end in clumps of five to fifty, hatch in the spring. The larvae resemble tiny, black, spiny alligators with orange spots, and they may eat about four hundred aphids as they grow up. An adult ladybug can go on to eat thousands, insinuating its body into tight little buds and other places sprays can't reach. It may produce several generations of predaceous offspring in one summer.

When you release ladybugs, do it in the evening in a well-sprinkled garden; they are less likely to fly away at night. Handle them gently, for too much agitation causes them to fly to safety. Place them at the base of plants, but not too many at one spot—a tablespoon per plant or shrub will suffice. They can be stored in the refrigerator for two weeks and doled into the garden a few tablespoons at a time—think of them as garden vitamins.

A lot of people faithfully buy ladybird beetles, bring them home, and release them, only to find no trace of them the next day. The trick is to get them to stay long enough to lay eggs, for their larvae will stick around and dine exceedingly well for you.

Provide them with something to eat immediately; spray the plants with a 10 percent sugar or honey solution or a commercial preparation like Control, Honeydew, or Wheast. Ladybugs require high humidity, with water droplets to drink, so keep the garden moist. If you have a plant that is infested with aphids, release the ladybugs on it and then tie a net over the plant to keep them in place. Be certain pests are on the plant, however, or your little friends will starve.

Ladybugs have few enemies because of their bitter taste, but they are highly vulnerable to poisonous sprays.

Ashy Gray Ladybird

MEALYBUG DESTROYERS
▼▼▼▼▼▼▼▼▼▼▼▼▼▼▼▼▼▼▼▼▼▼▼▼▼▼▼

An Australian relative of the ladybird beetle, the mealybug destroyer is, of course, a mealybug predator. In its larval stage it quite resembles a mealybug. The adult, a black, shiny insect with a reddish head, will eat other pests if there aren't any mealybugs around. If you order them, be sure to keep the ants away, or they can't do their job. Don't use toxic pesticides within a month of their releasing.

Mealybug Destroyer

BENEFICIAL NEMATODES
▼▼▼▼▼▼▼▼▼▼▼▼▼▼▼▼▼▼▼▼▼▼▼▼▼▼▼

It's a good thing nematodes are literally invisible, because these microscopic roundworms are incredibly fearsome looking. They're quite lethal, too—to their under-

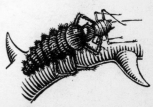

Ladybug Larva and Aphid

177

ground victims. In many areas they have become one of the most effective, as well as safest, ways to take care of pests like cutworms, armyworms, root maggots, borers, wireworms, cabbage loopers, as well as grubs in the ground, like Colorado potato beetles, Japanese beetles, and June beetles. In fact, beneficial nematodes will kill more than two hundred species of insects, but they will not harm earthworms or plants. (Other nematodes, such as root-knot nematodes, are harmful to plants.) Beneficial nematodes are also being used to control subterranean termites.

Nematodes can live in the soil for months. Like awful creatures out of science fiction, they enter their victims through their mouth or body openings. Some kill by introducing bacteria into their victims, others by slowly eating their tissue.

Building a healthy, humus-rich soil always leads to an increase in beneficial parasites. But now you can also buy these nematodes in a form that can easily be sprayed or poured onto the surface of the soil. A small package containing millions of these organisms will go to work ravishing and destroying harmful pests. Although they don't last in the ground forever, they're not that fragile, either. Don't spray them in direct sunlight, however.

PRAYING MANTIDS
▼▼▼▼▼▼▼▼▼▼▼▼▼▼▼▼▼▼▼▼▼▼▼▼▼▼▼

This is one of the silliest, most oddly affecting insects you will ever make friends with. It's also one of the insect world's great ambush predators. Lying patiently in wait for its victims, looking for all the world like the soul of religious contemplation, the mantis can suddenly attack with lightning speed and grasp its victim in a sawlike clamp. It consumes its prey alive and then delicately grooms and cleans itself. Aggressive and gluttonous, it can eat massive quantities of insects, including beetles, caterpillars, and grasshoppers. Some even attempt to attack small frogs, lizards,

Praying Mantis and Prey

and birds. It will also eat beneficial insects, like bees and others of its own kind, which is one of its chief drawbacks.

The female praying mantis constructs an *ootheca*; that is, she lays her eggs while secreting a foamy substance that hardens into a little protective case. Inside this case, which overwinters attached to a twig or a piece of bark, fifty to four hundred eggs lie cushioned within air bubbles. In Europe, women used to collect these cases under a full moon to use them for toothaches or chilblains. In Africa, it was even believed they could bring the dead to life!

If you get the praying mantis egg cases through the mail, attach them on low-growing twigs in the fall. It can be a lot of fun to watch them hatch, but the event is easy to miss. The young insects, looking like fairy ghosts, emerge in the spring when it turns warm, and disappear right into the vegetation.

If you do happen to see them hatch, you can then protect them by keeping the predators away until the air hardens their skin. Ironically, most fall prey when they first hatch, to ants, lizards, and other predators—themselves included. You can put the egg case in a paper bag secured with a paper clip. Place it in a sunny spot on a windowsill, but don't let it get hot. Check it daily to see if any are hatching (it could take up to eight weeks). As soon as they start to emerge, take them outside and let them go.

PREDATORY MITES

▼▼▼▼▼▼▼▼▼▼▼▼▼▼▼▼▼▼▼▼▼▼▼▼▼▼▼▼

Predatory mites, which are bigger than their prey and breed faster, too, can be ordered through the mail and released to control spider mites, especially in greenhouses. They can't be dispersed if residual pesticides have been used in the previous two or three weeks. The pest mite population should be controlled with insecticidal soap as much as possible before releasing the predators.

PARASITIC WASPS

▼▼▼▼▼▼▼▼▼▼▼▼▼▼▼▼▼▼▼▼▼▼▼▼▼▼▼▼

These are our tiny allies on the bug battlefields. They search out many of the pests (or their eggs or larvae) in the garden, lay their eggs in them, and force them to switch roles—from pests to terminal incubators of more wasps. All are available through mail order suppliers.

TRICHOGRAMMA WASPS

These insects are giving wasps a good name. With a wingspread of about one-fiftieth of an inch, they sting neither humans nor animals. But different species can kill as many as two hundred kinds of pests, mostly caterpillars, like armyworms, cutworms, corn earworms, hornworms, gypsy moths, leafworms, and bollworms. One wasp may parasitize as many as one hundred pest eggs during its lifetime. When the eggs hatch, they feed on the contents of their host eggs, killing them and later emerging as well-fed adults. Entomologists call parasites such as these *parasitoids*, since the host never survives but is completely consumed from within. And they effectively prevent the pest from even starting to do any damage.

You can purchase them by mail. They arrive inside the host eggs. Keep them in a warm and humid place. Timing is important when dispersing these beneficials, because it must be done when the moths are laying their eggs. Start releasing them in stages where the moths are doing their laying the moment you first see them in your garden.

ENCARSIA FORMOSA PARASITES

Another parasitic wasp is the whitefly parasite, also known as *Encarsia formosa*. This wasp lays its eggs right in the scales of immature whiteflies; as the wasp grows, it feeds on the whitefly and kills it. When an egg is laid on a scale, it turns black, so you can actually watch the process working.

BRACONIDS

These wasps can be observed as little white ricelike attachments of death on the backs of hapless caterpillars. The tiny silken bags are the cocoons of the next wasp generation. The larvae themselves have already spent some time inside the body of the caterpillar, consuming its tissue without quite killing it.

Braconid Wasp

181

Some are also avid aphid eaters; they leave the dead aphids with little holes in their backs.

CHALCIDS

Very tiny, and very vulnerable to pesticides, chalcid wasps are found all over North America. They strike against leafhoppers, scale, whiteflies, larvae of beetles, and caterpillars. They are shipped as adult wasps and proceed to lay eggs on the pests as soon as they find them.

ICHNEUMON WASPS

These insects, with very long ovipositors (egg-depositing devices), which look like formidable stingers, actually use them to bore through bark and lay eggs on caterpillars hiding deep within the bark or wood of a tree. They may find their victims by sensing them through vibrations.

FLY PARASITES

▼▼▼▼▼▼▼▼▼▼▼▼▼▼▼▼▼▼▼▼▼▼▼▼▼▼▼▼▼

These predators are very specific parasitoids that do in flies that hang out around livestock. People do not even notice their presence. They lay their eggs inside fly pupae, killing them before they can emerge. They are quite effective where flies are in abundance, particularly around manure in stables, kennels, feedlots, barns, and big composting operations.

These parasites have to be released continuously throughout the fly season because flies steadily move in from elsewhere. Just because you're using them doesn't mean you can give up good sanitation. Traps should be used along with the parasites, because the flies are much faster breeders than the parasites are. A program using fly parasites may take weeks or months to get going, but they do work, often quite dramatically. As with other biological controls, the parasitic flies are much more vulnerable to insecticides than their hosts are.

OTHER GOOD FLIES
▼▼▼▼▼▼▼▼▼▼▼▼▼▼▼▼▼▼▼▼▼▼▼▼▼▼▼▼▼

Though vastly outnumbered by their pestiferous relatives, it would not be fair to omit these insects from any good-guy list. Though they are not available through mail order, you should know them when you see them and not try to harm them.

ROBBER FLIES

Robber flies, some of which look like bumblebees, can act pretty ferocious. They attack flying wasps and bees. Some even run down their prey, such as small grasshoppers. The larvae feed on other larvae in the soil.

SYRPHID FLIES (HOVER FLIES OR FLOWER FLIES)

These colorful, yellow-striped flies are noted for their striking protective mimicry; some look like bees, some like wasps. Their appearance keeps them safe from birds and predators, though they are actually quite harmless. Some can be as large as half an inch and remain motionless in flight like a hummingbird; like hummingbirds, adults feed on nectar. The larvae eat aphids, scale, leafhoppers, and thrips, among others. That small green worm on your rosebud may well be a syrphid larva hunting for aphids, so take care.

TACHINID FLIES

Parasitic insects that closely resemble extra-large, hairy house flies, they glue their eggs onto many kinds of caterpillars or onto the leaves that the victim might eat. One species can parasitize a hundred kinds of caterpillars, including European corn borers and gypsy moths.

Many other beneficial bugs appear in the garden on their own without benefit of insectaries and postage. Learn to recognize and appreciate them, and leave them alone.

TRUE BUGS (*HEMIPTERA*)
▼▼▼▼▼▼▼▼▼▼▼▼▼▼▼▼▼▼▼▼▼▼▼▼▼▼▼

Some bugs, like bed bugs, plant bugs, and lace bugs, are definitely pests. Others, like assassin bugs, soldier bugs, ambush bugs, damsel bugs, and pirate bugs, are beneficial. Some have adhesive pads on their legs, covered with thousands of sticky hairs—like Velcro—that enable them to get a good grip on their victims.
  Assassin bugs are dark and oblong and almost look like spiders. They stab their prey, inject them with a dissolving agent, and suck them dry. They kill leafhoppers, caterpillars, and bed bugs, among others.

In the western United States and South America, a relative of the assassin bug—the conenose bug, also known as the kissing bug—does indeed bite. It can cause severe reactions and can transmit the quite dreadful Chagas' disease, a very serious illness in South America but of little consequence in the United States.

BEETLES

▼▼▼▼▼▼▼▼▼▼▼▼▼▼▼▼▼▼▼▼▼▼▼▼▼▼▼

Beetles make up the largest order of all living things—almost three hundred thousand species. There are so many kinds, it's often hard to determine which are good and which are bad. One rule of thumb from gardener lore says that if it's moving slow, stomp on it; if it's moving fast, it's probably after another bug, so let it go. You can always tell a beetle from the straight line going down the center of its back, where its hard front wings join.

BLISTER BEETLE

This is an example of a good/bad bug. We are including it here because its larvae eat grasshopper eggs, but the basic message is: Stay away from this beetle. Touching it can cause a painful blister. Ground-up dried blister beetles were used for medicinal purposes for years. The notorious and ignominious aphrodisiac, Spanish fly, is made from them.

FIREFLIES

Also called lightning bugs, although they are neither flies nor bugs, fireflies possess a luminous segment near the end of the abdomen, which is the basis of an elaborate

Ground Beetle

Rove Beetle

Soldier Beetle

mate-signaling behavior. As larvae (glowworms), they eat cutworms and small insects. They also have a way of eating slugs and snails by injecting them with digestive juices and then drinking the newly liquefied tissue.

GROUND BEETLES

There are twenty thousand species of ground beetles, but since they are mostly nocturnal, hardly anyone seems to be expert at identifying them. A bit horrifying and tempting-to-squash-looking, most are black, but some are iridescent. Their bodies may be shaped like a shield. Sometimes called caterpillar hunters, ground beetles are very valuable in any garden. They eat ants, aphids, cutworms, flies, gypsy moths, mosquitoes, slugs, snails, spider mites, termites, and many other pests. Some even climb trees to hunt their prey. One of these, the European ground beetle, was imported to help control gypsy moths in the East. Most ground beetles emit noxious vapors when attacked, so be careful about picking them up.

ROVE BEETLES

This slender insect doesn't look like a "real" beetle, but more like an earwig without the pinchers. Very active and quite speedy, it sometimes raises the back end of its body when running around. It scavenges in decaying material and is an important predator of cabbage beetles.

SOLDIER BEETLES

Soldier beetles, with their rectangular shape and brownish color, somewhat resemble fireflies with the light turned off. Their larvae are insect predators, but the adults no longer soldier and spend their days on flowers.

186

TIGER BEETLES

These master hunters are beautifully colored, iridescent blue, green, and bronze, and big—three-quarters of an inch long. A truly fast-moving beetle, it goes after ants, aphids, caterpillars, and others. Their larvae live in vertical tunnels in the ground. They position themselves with their head blocking the tunnel entrance, then they stretch out and grab passing prey.

OTHER PREDATORS

▼▼▼▼▼▼▼▼▼▼▼▼▼▼▼▼▼▼▼▼▼▼▼▼▼▼▼

DRAGONFLIES

Although fossils of ancient "dinosaur" dragonflies show them to have once been giant insects of the air, with up to twenty-nine-inch wingspans, they are still quite impressive today at around five inches. Also known as mosquito hawks, bee butchers, horse stingers, and devil's darning needles, they are magnificent fliers, with fabulous 360-degree vision. Tennyson called them "living flashes of light."

Dragonflies scoop up their prey with their hairy legs forming a "shopping basket."

Tiger Beetle

Dragonfly and Prey

187

They devour their victims in flight by sucking them dry and discarding the carcasses. They can eat their weight in food in half an hour. A dragonfly was once reported to have had as many as one hundred mosquitoes in its basket of legs at one time.

In one of the more amazing transformations of the insect world, the dragonfly changes from an underwater creature to one that spends most of its time in the air. The only thing that remains the same is its insatiable appetite for living, moving insects.

DAMSELFLIES

Damselflies are a smaller version of dragonflies, and they prefer insects with soft bodies. A damselfly can hover motionless in midair while picking off aphids, one by one, from a bud or leaf. Like dragonflies, they are daytime hunters and usually patrol near bodies of water. The nymphs of both dragonflies and damselflies eat mosquito larvae practically nonstop.

ANTLIONS

As an adult, this insect resembles the damselfly. The larvae, which are sometimes called doodle bugs, are wonderful hunters and trappers. They dig little pits in dry earth or sand and wait for their victims to tumble in. Then they throw up sand to confound them, pounce on them, paralyze them, suck out their insides, and toss their dry shell out of the pit. "Next!"

GARDEN PESTS

ANIMALS

Humans are such territorial animals. We're always deciding whom to allow on our property and whom to keep out. This is certainly true when it comes to animals—some we cherish and other we chase away. The writer Lee Eisenberg once summed up the situation, "Bring on the hummingbirds! Raccoons keep out! What am I, the doorkeeper at nature's disco?"

If you don't really know what or who is responsible for chewed up leaves and disappearing plants, put some white flour in a sifter and sprinkle a smooth coating over the ground. This will enable you to investigate the footprints of the plant nibbler, identify the culprit, and take suitable measures.

The persistence of small garden marauders—woodchucks, rabbits, raccoons, opossum—may force you to build a fence. The best ones are made of loose chicken wire, forty-eight inches high, that flops precariously when the animals start to climb it, forcing them to give up. Spacing the fence posts far apart—eight feet—will cause the fence to sag in a way the animals don't like. The chicken wire must go down into the soil at least twelve inches to keep some of the animals from tunneling underneath.

An electric fence will almost always work, but it smacks (and jolts) of supreme isolationism, and it's expensive. It does, however, have only one or at the most three

189

strands of wire. We recommend getting professional help when it comes to harnessing electricity in a garden war.

Wormwood is said to be a good border plant to use around the garden, because animals don't like it. Some say a border of onions or any member of the garlic family deters rabbits and other small animals.

Repellants have always been used against animals encroaching on domestic produce. Many of these rely on smells that bring up bad associations for the animals. Human hair is recommended for deer, and we suspect it offers a panoply of bad smells for all kinds of animals. (More on this under *Deer.*)

Another repellant that seems to work for (or against) animals is a border of wood ashes sprinkled around the plants. After it rains, however, the ashes lose their efficacy and must be replaced.

Some people take a portable radio, put it in a protective covering like a plastic bag to keep the dew off, and tune it to an all-night talk radio station. The sounds of human voices keep the animals at bay. Other people rig up lights for the same purpose. We do not recommend this method, as shining lights on growing plants at night can interfere with their growth patterns.

SKUNKS

Not all animals are unwelcome in the garden. If you're lucky enough to play host to a fox, it's looking for rodents, so let it alone.

Skunks are also great rodent hunters, and they live on insects as well. They like armyworms, grasshoppers, tobacco worms, grubs, cutworms, and potato beetles, among others. New York State even passed a law protecting them because they were helping the hop growers by eating hop grubs. We feel amiable toward skunks unless they take up residence under the house. Then we feel nervous.

Animal control officers will come and trap a skunk for you, but they may also destroy it because of the fear of rabies. It is better to trap your trespasser carefully on your own and release it a good two miles away from the premises.

The trick with skunks is to put the cage inside a big dark plastic garbage bag, open at the trap opening. Bait it with cat kibbles—they love them. When you have caught the skunk, slip another plastic bag over the other end of the cage, and you should be home free—spray free, too.

Don't be surprised if you come back to the house and find the skunk's mate and have to do the whole procedure all over again. When all trespassers have departed, close off their entranceway.

SQUIRRELS

Squirrels and chipmunks don't usually do much damage to a garden. If you find that chipmunks—or any animals—seem to be digging up your plants as soon as you put them in the ground, put screen covers secured with stones over them for a week or two.

If the squirrels are getting into fruit or nut trees, tie aluminum pie pans—real aluminum not foil—to the lower limbs of the trees. Hammer a nail through the pan to make a hole to attach the string.

You may have to build a barricade to keep squirrels out of trees and bird feeders. Sticky products like Tanglefoot or a good coating of Vaseline make the climbing surface off-limits. Or make a barricade by taking a number of plastic milk cartons with little handles and stringing them together through the handles. Tie as many bottles as possible around the tree trunk to create a bubble skirt barricade without any space for the squirrels to get through. It may look silly, but you can take it down when the fruit has been harvested. Another barricade can be made by cutting the top half off plastic milk bottles and then stapling or nailing them with the open ends down, right onto the tree trunk and touching each other.

DEER

If you have deer encroaching on your property, it is probably because your property is actually encroaching on the deer. By eating ornamentals (they even eat roses), sampling vegetable gardens, and nibbling at tree bark, they can do a lot of damage to a garden.

One deer repellant can be easily made from mixing 4 raw eggs into 1 gallon of water, blending it well, and spraying on vulnerable plants. Another repellant is hot pepper/onion/garlic spray. (See chapter on *Tactics of Tiny Game Hunting* for formula.) Manure from the zoo from members of the cat family—lion, tiger, cheetah, etc.—makes a terrific repellant as long as the smell lasts. Spread it on the ground near plants or at the edge of the garden.

Nylon stockings stuffed with human hair are a classic deer repellant. Hair really does absorb odors. Go to a beauty parlor and ask for the day's supply of haircuttings, then make a good number of little bags of human-scented potpourri to hang on the plants. Place the bags about two feet high every eight to ten feet around your property. Or dig a shallow trench around the perimeter of the garden and fill it with hair. (The birds will love it for their nests.) Later, the hair, which is full of nitrogen, can be worked into the soil.

Soap has received high ratings as a deer repellant. Use nylon stockings filled with Ivory soap flakes, or tie bars of strong smelling deodorant soap right onto the trees and bushes. Insert a wire through the soap bars to hang them, or put them into nylon stockings and tie them onto branches. Hang the bars about two to three feet from the ground.

Spread wire mesh fencing or chicken wire around on the ground. Deer do not like stepping on it, nor do other animals. People don't either, actually. Another tactile tactic consists of planting tomato or squash vines and letting them spread out over the ground at the perimeter of the garden. Deer don't like to step on these either. Of course, you have to wait until the vines mature for this to work, by which time the garden may have been consumed! Try planting these vines before the plants you want them to protect to give them a head start.

Some people put blood meal in bags and or sprinkle it around the yard to repel the vegetarian deer. So does this: Take ¼ to ½ pound of fresh beef liver and put it in a food processor with 1 quart water. Sprinkle or spray onto plants. It will also repel rabbits, but you may find the dogs going crazy over your corn. Of course, a dog with a good sense of guardsmanship can be an excellent deer repellant.

Note: All organic or spray repellants must be replenished after a good rain.

Fences that are not electric must be at least six feet tall to keep deer out, and if the deer can see through them, even eight feet may not be tall enough. One effective way to fence out deer is to build two fences about five feet apart. Although deer can jump quite high, they are not broad jumpers. The two fences don't have to be any higher than five feet, which makes them much more ornamental. If a fence is out of the question, set up a barricade of planted-just-for-the-deer crops, like corn or soybeans, and hope they don't get too greedy.

To protect trunks of trees that are being nibbled, wrap netting or chicken wire around them. In the winter you can use heavy aluminum foil or fiberglass insulation.

193

Commercial tree guards are also available. Some people wrap the trees in plastic pipe that has been slit with a saw. This barrier will also protect trees from the nibbles of rabbits and mice, is easy to remove, and lasts a long time.

RABBITS

Rabbits have always loved our gardens, but gardeners have not always loved rabbits. Sprinkling blood meal on the ground around plants will sometimes repel rabbits, as will powdered lime and sulfur. They also dislike the smell of manure, tar, and kerosene. Sprinkle hot red pepper, black pepper, or garlic powder on the dampened leaves of plants to make them unpalatable as rabbit food.

The smell of fish is also said to be offensive to rabbits. Mix 2 tablespoons of fish emulsion in a gallon of water and spray it on the plants. Be warned, however—cats love it. Planting onions throughout the garden may deter rabbits. The short sections of garden hose you put around your garden to scare off birds may also scare away rabbits.

If rabbits are nibbling around the tender trunks of saplings, wrap them with fiberglass insulation or plastic pipe that has been slit lengthwise with a saw. Commercial tree wraps made of paper or heavy grade aluminum foil can also be used successfully. Chicken wire makes another good barrier against rabbits and mice chewing on bark. Some people smear bacon grease or other animal fat on the trunk.

When rabbits go after young seedlings, protect them with row covers or aluminum screens bent in half over the plants. Seal off the ends with more chicken wire.

We know a gardener who always plants a patch of lettuce especially for the rabbits, well away from her own lettuce. Sometimes she even steals from the rabbits' patch.

RACCOONS

Raccoons inevitably go after the garbage cans. No matter what you do to discourage them—bright lights, scarecrows, clattering pie pan traps—they always seem to be able to get at the goodies. Their dexterity and persistence with a garbage can lid is legendary. Still, there are a few things you can do.

While putting a heavy rock on top of the garbage can lid may or may not keep them out, here are a few repellants to try:

Sprinkle hydrated lime around the cans—on the ground and on the lids.

Try liberal doses of ammonia, Lysol, or hot Tabasco sauce on the tops of the cans.

If you find that raccoons are climbing over the fence into your garden, try hanging a few articles of dirty clothing (the greater the body odor the better) over the fence. The all-too-human smell should keep them away. As the clothing airs out, replace it with others from the dirty clothes hamper.

Raccoons just love corn, and rows of these tasty vegetables can become the site of a real battle of the taste buds. Sprinkling hydrated lime on the ground around the vegetables may keep them away. Or take a spray bottle and spritz the corn with water, then sprinkle with hot red pepper. It has to be really hot to work. Another red pepper concoction consists of ½ cup cayenne, 1 tablespoon liquid soap, and 1 pint water. Mix and let stand overnight, then strain and spray on the ears of corn.

You might have to resort to putting a paper or plastic bag over each ear of corn and securing it with wire string. A reader of *Organic Gardening* magazine wrote that running her hands over each ear of corn gave it a smell that the raccoons did not like.

Some gardeners plant pumpkin seeds among the corn plants. The raccoons seem to like eating the corn while standing up so they can look around; the big pumpkin leaves keep them from doing this. They don't seem to like cucumber plants among the corn, either. Thin black plastic spread flat around plants on the ground may also deter them. Or if you know a house painter, ask for all the used plastic drop cloths.

Go to a pet groomer and get the hair trimmings from the dogs. Put them in mesh bags and set them around to keep the raccoons and other animals away. Hopefully, they'll get the idea that an army of dogs is on duty.

Here is a way to trap a raccoon (or any small scavenger) inside an empty metal

Raccoon and Small Animal Trap

garbage can: Place the can near a railing, or put a stepladder next to it—just far enough away so that the animal has to leap to get to the can. Set the lid upside down on the can with a few enticing morsels of food to induce the animal to leap for the can. The lid will swing over and deposit the critter right into the can, in which you transport it far away from your yard to release it.

Remember, the humane society or animal control officer in your area will have live traps that you can borrow and use. Havahart traps and Safe-N-Sound live traps are available from mail order sources. (See *Mail Order*.)

DOGS

We have always wondered about the motives of people who let their dogs invade and befoul other people's yards. If the dogs in the neighborhood are getting into your garbage, sprinkle ammonia around the bases of the cans. And make sure the lids are always on tight.

A repellant spray for dogs can be made by mixing 2 cups rubbing alcohol and 2 teaspoons lemon grass oil; spray it on the areas where you don't want the dogs. Rotten potatoes placed along their route will also keep the dogs from lingering for very long.

Another repellant—if you can bear to handle it—is to soak a package of chopped-up cheap cigars (or several packages of torn-up cigarettes) in a bowl of water overnight. Dribble it where the dogs show up and lift their legs. Or dip strips of rags in it and hang them from the bushes. This is very toxic, however, and must be handled with great care.

If your own clunk of a dog refuses to show any respect for your new little seedlings and keeps stepping on them, protect them with upside-down strawberry baskets or cans with both ends cut out.

To keep the dog from digging itself a nice napping spot in the dirt among your plants, take croquet wickets, grape stakes, or wooden stakes (an old broomstick cut into twelve-inch lengths works well), and pound them into the ground at intervals of about one foot.

ANTS

▼▼▼▼▼▼▼▼▼▼▼▼▼▼▼▼▼▼▼▼▼▼▼▼▼▼

See under *Household Game Hunting*.

APHIDS

▼▼▼▼▼▼▼▼▼▼▼▼▼▼▼▼▼▼▼▼▼▼▼▼▼▼

Aphids

Aphids are probably the commonest and most numerous pests in your garden. Small—about one-tenth of an inch—and soft bodied, aphids come in many colors: white, green, pink, gray, red, brown, and black. They love the tips, buds, and tender stems of plants, and the four thousand or so species will happily infest a wide variety of plants. Indeed, there are few plants that are not attacked by one kind of aphid or another. They are often called plant lice (or green fly). Even though it seems that no one ever sees fewer than hundreds of aphids on a single plant, with a little diligence—and an eye out for the ants— aphids are really not that hard to control.

There are two main reasons for their great proliferation: Pesticides readily kill off the beneficial insects that prey on aphids. For instance, the aerial sprayings of malathion in Los Angeles County in 1990 to kill the medfly (good luck) led to tremendous and discouraging aphid proliferations in people's gardens.

The other reason is their amazing reproductive system. Aphids may be the most prolific of all insects. Thomas Huxley once announced that at the end of one summer the descendants of a single aphid might amount to a bulk equal to that of the population of China.

When aphids go to work on a plant, they insert their piercing mouth into the stem or onto the underside of a leaf. The sap starts to flow, and they just suck the day away. The leaves become curled or turn yellow, growth stops, and the plant can die. But the worst thing aphids do to your plants is transmit diseases through their salivary secretions.

Aphid

To extract the nutrition they need, namely nitrogen, aphids have to draw out huge amounts of the plant's juices. (Using a high-nitrogen fertilizer to induce quick growth is often an open invitation to aphids.) They excrete the excess in the form of a sticky-sweet liquid called *honeydew*, often producing many times their own weight of the stuff in one day. Honeydew coats the leaves of the plants, making them look slightly silvery in the light. Sometimes the honeydew nourishes a black sooty-looking fungus.

Ants love aphids because of this sweet honeydew. They even have a way of stroking the aphids' abdomens to get them to release more of it. Ants assiduously guard their aphid cows from their natural enemies. They move aphid nymphs to new plants and into their own nests during bad weather. If you see aphids or signs of aphids, look for ants traveling up and down the stem of the plant, and then keep the ants away. Use a barrier like Stikem Special or Tanglefoot to stymie them. Or spread diatomaceous earth around the base of the plant.

When ants aren't keeping them away, the best natural predators for aphids include ladybugs, ladybug larvae (which look like little monster alligators), birds, lacewings, lacewing larvae (called aphid lions), daddy longlegs, hover fly larvae (Syrphidae), and parasitic wasps.

Aphidius Wasp

199

Winged Aphid

If you observe an aphid that is swollen and metallic, dull brown or blackened, it is a *mummy*, an aphid that has been parasitized by a wasp. Leave it alone so the wasp larva can develop. Don't forget: If you don't have any aphids, there won't be anything for the predators to eat and they will go elsewhere. Even the FDA considers forty to sixty aphids in a serving of brussels sprouts to be perfectly acceptable.

CONTROL

Plant nasturtiums around plants that tend to get aphid infestations. Or plant garlic, which works well as an aphid repellant.

One preferred deterrent is to place strips of aluminum foil underneath plants particularly susceptible to aphids. Along vegetable rows, use the full width. Light reflecting off the foil confuses them and prevents them from landing on the plant. You'll get the added bonus of both weed control and moisture retention.

Sticky yellow traps can be used for aphids but only flying aphids; if aphids are on the wing, they will likely alight on these traps. Or place bright yellow bowls filled with soapy water around the plants, and the aphids will fly into them.

If you have an aphid infestation, the first thing to do is direct a strong stream of water at it. This is called artificial bad weather. Once knocked off the plant, aphids

Waterworks

don't usually have the strength to get back on. You can also simply brush them off or crush them with your hands, or use a little rubbing alcohol to kill them.

Other methods include spraying with homemade soap spray, insecticidal soap, garlic/hot pepper spray, tomato leaf spray, diatomaceous earth spray, quassia spray, sabadilla, ryana, or rotenone. (See *Tactics of Tiny Game Hunting*.) We think the last three sprays are overkill, considering that water alone will often do the trick. Try the simplest and weakest remedies first, moving onto stronger ones only if they don't work. For fruit trees, spray in early spring with dormant oil spray.

BORERS

▼▼▼▼▼▼▼▼▼▼▼▼▼▼▼▼▼▼▼▼▼▼▼▼▼▼

Borers can be either caterpillars that plague annuals or the larval stage (grubs) of beetles that mostly go after trees. They are called borers because this is how they perpetrate their worst damage—boring into plant stems or stalks or tree trunks and then eating their way merrily inside—in an upward direction. Because they may go unnoticed for so long, they can utterly destroy plants and trees. Diseases in trees often get their start through borer holes.

Borers seem to prefer plants that are weak and undernourished and trees that are stressed from lack of water or those with wounded bark. Watch that lawn mower around the trees! Wood-pecking birds (woodpeckers and flickers) are important allies, because they are often searching for borers.

If you can pinpoint a borer's hole, go after it with a piece of stiff wire or the pointed end of a knife and try to impale the little sucker. Trees can be wrapped in cardboard or other barriers to stop larvae from starting up the trunks. Mix wood ashes and water to make a thick paste, then paint it on tree trunks to control borers.

When a plant starts to look wilted from a particular spot on the stem upward, check for the borer's hole, which you can usually see, along with the "sawdust" that gives them away. When you find it, slice the stem upward from the hole to find the fat, well-fed borer and remove it with tweezers or a small crochet hook. Or inject a little shot of *Bacillus thuringiensis* (*B.t.*) into the hole with a syringe or medicine dropper to infect the borer with a deadly disease. Cover the damaged stem well with piled up, damp dirt. Or gently wrap the plant stem in dampened cloth strips covered with tape to bind up the slit. The plant may or may not survive this mauling, but it can surprise you and bounce back.

Plant early or late to foil the borers' schedule, or plant resistant varieties.

Clearing all the plants from the garden right after harvesting helps eliminate borers who may have set up housekeeping in them. And tilling the soil well in the fall will help, too.

Squash Vine Borer

Squash vine borers go after squash, gourds, pumpkins, and sometimes cucumber and melons. Using fabric row covers for those plants will prevent the moths from laying eggs on them. The clear-winged moths look like colorful, beautiful wasps and excite admiration with their zippy flight patterns.

An aluminum foil mulch may confuse the moths and keep them from laying eggs on the plants. Wrapping the stems with aluminum foil or cut-up panty hose may also keep the borers out.

Some people advise planting radishes around the susceptible plants or sprinkling black pepper or wood ashes around on the soil. Others say to place a couple handfuls of cigarette ashes on the hill when the seeds are planted.

*European corn borer*s are great pests of corn, but they go after other plants, too—over two hundred kinds. They generally feed on the leaves for a while before entering the stalk. Look for little holes with sawdust around them.

By using a light trap around May, you may be able to kill the moths before they can lay eggs on the leaves. Spraying *B.t.* may also control them before they start to bore into the plant. Lacewings, ladybugs, and braconid wasps all prey on this pest.

Peach tree borers, a close relative of the squash vine borer, are found throughout North America in several kinds of fruit trees besides peach. They do their damage around the bottom ten inches of the tree trunk (starting initially at the soil line or just below it). Trees are rarely infested with just one solitary borer.

CONTROL

If you see the tell-tale gum and sawdust mixture, break off the bark and try to locate the borers. Scrape them out and impale the creatures with something sharp. You can inject shots of *Bacillus thuringiensis* into the holes; repeat this procedure every ten days. Also dig around in the soil and look for the dark brown, large cocoons and destroy them.

Gardeners used to hang bars of soap on the trunks of trees. When it rained the soap would run down the tree and the borers would be repelled by the taste. Squirting a line of liquid hand soap around the tree and letting it run down the bark would accomplish this same purpose.

To prevent borers from getting a start in the tree, surround the trunk in the spring with a good wide barrier of diatomaceous earth or tobacco dust, digging it into the soil and replenishing it after a rain. You can also wrap the tree with a barrier and cover the wrap with sticky trapping compound like Stikem Special or Tanglefoot.

Pheromone-baited traps are available for many moths. Predators of the borers include ants, spiders, moles, birds, mice, and skunks. Keep the trees as healthy as possible, because borers attack the weakest trees.

CABBAGE LOOPERS AND
IMPORTED CABBAGEWORMS

▼▼▼▼▼▼▼▼▼▼▼▼▼▼▼▼▼▼▼▼▼▼▼

Although separate species of insects, one being a moth and the other a butterfly, these two caterpillars have many similarities. In addition to cabbage, they attack almost any vegetable you care to grow: broccoli, cauliflower, beans, radishes, turnips, lettuce, parsley, peas, mustard, potatoes, tomatoes, brussels sprouts, and even a few flowers. They chew big holes in the leaves and then bore right into the vegetables.

The cabbageworm, a pretty green color, comes from a white butterfly with black spots on the wings. It's not hard to catch in a butterfly net. Or take out an old tennis racket and whack it to death before its offspring start whacking at your plants.

The cabbage looper moth is brown and gray and has a couple of silver spots on its wings. The caterpillar gets its name from the funny loopy way it draws itself up as it moves, which is why it is sometimes called the measuring worm or "inchworm." For once, we have a pest that lays its eggs (little white ones) on the tops of leaves. Because both these caterpillars have several generations a year, they can be summer-long nuisances. The following controls work for both of them.

Cabbage Looper

204

CONTROL

If you find that these pests have infested the heads of cabbage, pour sour milk into them. You can make milk sour by adding a little vinegar to it (4 teaspoons per cup of milk). Mish-mash spray (See *Tactics of Tiny Game Hunting*) makes another good repellant.

For another tried-and-true repellant, mix ¼ cup salt with ½ cup flour and dust the plants lightly with it. Ruth Stout (*Gardening Without Work*) simply marched between her rows of cabbage, sprinkling them with a saltshaker a couple of times during the growing season. Wood ashes sprinkled on the leaves act as a repellant. If you don't believe this, try sprinkling ashes on your own salad.

Keep an eye out for their eggs under or on top of leaves. If the caterpillars are at work already, you will see chewed-up leaves and even their green droppings at the bottom of the leaf. They can be knocked off the plants into jars of soapy water, alcohol/water, or ammonia/water. Or knocked off and stomped on.

Some people spray the plants with water from the ocean. (Plants in the cabbage family can tolerate a little bit of salt.) The saltwater kills the eggs and keeps the caterpillars from eating the leaves.

A homemade dust attack consists of taking 1 cup of lime and mixing it with 1 tablespoon black pepper. If you sprinkle cornmeal or rye flour on the plants, caterpillars will eat it and die. Diatomaceous earth can also be sprinkled onto the plant. All these dusts must be reapplied after rain or watering.

As with hundreds of other pestiferous caterpillars, *Bacillus thuringiensis* (*B.t.*) is a most effective treatment. Start spraying it once a week after the butterflies or moths appear. Try *B.t.* before using botanical sprays like sabadilla or rotenone, which will also kill them. *B.t.* is a pathogen that only attacks leaf-eating caterpillars, so it doesn't pose any risk of harming other beneficial insects.

Cabbage pests tend to get worse year after year, so be sure to rotate the plants around the garden. Clear away all garden and crop debris in the fall, because this is where the eggs will overwinter. When you put in new crops, watch for the butterflies. As soon as you see them, cover the plants with fabric row covers or other protective barriers.

Parasitic wasps are natural parasites of caterpillars. And yellow jackets and ground beetles will eat great numbers of them. Although many gardening experts advise keeping weeds out of the garden, ground beetles like a few weeds around. Plant some ragweed or lamb's quarters just for the beetle predators.

Cabbageworms can also be deterred by placing geranium leaves over the growing cabbage, but you run the risk of having the cabbage plant die from embarrassment.

CODLING MOTHS

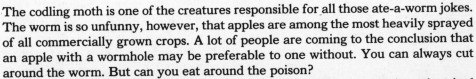

The codling moth is one of the creatures responsible for all those ate-a-worm jokes. The worm is so unfunny, however, that apples are among the most heavily sprayed of all commercially grown crops. A lot of people are coming to the conclusion that an apple with a wormhole may be preferable to one without. You can always cut around the worm. But can you eat around the poison?

The little gray-to-brown codling moth is not one of nature's great beauties. And the worm is even worse—a plump white body with a pinkish tinge. In the spring, the moth lays her eggs on the branches of fruit trees, mostly apple, but also pear, quince, and walnut. When they hatch, the caterpillars tunnel into the middle of the fruit, where they live and eat in the core, leaving our preferred part of the apple

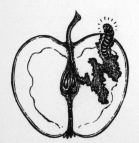

Codling Moth

for us—if only we weren't quite so squeamish. Later they tunnel out to pupate down at the base of the tree. The only sign of their presence on the apple is a little puncture on the skin with some brown excrement. As moths, they lay more eggs, and the cycle starts all over again. Thus the tree is under siege all summer.

CONTROL

Codling moths spend the winter as cocoons under tree bark, down in the lowest three feet of the tree. To get at them in the spring, scrape off the bark and kill them. In late winter, spray the tree with horticultural oil.

If you fail to get the cocoons, try to get the moths by hanging traps in the trees. These traps are containers filled with a sweet substance that attracts the moths, which fly right into it. You can use paper cups, glass jars, or plastic milk bottles with an opening cut in the side. (Their handles make it easier to tie them to the tree.) The bait can be a mixture of molasses and water in a 1:8 solution, or a mixture of 2 parts vinegar to 1 part molasses. People use a wide variety of formulas with success, for instance, putting a banana peel, 1 cup sugar, and 1 cup vinegar into a gallon bottle, filling it with water, and hanging it from the tree. Another sweet bait can be made from 1 gallon of water, 3 cups molasses, 1 tablespoon yeast, and ½ tablespoon oil of sassafras. Empty the traps every few days. If you are getting honey bees in the traps, put a one-eighth to one-quarter inch screening over the opening.

Pheromone traps can also be purchased from suppliers. These traps attract the male moths and can be quite effective in the home orchard (or tree), although it usually takes two or more years to get a good result. Two pheromone traps should be placed in each tree several weeks before the buds open.

Codling moths can have two or three generations in a summer. Since the caterpillars will make one trip down the tree to complete their cycle in midsummer, in early

Corn Earworm

summer wrap the tree trunks with burlap or corrugated cardboard (bumpy side inward) or use a sticky barrier. Pick off this generation of caterpillars as it crawls down the tree and destroy it. You can also use a sticky barrier to trap the caterpillars. Keep the trees wrapped all summer and check them every week or so.

A hundred years ago, bars of soap were tied to the trunks of trees to keep caterpillars from traveling up and down. Try using liquid soap on the tree trunk to get the same effect.

Farmers used to burn big bonfires in the orchards believing that the moths flew into the flames. You could try this on a small (and cautious) scale by burning a small fire between 6 and 10 P.M. in a barbecue grill near the tree. Or you can set up light traps at night to capture the moths.

Woodpeckers are the apple grower's best friend when it comes to controlling codling moths, so place suet in the trees for them. Trichogramma and brachonid wasps also parasitize them.

CORN EARWORMS

▼▼▼▼▼▼▼▼▼▼▼▼▼▼▼▼▼▼▼▼▼▼▼▼▼▼

This insect is also known as the cotton bollworm, a name we like because it sounds so rowdy, and the tomato fruitworm, which we don't like because it brings up the argument about whether a tomato is a fruit or not. (Well, is it?)

Although most famous for its corn expeditions, you'll find this pale green or brown caterpillar ruining tomatoes, grapes, peas, beans, peppers, squash, and okra. The only nice thing about this little worm is that, unlike the corn borer, it enters the corn at the tip, and only one worm inhabits an ear. So long as the kids don't see what you're doing, you can always cut the wormy end off and serve it anyway.

It's a lot less nerve-wracking to eliminate these pests before they get to the table, however. The classic repellant for corn earworms is a squirt of mineral oil, which smothers the worms, applied with a medicine dropper (half full) inserted into the tip of each ear of corn. Do this after the silks have started to wilt and turn brown. Some people add hot pepper to the oil. Beneficial nematodes can also be injected into the ears. If you're going to all this trouble, however, you may as well handpick the little suckers.

Bacillus thuringiensis (*B.t.*) works very well against corn earworms. Spray it on the plants every two weeks or inject into the ears of corn. A number of parasitic wasps will lay eggs in earworms, and green lacewings make excellent predators, too.

Healthy, hearty corn plants are more resistant to these caterpillars, so be sure to give your plants a decent organic, well-fed soil in which to thrive. Rotating the location of the corn every year will also give the plants an advantage, because these insects pupate in the soil right under the plant. Many varieties resistant to this pest have been developed.

CUCUMBER BEETLES
▼▼▼▼▼▼▼▼▼▼▼▼▼▼▼▼▼▼▼▼▼▼▼▼▼▼

Is it cucumber beetle's fault if the plant it feeds on starts to wilt, stem by stem, until the whole thing collapses in a dead heap? It certainly is. These beetles carry the dreaded bacterial wilt and other plant diseases in their digestive tracts.

If you want to know whether your wilted plants have been infected, cut one of the vines in two and hold the ends of the two parts together, squeezing slightly to release the plant juice. Pull them apart slowly; if they have a white gooey substance that you can draw out into a thread, that's it. Good-bye, plant.

A number of beetle species share the name cucumber beetle. The *spotted cucumber beetle* (also known as the Southern corn rootworm) is found east of the Rockies, whereas the *banded cucumber beetle* makes its home in the West. The *striped cucumber beetle*, yellowish orange with black stripes, can be found virtually everywhere and gets the award for being the biggest pain of all for the cucumber.

All cucumber beetles and their bacteria hibernate over the winter months in garden debris or weeds or under logs or leaves. Although the adults feed on just about any plant, their larvae are more picky; they need cucurbit plants to develop. In addition to cucumbers, cucurbits include vines like squash, pumpkin, melon, and gourd, so they have plenty of choices in a well-stocked vegetable garden. They lay their orange-yellow eggs in the soil at the base of plants. Little whitish wormy grubs hatch and go after the plant roots. Both the grubs and the adults pass along incurable diseases to the plants. Tilling or cultivating the ground in early spring or late fall helps kill the eggs in the soil. And use a good mulch to prevent these beetles from laying their eggs there in the first place.

CONTROL

Radishes, marigold, catnip, and nasturtiums repel cucumber beetles as well as Japanese beetles. Some gardeners literally ring their plants with radishes.

The bitter essence (curcurbitacin) of the cucurbit family strongly attracts cucumber beetles. Although repellant to other insects, it's like a drug to these beetles, and they eat compulsively when they get around it. Certain varieties of plants have had the bitterness bred out to some extent, providing some resistance to the beetles. You can disguise the bitter essence of the plants by making a spray out of water and artificial vanilla flavoring and spritzing the plants with it.

You can also take advantage of the beetles' addiction to this particular flavor and use it to make traps. Take the peels of some cucumbers and put them in a pile,

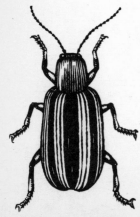

Striped Cucumber Beetle

sprinkling them with rotenone or pyrethrum, which will poison the beetles, or with diatomaceous earth, which will puncture their outer membranes. The nice thing about this trap is that other insects will not be attracted to it, although there is always the possibility that you could attract the neighbors' beetles.

The beetles' frenzy for the bitter quality in these vegetables (especially for the buffalo gourd) can make experimenting with these traps kind of fun. Try coating a piece of yellow board with a sticky substance (motor oil, Vaseline, Stikem Special, etc.) and placing some cut-up cantaloupe rinds on it. Or use a shallow bowl with water, a little liquid soap, and some cantaloupe rinds or cucumber peels. Another tactic is to place cantaloupe rinds or cucumber peels in a blender with water and liquefy them.

Some suppliers now carry a pheromone trap for these beetles. These traps will not rid you of the entire beetle population, but they can give you a good idea of how serious your problem is, and you can proceed from there. If your situation is desperate, spray the plants with rotenone as a last resort. You can handpick these bugs, and you should, too. But they are really small, only a quarter of an inch long. One of the best places to look for them is inside the blossoms.

A traditional treatment for cucumber beetles is to mix ¼ cup wood ashes and ¼ cup lime in 1 gallon of water and spray it on the plants. Make sure the undersides of leaves are sprayed, too. The plants can also be sprinkled with hot red pepper, lime, or chalk powder. Be sure to mist the plants first so that the dust will adhere.

In the spring, cover your seedlings with barriers like cheesecloth, floating row covers, or screen covers to keep the beetles away. Bury the edges well—don't leave a single spot where the little marauders can crawl under and get to the plant. But be sure to plant extra as insurance against losing your produce.

These beetles may be formidable, but they're not without enemies. Lacewings, ladybugs, soldier beetles, and beneficial nematodes will all consume them; tachnid flies will parasitize them.

CUTWORMS

▼▼▼▼▼▼▼▼▼▼▼▼▼▼▼▼▼▼▼▼▼▼▼▼▼▼▼

These obnoxious, greedy little devils can be black or gray-brown to yellowish in color. Look for them on the ground curled up plump and comfy under bits of leaves or dirt. They curl up on purpose; perhaps you'll think they are dead. Don't be fooled. At night they go around biting off the stems of plants just above or just below the soil line. They are really vicious and not too smart, since they kill off the poor plant entirely and have to go find another one the next night.

Cutworm collars, a good, sensible line of defense, can be made from toilet paper tubes, lightweight cardboard, or tar paper cut in a band and stapled around the plant stem. Press the collars down into the dirt around the plant at least an inch or two. Several layers of newspaper or even aluminum foil can also be wrapped around the stem. The newspapers will eventually disintegrate into the soil.

Milk cartons or tin cans with the tops and bottoms cut out will protect the plants. In the nineteenth century, before the advent of tin cans, stems were wrapped with hickory or walnut leaves, which probably acted as both repellant and barrier. Some people still like to anchor the ends of a couple of long onion or garlic tops in the hole before setting the plant in, then take the tops and wrap them around and around the stem of the plant.

Another cutworm foil consists of placing a little twig, nail, straw, or wooden coffee stirrer next to the stem and sticking it down into the dirt. It keeps the cutworm from doing its boa constrictor number on the plant. When the plants get older and tougher, they aren't as appealing to cutworms.

Cutworm at Work

Take a flashlight out at night and look for these caterpillars. Sometimes you'll even find them chewing on the edges of leaves. During the day you may find them resting under the soil right next to the stem—especially if they've just mangled that plant. Scrape away a layer of dirt or poke viciously around the soil with a sharp skewer or knitting needle. If you find one, put it in the bird feeder, because birds like cutworms a lot. So do toads, moles, and predatory beetles. They can also be parasitized by tachinid flies, trichogramma and braconid wasps, and nematodes.

Cutworms dislike the prickly quality of an oak leaf mulch. Eggshells are another sharp deterrent. Crush them and mix them into the soil near the plant. Or sprinkle diatomaceous earth or wood ashes in a circle around the plant. Ruth Stout, author of *Gardening Without Work*, wrote that if her thick hay mulch was close enough to the stem of the plant, she was never bothered by cutworms.

Onion plants and tansy are said to repel cutworms, but a dusting of *B.t.* will really kill them. An old standby is to sprinkle cornmeal around the plants, which will bloat them to death if they eat it. Gardening literature from the early part of the century advised putting soot and lime around the plant; this probably worked, not because it hurt the cutworm, but because it enabled the plant to outgrow it. (Soot can be collected by scraping the inside of the fireplace chimney.)

We especially like the idea of turning cutworms into little wooden mummies. This can be done by concocting a mixture of equal parts molasses, wheat bran, and saw-dust from any hardwood. Ask for it at a lumberyard. Mix these ingredients together, thinning them with water. Spread the mixture around the plants. Cutworms crawl into it, and it dries on them, turning them into candied worms.

213

FALL WEBWORMS AND EASTERN TENT CATERPILLARS
▼▼▼▼▼▼▼▼▼▼▼▼▼▼▼▼▼▼▼▼▼▼▼▼▼▼▼▼

Fall webworms behave quite gregariously, in that all the caterpillars that hatch from eggs laid by one moth on a tree stay together and spin a kind of waterproof tent/awning/pavilion for themselves. They travel back and forth between this home base and the leaves of the target tree. There may be between fifty and three hundred caterpillars in a single web. They can completely defoliate a tree in a very short time.

Tent caterpillars also spin cozy webs for themselves in the crotches of trees or forks of branches. Unlike webworms, their webs do not cover leaves and the ends of branches. With both of these caterpillars, however, the combination of insects and web makes for the essence of infestation. But at least they're easy to spot.

An old method used by gardeners in the 1790s was to hang wet seaweed, taken from rocks on the beach (called rock weed), in the crotches of trees in the spring. It probably repelled the moths. And the seaweed would also make a good mulch as it disintegrated.

Look for the egg masses on the trees during the winter months and cut off or scrape away any you find. The tents or webs can be torn out manually and viciously with a stick or long pole, and then the caterpillars can be stomped upon. If the caterpillars are already crawling about on the tree, spray them with *Bacillus thuringiensis.*

Because they crawl down the tree trunk before they pupate, you can set up traps for them around the trunk. Wrap the trunk in burlap or flannel, check it daily, and pick out the caterpillars.

Both tent caterpillars and webworms share a number of predators, including birds, praying mantids, and parasitic wasps. They are even eaten by some species of beetles bold enough to climb the tree and invade their nests.

FLEA BEETLES

▼▼▼▼▼▼▼▼▼▼▼▼▼▼▼▼▼▼▼▼▼▼▼▼▼▼

When disturbed, these little shiny black bugs jump just like the fleas they're named after. For such a little pest (one-sixteenth of an inch), they make an awful lot of distinctive round holes in the leaves. These beetles generally won't kill your plants; they just ruin their looks. Some people actually tolerate them with a good deal of equanimity. It's such a relief sometimes to deal with a pest that maims but doesn't murder.

They feed on the leaves of dichondra, broccoli, cabbage, and cauliflower, among others. Many vegetables have their very own species of flea beetle. On the West Coast, they've really taken to California cuisine—they just love arugula.

Friendly plants that seem to repel these beetles include elderberry, mint, catnip, and wormwood.

Flea beetles are said to be attracted to traps baited with beer. They can also be trapped with white cards smeared with a sticky substance.

These hopping beetles dislike moisture, so first zap them with a hard spray of water. Other sprays that can be used against them effectively include garlic spray, onion spray, wormwood tea, or soap spray.

Flea beetles have several generations a year in the South. Cultivate around the plants regularly to kill or expose their eggs. Like other pests, they seem to favor the weakest plants, so be sure that your plants have the advantage of a rich soil with a high organic content.

The plants flea beetles have infested can also be dusted with wood ashes or soot mixed with lime. The dusts adhere better if the plant has been misted first.

Adult beetles lay eggs on the soil when they "awaken" (emerge) in early spring. The fewer the weeds and garden debris left in the garden from last fall, the fewer

215

the beetles this spring. Tilling the soil also helps get rid of the grubs. When the larvae emerge, they feed on the roots. The adults feed on weeds while waiting for the good stuff to appear in the garden. They especially like young plants, so in the spring cover new plants with fabric row covers or screen covers.

GOPHERS

▼▼▼▼▼▼▼▼▼▼▼▼▼▼▼▼▼▼▼▼▼▼▼▼▼▼▼▼

Our backyard battles with these subterranean scavengers fluctuate between farce and tragedy, frustration and triumph.

Early French settlers gave the animal they found burrowing in North America its name after the French word *gaufre*, which means "honeycomb." Because the word is often used to describe a variety of burrowing animals, there is some confusion about what we mean by *gopher*.

When you see a raised ridge of earth in your garden or yard, the culprit is likely a mole, not a gopher, and moles are mostly beneficial in that they eat subterranean insects as they burrow. (See *Moles*.)

When we say gopher, we mean the *pocket gopher*, rodents that eat a wide variety of plants, starting with the roots, including roses, tomatoes, peppers, carrots, gladioli, fruit trees, grape roots, dahlias, delphiniums, hollyhocks, garlic, squash, cucumbers, melons, tulips, lilies—to name just a few. Of course, the plants they usually strike are the ones you cared about the most.

Described as "all mouth and no heart," the gopher doesn't just nibble on a little bit of the plant, or even allow it to send out calls for help in the way of limp or yellow leaves. There's no time given for negotiation. One minute the plant is upright and looking fine, and suddenly, with the slightest tremor of a breeze, it topples over, gone, never to be resuscitated. Even more outrageous is the sight of a plant being pulled into the ground, leaf, stock, and stem. Then you know you have a pocket gopher and not a mole or a ground squirrel.

The only way to keep the gopher from getting the next plant is to get the gopher. First study the earthen burrows to locate it. Both gophers and moles push out dirt mounds from lateral runs off their main tunnels, and these are often important clues to their presence. Mole runs go along just under the surface, whereas gopher runs are deeper. Furthermore, a molehill is circular, and a gopher hole has a fan-shaped pile of dirt. Sometimes a gopher will plug its hole after pushing out the dirt onto the mound, but one can still see the fresh dirt.

Busy workers, gophers can dig a hundred-foot tunnel in a day. Although they lead solitary lives and will fight with other gophers whom they happen to meet, a number of gophers can cohabit a plot of land together, living entirely alone in separate tunnels. A gopher can have from one to three litters a year, with usually five or six young.

The most bothersome to gardeners, pocket gophers are so called because of the fur-lined pockets on their cheeks in which they carry roots and other foods back to their storage chambers. The teeth never wear out because they continue to grow—up to fourteen inches a year. Remarkably, they never get dirt in their mouths.

CONTROL

In their impotence against this wily adversary, people have resorted to poisons that could kill armies. They inject them with special applicators into the soil, and these toxins eventually make their way to the water table. Poison's disadvantage is that you never really know if you got the gopher—unless, of course, your dog dies from

217

eating the animal. Strychnine, a poison used against gophers, is extremely poisonous to mammals (including people) and fish.

In gopher territory, one of the best systems of defense is a barrier. Dig up the planting bed and line it with half-inch galvanized wire fencing mesh buried two feet under the soil. Around the edges, make sure the wire comes all the way up to the surface of the soil and even a few inches above it. Young trees can be planted into large holes lined with light wire mesh. Once mature, the trees will not be as vulnerable to attack.

We know a person who grew flowers commercially in a large outdoor field. He always planted several rows of bulbs, such as tubers, amaryllis, and lilies, at the edges of the field. He claimed these satisfied the gophers and kept them out of his flowers but admitted they were an expensive way to buy them off.

Do not underestimate the gopher's own predators, which include owls, hawks, skunks, cats, dogs, badgers, coyotes, and snakes. Try putting a gopher snake or king snake down the gopher hole and let it do the killing. Local pet stores sometimes have these snakes. Build a nesting box for barn owls, which can eat several gophers apiece every night.

Another tactic consists of rolling up pieces of Juicy Fruit gum and putting them into the gopher holes. If they eat it, the gum plugs up their intestines. Put on gloves when handling the gum to eliminate your human smell.

Repellants

Gophers reportedly avoid garlic plants. A garlic-and-onion-smelling rock can even be purchased and buried in different spots in the garden. The crown imperial plant has a skunklike smell that gophers supposedly dislike. They are also said to avoid oleander and scilla bulbs, also called squill.

Some feel it's possible to use noisemakers to discourage gophers, which have acute hearing. Try placing a plastic pinwheel (or several of them) in the ground near the tunnel. A small windmill, attached to a stake driven deep into the ground, can be augmented with pieces of wood or clothespins attached to the propellors, making it clatter as it turns. This system requires wind.

We once saw a homemade "gopher wind chime" made from pieces of short metal galvanized pipe hung from cords attached to a pie pan. The pie pan was affixed to the top of a big metal pipe driven deeply into the ground. Hitting against this pipe, the metal "chimes" caused an underground vibration.

You might even want to try a small battery operated radio, securely wrapped inside a plastic bag, set on loud static and placed inside the tunnel.

Other items that can be placed in the tunnel are dead gophers, dead fish or fish heads, canned sardines, rotting garbage, paper towels soaked in rancid oil, urine, sponges saturated with ammonia, and thorny branches. Make sure that all the holes are closed so that the tunnel gets as smelly as possible. All these materials decompose in the soil. We do not recommend broken glass or barbed wire because it will remain in place and may pose a future hazard.

Trapping

The best way to get rid of gophers is by trapping. A good gopher trapper embodies the best of the tiny game hunter: keen observation, great persistence, and creative flexibility. Some areas have professional gopher trappers, people who come to your place and get paid by the body count. They can also teach you how to do the trapping properly.

To be effective, gopher traps must be placed correctly. Study a fresh mound to locate the main tunnel. Determine which portion of the mound is the base of the fan—the most recent site of earth ejection. Take a sharp spade and cut through it at that point. With some luck you will expose the tunnel.

Set *two* traps facing in opposite directions inside the tunnel and cover them well so that no light enters the tunnel. Attach the traps to a rope or chain on a stake or the gopher may drag them off. Wear gloves when handling the traps, because human odor is a great repellant. Wash traps in hot soapy water before using.

Traps can be baited with potatoes, green onions, leeks, handfuls of grass, bamboo sprigs, pieces of raw vegetables, grains, or nuts. Check the traps daily; if you don't catch anything in a day or two, move them.

Old-fashioned metal gopher traps and wooden bottom rat traps are considered to be among the best, although setting them can be a little tricky.

Flooding

If you need to deep water your trees anyway and can afford the water bill, stick a garden hose down into the tunnel and flood out the gopher. Two hoses at opposite ends of the garden work even better. It may take a while if the tunnels are extensive. Sometimes you can detect movement going along a tunnel. Take a shovel and stick it in the ground to block the gopher's progress. Some people lay in wait and whack the gopher with a shovel when it appears. Others merely pray that it moves next door.

Fumigation

The gopher can often be smoked out of its tunnel or driven back into the neighbor's yard. One of the easiest ways is to stick lighted "gopher bombs" or highway flares into the tunnel and close it off carefully with dirt so that the gas doesn't escape. Another method is to use flexible metal exhaust pipes, garden hoses, or vacuum

Smoking Out a Gopher

cleaner hoses—and lots of duct tape—and fill the tunnels with exhaust from either the tail pipe of a running car or a gas-powered lawn mower.

GRASSHOPPERS

▼▼▼▼▼▼▼▼▼▼▼▼▼▼▼▼▼▼▼▼▼▼▼▼▼▼▼▼

Grasshoppers have plagued us through history, devouring millions of acres of our crops. But this is one pest on which we've taken a similar revenge: the Bible describes the eating of grasshoppers with honey, and American Indians used to dip them in saltwater, then bake them and eat them or make flour out of them.

Grasshoppers and locusts were once thought to be two separate creatures, until the startling discovery was made that under certain circumstances, including food shortage, some species of solitary grasshoppers actually metamorphosed into gregarious locusts, multiplied unbelievably, and took off in swarms of inconceivable numbers.

221

Before the twentieth century, the arrival of these locusts (sometimes described as "grasshoppers gone crazy") meant that famine and great mortality were sure to follow. The desert people called them "the teeth of the wind." The American settlers in the 1800s called them hoppers, fighting them off with small success and great losses. Locusts would literally darken the sky as they appeared, accompanied by a great roaring, crackling sound. Where they landed they ate everything except native grasses—including the paint off houses. Locusts have done much to contribute to the idea that insects are our enemies, and every year is the year of the locust somewhere in the world.

Grasshoppers in the home garden can be big pests because they eat so much. They range from an inch to two-and-a-half inches long and are dark gray, green, yellowish, brown, or black. Powerful hind legs let them jump a whopping twenty to thirty inches, and they can also fly for very long distances. Their powerful jaws and teeth are great for chomping.

Grasshopper

CONTROL

Look for clusters of creamy or yellow eggs in the shape of rice. Destroy them by digging up the soil in the fall; you will kill the eggs or bury them so deeply—at least six inches—the hatched grasshoppers can't make it to the surface in the spring. A good thick mulch will also make it hard for them to come above ground.

Grasshoppers can be picked off at night by going out with a flashlight and getting them while they sleep. Or you can handpick them in the early morning while they are still lethargic. Wear gloves or use an extra pair of kitchen tongs and drop the bugs into a jar of soapy water.

Here is a lazy way to get rid of grasshoppers: Make a solution of molasses water using 1 part molasses to 10 parts water. Fill widemouthed containers or dishes half full with this solution and set them around the yard. The grasshoppers will go after the sweet concoction, and the birds, especially jays, will go after the grasshoppers. Birds love grasshoppers. (See *Wild Tiny Game Hunters* for ways to attract birds to the garden.) Other predators include praying mantids, spiders, if they get them in their webs, snakes, toads, coyotes, skunks, and chickens. Ground beetles and blister beetles will devour grasshopper eggs—another reason not to use pesticides.

In addition to using molasses in water to trap them, you can also try other ingredients such as citrus juices, vanilla, beer, and vinegar.

An old-fashioned grasshopper trap, called a hopper trough trap or hopperdozer, dates back to the days of the American settlers. To make one, take a long narrow wooden box, shaped like a planter box, and nail a three-foot-high piece of wood to one side. Put a little soapy water in the box and drag it between rows of vegetables. When grasshoppers try to jump over the box, they hit the "backboard" and fall in. Putting sticky substance on the wood will make this trap even more effective.

Spray hot pepper spray or onion/garlic/pepper spray right on the plants to keep grasshoppers from eating them. (See *Tactics of Tiny Game Hunting* for recipe.)

Covering plants with cheesecloth or fabric row covers will also keep grasshoppers from getting to them. Leave enough room for the plants to grow under the fabric, securing it well around the edges with dirt and rocks.

An effective biological control for grasshoppers is with a naturally occurring spore or parasite called *Nosema locustae*, which infects the insects with a killing disease. It has to be ingested by the grasshoppers and comes in the form of baited wheat bran under the trade name Nolo Bait. When a grasshopper eats the bait, the spore is activated inside its digestive system, slowing its ability to feed and eventually killing it. The disease spreads from grasshopper to grasshopper, as they are cannibalistic. Timing is important; starting in early summer is best, as grasshoppers should still be young and between one-quarter to three-quarter inch in length when it is applied.

GYPSY MOTHS

▼▼▼▼▼▼▼▼▼▼▼▼▼▼▼▼▼▼▼▼▼▼▼▼▼▼▼

After the accidental release of gypsy moths in Medford, Massachusetts, in 1869, by an astronomer who should have known better, the voracious caterpillar descendants of this prolific moth went on to defoliate millions of trees. The Frenchman who brought them to this country had been hoping to breed them with silkworms to help the French silk industry.

It took twenty years for the infestation to build to truly grandiose proportions. By the 1880s, the caterpillars in Medford were described as coming down the street in a black tide. They fell off the trees onto people and covered their hats and clothing, and they defoliated the trees like mad.

The female moth lays her eggs in large clusters of several hundred to a thousand, covered with hairs from her body. These clusters overwinter under stones, on tree trunks, and on many other kinds of surfaces—patio furniture, planters, cars, trucks, and campers. People have unknowingly transported many an egg cluster to a new location. When the eggs hatch, the caterpillars climb the trees.

The female moths themselves don't fly. The hairy little caterpillars travel by hanging themselves from the trees on silken threads they spin, until the wind picks them up and carries them aloft. They can easily go half a mile, and a strong wind will take them farther.

Although they completely devour all the leaves on a tree, gypsy moths kill few of the trees that they infest; but they do weaken them. Also, when a forest loses its leaves in the summer, the ecology of that landscape changes. Furthermore, certain trees do not fare as well as others, changing the makeup of the forest. Although the moths prefer oak and other hardwoods, they will feed on over four hundred plant species.

Over the years, an incredible barrage of pesticides was sprayed but failed to control them or even stop their spreading. In the 1950s three million acres were sprayed with DDT in the Northeast, killing songbirds, fish, and crabs and forcing beekeepers out of business. This spraying may have made the problem even worse by getting rid of the moths' enemies.

Infestations seem to come and go and have peak years—in 1981 this amounted to almost ten million acres of defoliated forests. Ultimately, when the moths reach peak populations, a virus kills off most of them, quite spectacularly, and then the cycle starts all over again. Numerous predators have been imported against this moth from all over the world, including flies, wasps, a white-footed mouse, and a large ground beetle that, despite its name, climbs trees and feeds on larvae and pupae. Brachonoid wasps and tachnid flies are among those who parasitize them.

CONTROL

These moths have been called "pests of people," not of trees, mainly because they do not destroy forests so much as they outrage homeowners by crawling all over their backyard, causing skin rashes and ruining the looks of the best trees. The best solution is for each person to fight his or her own moths to bring them within a personal tolerance level.

Eggs can be scraped off surfaces and dumped into ammonia or soap solutions. Banding the trees in late May and June may capture many of the caterpillars. Tie a piece of burlap or wool to the tree and fold it over to make a double layer, with the fold at the top. The caterpillars, who are nocturnal, will crawl under it, seeking shade in the daytime. Then you can shake them out over a large pan of soapy water.

To keep the caterpillars out of the trees, band the trunks with a sticky substance. (See *Tactics of Tiny Game Hunting.*) Remember, these caterpillars are travelers; if kept out of one tree, they will simply move to another.

Bacillus thuringiensis sprayed on the caterpillars will be effective if done at the right time. Use a commercial sprayer available from garden catalogues—or hire a tree company. Apparently, it is not used widely on forests because it has to be reapplied every two weeks and hence is too expensive. The insecticide neem has also been used successfully against them.

Pheromone or sex attractant traps are available for these moths. They are usually coated with Dispalure or Gyplure, which lure the males. These pheromones can also be sprayed to cause general mayhem, confusion, and nonperformance among the male moths.

Birds are wonderful predators of these caterpillars, and they should all get medals for eating such hairy creatures. Moles, shrews, skunks, chipmunks, and squirrels are also predators, so the more such animals live in the yard, the better off you are.

If your trees are attacked and turned into the ugly ones on the block, do not abandon them. In order to bounce back they will need nurturing—adequate water and good feeding of the soil.

JAPANESE BEETLES

▼▼▼▼▼▼▼▼▼▼▼▼▼▼▼▼▼▼▼▼▼▼▼▼▼▼▼▼▼

What a mess these beetles can make of people's gardens. They are about as popular among gardeners in the Eastern United States as Japanese cars are in Detroit.

The Japanese beetle invasion took place in New Jersey in 1916, when they hitch-hiked in on some plants from Japan. That has been the time-honored way that some of our worst pests got their start here, while their natural predators missed the boat. After their arrival, the Japanese beetle flourished far better than they ever did in Japan.

The infestation began in the East, but they have been gradually spreading west. The beetles devour a wide variety of plants, around three hundred of them, including your favorite roses. They chew on leaves, going for the choice meat between the veins and leaving the leaf in lacy shreds. They also feed, often in clusters, on flowers and ripe fruit. Later they lay eggs in the grass, and the C-shaped grubs root around under lawns and do a great deal of damage. If you start getting brown patches of dead grass, suspect Japanese beetle grubs. You can dig up the sod and look under it. If the grubs are there, you'll see them.

Japanese Beetle

CONTROL

The adult beetles are fairly easy to handpick. In the early morning before the sun makes them active, they can be shaken out of bushes and plants onto a cloth or opened umbrella laid on the ground. Later in the day, they are so busy eating that they will hardly notice when you pick them up and throw them into a can of liquid end-of-the-road. (Soapy water or water and rubbing alcohol.)

Japanese beetles are easy to trap, so easy that placing some of the commercial traps in your yard may draw beetles from all over the neighborhood. Put them downwind and well away from the plants you want to protect so that the newcomers heading upwind will reach the traps first. These traps generally are made of a funnel over a jar or bag that has been baited with a pheromone or a scent the beetles find attractive. Since many people believe the pheromone traps are too effective, you

227

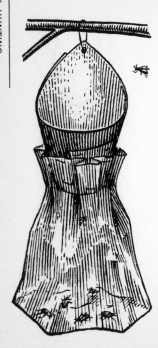

Japanese Beetle Trap

could try experimenting with some less potent ones. Make your own trap by taking stiff yellow construction paper and folding it into a cone with a hole at the bottom. Staple or tape it to a plastic bag (preferably not a clear one) into which you have poured a little geraniol oil—a rose scent used in soaps.

This trap appeared in *Consumers' Research* magazine: Take a small can of fruit cocktail, open it, and let it sit in the sun for a week until it ferments (keep the ants away). Then place it on a block in the middle of a yellow bowl or pail filled with soapy water to just below the top of the can. Place it about twenty-five feet from the plants that need protection. The beetles zero in on the smell of the fruit, fall into the water, and drown. To make your own fermenting mixture, simply combine mashed ripened fruit, water, sugar, and a little yeast.

Another trap is made by suspending a can of grape juice inside a pail of soapy water. Drill holes in the top of the can so that you can tie it to the bucket handles. The beetles will fly right for the aroma of the juice, miss, and fall into the water. These traps will work better if they are set at least a foot off the ground.

Extracts from the neem tree are said to be quite effective at keeping these pests away. Parasitic wasps and flies can also be used to control them, and spiders do an excellent job. Nematodes can be purchased and applied to the soil against the grubs. Moles, skunks, and birds will devour them. Dry weather and an alkaline soil tend to keep the population down.

Because Japanese beetles spend ten months out of their one-year life cycle as grubs in the ground, the best control is milky spore disease (*Bacillus popilliae*), which attacks them at this stage. It can be easily applied to grass by the teaspoon (it comes in a powder) and then watered into the soil. Once in the ground, it infects the ground-dwelling grubs with a disease that turns them white and kills them. Although it takes several years for the spore disease to accumulate in the soil, it will last for several decades. Milky spore disease is harmless to humans, animals, and plants. It also kills June beetle grubs, but that is all for the good. If you have a problem with Japanese beetles, try to get all your neighbors to apply treatment, too. That way their beetles won't show up in your yard. If they won't cooperate, you may need to stage secret midnight milky spore attacks on their yards. If you don't wish to be arrested as a Peeping Tom, try lobbing a burstable packet over the fence or hedge.

MEALYBUGS

▼▼▼▼▼▼▼▼▼▼▼▼▼▼▼▼▼▼▼▼▼▼▼▼▼▼▼▼▼

These plant-sucking insects look like little fluffs of white, greasy or waxy cotton snuggled down into the crevices between stalks and stems or clamped onto the undersides of leaves. These may look wimpy, but they are one tough little bug. They don't move around much, just stick their mouthparts into the plant and suck out its juices.

Mealybugs can be found all over the United States but are especially common in the South and on houseplants—probably because their predators can't get into the house. Some give birth to live young, whereas others lay hundreds of eggs, which they cover with a white coating similar to the one they hide under.

The more water and nonorganic fertilizer a plant gets, the higher its nitrogen content, and the more this pest is attracted to it. Furthermore, a small infestation can rapidly become a large one, and if unchecked they will kill the plant.

Like aphids, mealybugs excrete honeydew, so ants may be protecting them from predators. Keep ants away from these plants with sticky barriers. (See *Ants*.)

If the infestation is not too severe, pick them off with a toothpick or a pair of tweezers, a procedure that can be fun. Or use a small paintbrush or cotton swab dipped in rubbing alcohol (or fingernail polish remover) and swab the mealybug.

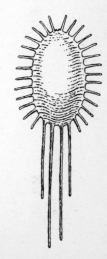

Long-Tailed Mealybug

229

The alcohol or acetone destroys the insect's protective waxy cover, then kills the bug itself. Sometimes it takes more than one treatment to really get them. Try not to get any of the liquid on the plant leaves.

A strong jet of water can be used against mealybugs outdoors. Homemade soap spray, Safer's insecticidal soap, or horticultural oils can be also be used, as can quassia spray, an old remedy. As a very last resort, use a nicotine or a pyrethrum spray.

Increase the predator population in your garden. Buy and disperse ladybug beetles or mealybug destroyers, a kind of ladybug beetle. Lacewing larvae also make wonderful mealybug predators. Syrphid flies and chalcid wasps search them out and destroy them by laying eggs on them.

MEXICAN BEAN BEETLES

▼▼▼▼▼▼▼▼▼▼▼▼▼▼▼▼▼▼▼▼▼▼▼▼▼

The Mexican bean beetle is known as the rotten relative of the beneficial, insect-eating ladybird beetle. It doesn't seem quite fair that it got this bad reputation just for being a vegetarian in a family of meat eaters. You can distinguish it by the sixteen—no more, no less—spots on its copper, rounded body, one-quarter of an inch long. True to its name, this insect loves the members of the bean family, specifically the leaves, which it eats until nothing is left except useless, limp skeletons.

Usually a female lays around four hundred eggs, but she can lay as many as fifteen hundred, so a small problem can rapidly escalate into a large one. Even before it turns into a hungry adult beetle, it does a lot of damage as a weird yellow grub, one-third of an inch long and covered with spines. Commonly found east of the Rocky Mountains, the Mexican bean beetle overwinters right in your garden under woodpiles or among plant debris.

Mexican Bean Beetle

You may mistake a bean leaf beetle for this one. That's okay. Even though it belongs to an entirely different family, the bean leaf beetle looks and behaves quite a bit like the Mexican bean beetle and deserves the same treatment.

Interplanting potato plants with bean plants helps keep the beetles away. This planting arrangement also protects the potatoes from their nemesis, the Colorado potato beetle. Marigold, summer savory, rosemary, nasturtiums, and garlic are also good companion plants for bean protection.

Don't hesitate to handpick this beetle and crunch it or drop it into a can of soapy water. Even more important, try to get at its orange-yellow eggs laid on the undersides of leaves in groups of about fifty.

Garlic spray will repel it, and pyrethrum or rotenone will kill it. Insecticides made from the neem tree are also effective.

You can order from a supplier a parasitic wasp, the *Pediobius* wasp. Praying mantids, ladybugs, and the spined soldier bug will also eat these bugs. The nymphs of spined soldier bugs eat hatching bean beetles, and the adults move over to eat cabbageworms. What a good bug!

MITES OR SPIDER MITES
▼▼▼▼▼▼▼▼▼▼▼▼▼▼▼▼▼▼▼▼▼▼▼▼▼▼▼

We have good reason to hate mites. These distant, no-good relatives of spiders cause an amazing lot of damage. Like their other relative, the tick, they can be quite frustrating because they're so hard to see. A magnifying glass (10X or 15X hand lens) comes in handy when searching for these pests, although their presence eventually becomes quite obvious. Some feed on plant stems and the undersides of leaves with their piercing/sucking mouthparts, causing stippling or yellowing of the leaves, which then drop off.

If your plant looks discouraged with life, look for spider mites. Gossamer strands or webbing between the leaves gives a clue to the mites' presence. Or hold a piece of white paper under a leaf and tap it. If you see tiny, moving little dots on the paper, you have mites. Red spider mites (or two-spotted spider mites), the most common garden spider mite, may look like specks of red pepper.

Mites do not thrive in high humidity or under frequent watering. The hotter the weather and the dustier the plant, the more they flourish and the more eggs a female will lay. Quick regeneration is the root of the problem, with the worst damage occurring during the hot summer months.

Although pesticides have destroyed many of their natural enemies, the mites themselves have become quite resistant to pesticides. According to *National Gardening* magazine, they have become "epidemic around the country."

CONTROL

A number of essential oils that are said to be useful as repellants—at a dilution at 1:50 with water—are coriander oil, oil of lemon grass, lavender oil, or geramium oil. Mites are also repelled by members of the onion family, including chives and garlic.

Spraying frequently with strong jets of water during the morning and evening not only knocks the pests off the leaves, it also improves the humidity around the plant. Be sure to aim the jet of water at the undersides of the leaves. Mites are another good reason to mulch, because when a plant is water stressed, mites seem to do even more damage.

Soap sprays will kill the adult mites but have to be resprayed to kill the eggs as they hatch. Use a soap spray once every four or five days for three weeks.

Another effective spray consists of mixing 2 cups wheat flower, 2 gallons water, and ¼ cup buttermilk; spray this mixture on the infested plants. Glue spray (see *Tactics of Tiny Game Hunting*) will also impale and clog up the pests.

If the weather is over seventy degrees and under ninety, you can dust the plants with sulfur. This is a very old and fairly reliable technique, but wear a mask when applying the dust.

A weak solution of saltwater, very weak, can be used against mites—1 tablespoon to a gallon of water. Seawater has also been used with good results, but take care, as some plants cannot tolerate salt. Test the plant by spraying one small section first, then observe for damage.

A dormant oil spray can be a good defense when used in the fall or spring. During the growing season, spray with a lighter oil. Diatomaceous earth can also be dusted around the soil and onto the plants. Use a face mask and goggles.

Natural predators can be very important in their control. Tiny black lady beetles, known as spider mite destroyers, lacewing larvae, ladybugs, and predatory mites (we refer to them as mighty mites), all can be ordered from suppliers. Predator mites are almost as invisible as the mites themselves, but they move a lot faster and don't spin webs. All these predators are highly vulnerable to pesticides, so using poisons only leads to greater problems with the harmful mites.

NEMATODES
▼▼▼▼▼▼▼▼▼▼▼▼▼▼▼▼▼▼▼▼▼▼▼▼▼▼▼▼▼

They may not be bugs or insects, but bad nematodes are really bad. These miniscule-to-microscopic roundworms attack the root systems of plants, making it possible for bacteria and fungi to invade. Fortunately, only a small percentage of all

233

nematodes are harmful. Most are quite beneficial and attack grubs and other harmful pests in the soil.

You won't know you have nematodes until the plant shows signs of damage—stunting, wilting, or yellowing leaves. Root-knot nematodes cause galls or bulbous swelling or small growths along the roots. Others are harder to identify. You may have to pull out the plant, put it in a bag along with some of its soil, and take it to an agricultural extension plant expert or send it to the nearest agricultural experiment station.

It seems that the smaller the pest, the better it can reproduce; nematodes are no exception, for a female root-knot nematode can lay from three hundred to three thousand eggs in one gelatinous mass near the roots.

CONTROL

Fumigants and nematode-killing chemicals are extremely toxic. Many that were used for decades have now been removed from the market. One of these, DBCP, was banned in 1977 after being linked to sterility in the workers who manufactured it and to cancer in laboratory animals. This same chemical has now been found in 428 wells across the state of California. Furthermore, using these kinds of chemicals also kills every beneficial organism.

During hot and sunny weather you can heat nematodes out of your garden with solarization. The best time to do it is during July or August, when the temperature is high and the chance of rain is low. Prepare the soil for cultivation, then water thoroughly until the ground is saturated. Cover the soil with heavy-duty clear plastic and secure the perimeter with dirt and rocks. The temperature under the plastic can heat up to 140 degrees. In about four to six weeks, this heat will cook out the nematodes, as well as many insect larvae and a significant amount of weed seeds.

Some people advise clearing all plants from a nematode-infested area and keeping anything from growing there for at least three years. Who wants to do that? A much more ornamental, but still drastic, treatment consists of planting the entire area in French or African marigolds. The marigolds give off a chemical from their roots that is toxic to nematodes. When the marigolds have finished blooming, dig them into the soil.

Asparagus plants also produce chemicals that are inimical to nematodes. Every time you cook asparagus, pour the cooking water back into the garden. Other plants said to discourage nematodes are dahlias, salvia, calendula, hairy indigo, velvet beans, and garlic.

Sugar apparently draws moisture from the soil and dries out the nematodes. To kill them with sweetness, dissolve 1 cup sugar in 2 cups boiling water, add it to 1 gallon of water, and pour into the soil.

Rotating plants regularly and planting cover crops will also help. Nematodes are both host specific and homebodies, so they will starve if you move their favorite plants to another spot in the garden.

The higher the organic content of the soil, the better protected your plants will be. In nature, nematodes have plenty of enemies, including other cannibalistic nematodes and worm-catching, nematode-trapping fungi. These will all be found in a soil that is rich in organic matter. Use lots of good compost and heavy mulch in the garden. Apply fish emulsion, and don't forget to try seaweed, which is said to make plants more resistant to nematodes. Seaweed (extract or dried) can be added directly to the soil or used as a foliar spray.

ROOT MAGGOTS

▼▼▼▼▼▼▼▼▼▼▼▼▼▼▼▼▼▼▼▼▼▼▼▼▼

Cabbage Root Maggot

Gardeners can develop a real distaste for these pests. The fly, which looks all too much like a house fly, lays its eggs in the dirt. When their young hatch, the white worms (maggots) burrow down among the roots and feed voraciously. By the time the plant starts to wilt, it's usually too late to save it. Pulling it up by the roots and finding the little white worms will convince you that, with this pest, the best defense should have been started a good deal sooner.

Two common root maggots are the cabbage root maggot and the onion root maggot, but others attack the roots of cabbage, broccoli, cauliflower, radish, turnips, onions, leeks, shallots, and chives. Still another fly, the carrot rust fly, attacks carrots in the same manner. Root maggots are more likely to attack young seedlings, but they will produce several generations and torment the plants throughout the season.

CONTROL

Save used tea bags and mix the tea leaves into the planting mix as a repellant to the maggots. We have also heard of people who mix fresh, unused coffee into their planting mix to deter carrot root maggots.

The traditional means of control is to make root maggot mats. Pieces of tar paper or old sections of carpeting, cut into squares with slits to slip around the plant stem, will keep the maggots from penetrating the soil. Cover the slits with waterproof tape. Little bits of torn-up tar paper will repel them, as they don't like the smell of tar. (Who does?)

Some people take a big container to their favorite restaurant and ask the cook to throw all the eggshells into it for them. You can crush those shells into sharp little fragments and mix them into the soil to keep the maggots from getting through in one piece. A good mulch of oak leaves will do the same thing, as will mixing diatomaceous earth into the soil. Another mulch that acts as an impassible barrier is sawdust. It has to be at least two inches thick and extend six inches out from the plant. Pile the sawdust right up against the stem.

Or sprinkle wood ashes around the base of plants. Some people dust wood ashes right onto the plants, too. If you want to get fancy, make a mixture of equal parts lime, rock phosphate, and bone meal. To this mixture, add an equal amount of wood ashes and mix into the soil around the plant and even put it into the hole when planting. Besides being bad for the maggots, it is good for the plants.

Others soak a third of their seeds before planting them with the unsoaked seeds. The soaked seeds will sprout first, get eaten by the maggots, and leave the later plants to flourish. This sounds quite clever, but it does amount to feeding the enemy.

Another method of control is to cover plants with fabric row covers or cones made of window screens to keep the flies from laying eggs on the plants in the first place.

A more up-to-date treatment consists of using parasitic nematodes. Chalcid and trichogramma wasps can also be released. Rove beetles are the great unsung heroes in the cabbage maggot root wars. If pesticides are used, of course, there won't be any beetles to do battle for you.

Onion Root Maggot

237

SCALE INSECTS

▼▼▼▼▼▼▼▼▼▼▼▼▼▼▼▼▼▼▼▼▼▼▼▼▼▼▼

There are many kinds of scales, around seventeen hundred species, and all can be tricky adversaries. Using their own discarded skins from molting, along with fine waxy threads, they construct little domelike shells, or scales, under which they carry on as unobtrusively as possible, often blending in with the plant. Some are no bigger than a pinhead. By the time you notice them, the infestation may already be out of hand, and they are difficult to eradicate.

Scale insects can be classified as either hard (armored) or soft (tortoise-shelled), depending on their hideouts. They come in a great variety of colors from black, brown, yellow, or white, to transparent, gray, green, and even pink. A scale insect sucks out plant juices with mouthparts like a fine filament, often injecting toxic substances or viruses. It lays its eggs (hundreds of them) under its protective coating. When the eggs hatch, the young crawl away and find their own sucking spots. Once they find a spot, their legs actually fall off, and they're set for life. The plant under siege loses vigor and begins to wilt or show growth distortion.

CONTROL

Insecticides work only if the spray happens to catch the insects at the odd moment when they are still crawling around. When scale insects are hidden under their shells, they are for the most part impervious to pesticides.

In the eighteenth century, gardeners used to sponge off scale manually with tobacco tea. Now people use a soapy solution or an oil emulsion for this task. To do this, take a plastic scouring pad or a soft toothbrush and go at them. If there are only a few, a fingernail will do the trick. So will swabbing them carefully with alcohol or turpentine.

Horticultural oils, sprayed in the late winter before new growth, will suffocate them. Glue spray (see *Tactics of Tiny Game Hunting*) will also smother them. Insecticidal soap or soapy water can be used later; they work by dissolving the waxy covering.

When it comes to scale, you need predators! Ladybugs are excellent, but you will have to keep the ants away. Because soft scale insects produce honeydew, they are often tended by ants, who guard them from predators. The ants can actually lead you to a scale infestation you may not have noticed. Ants can be kept away by sprinkling bone meal or diatomaceous earth around the base of the plants and by wrapping and banding the tree trunk or plant stem with a sticky substance. (See *Ants.*)

Regularly spraying the plant with water will rid it of dust that may inhibit many of the potential parasites and predators. Other predators include parasitic wasps, aphid lions, predaceous mites, and syrphid flies.

SLUGS AND SNAILS
▼▼▼▼▼▼▼▼▼▼▼▼▼▼▼▼▼▼▼▼▼▼▼▼▼▼▼▼▼

What a perfect pest. Deeply unloved and often ridiculed (*gastropod* means "stomach foot"), they're fun to hate, easy to kill, and maddeningly frustrating to control. Slugs and snails eat large ragged holes in plants. They'll even eat the whole plant if it's young and tender. Both their destructive plant chomping and their silvery trails are dead giveaways to their presence.

These creatures of slime, who destroy by night and hide out by day, bring out the tiny game hunter in everyone. Because many species came from other countries, they don't have a good supply of natural predators in the United States. Thus we humans must be the predators.

The chief difference between a slug and a snail is that the slugs lack the spiral shell that snails tote around. The brown garden snail was introduced in this country in San Francisco in the 1850s by a Frenchman who thought he could get Americans to eat them. He was wrong, largely because he picked the wrong species. If people wouldn't even try them in San Francisco, it was surely hopeless for the rest of the country. Undaunted, the snails set out on their own to conquer the country and have succeeded so far in becoming the most common snail pest in California.

Several species of pest slugs range from a quarter inch to six inches in length and are gray, brown, yellow-ochre, and spotted. They are capable of eating thirty to forty times their body weight each day, and they range throughout North America.

Snails are mobile creatures and can travel a mile in about fifteen days. Slugs are almost twice as fast, traveling the same distance in eight days. In your garden, a snail may travel a hundred feet for a meal.

Both slugs and snails hide during sunny days in shady, preferably moist, spots under leaves, rubble, stones, and garden debris. They also favor certain plants for living quarters, among them agapanthus, lilies, irises, ice plants, ivy, nasturtiums, jasmine, and strawberries. You may consider thinning out plants like these where snails congregate and breed.

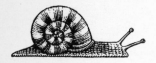

Snail

Slug

BARRIERS

The tender, soft, slimy bodies of slugs and snails need a fairly smooth surface on which to travel. (Can you imagine trying to navigate your garden on your tongue?)

Their trails, in fact, are self-created roadways laid down with mucus, which is why barriers are effective against them. They can be laid down around individual plants (bedding plants are particularly vulnerable), the perimeter of a planting bed, or even an entire garden.

Good barriers consist of wood ashes, hydrated lime, ammonium sulfate, marble dust, crushed oyster shells (from feed stores), crushed eggshells, diatomaceous earth, or sawdust. Sand is less effective. Make sure the barrier is at least three inches wide, the wider the better. If the barrier gets wet, it will need to be replenished.

A good mulch of oak leaves will also repel slugs and snails, as will drenching the soil with wormwood tea. Gather seaweed from the beach, and spread it around as a mulch. Not only does it makes a good barrier, it will also be good for the soil.

Some garden supply centers sell different kinds of fabricated barriers, some of which resemble strips of sandpaper; others have salt imbedded in the material.

Copper strips, available through mail order, make excellent barriers. Apparently slugs' and snails' moist bodies react with the copper and set up an electrical charge that shocks and repels them. These strips are also effective as barriers on trees. Snails love citrus trees and can be real pests in orange groves.

TRAPS

One of the most time-honored ways to get slugs and snails is the beer trap. We just love to see our enemies brought down by vices that resemble our own.

Get a small container, like a saucer or lid, or—if you are convinced you are infested with giant snails—a pie tin. Transparent plastic saucers (the kind used under potted plants) are even aesthetically pleasing. Hollow out the dirt under the con-

*Beer Trap for Slugs and
Snails*

tainer because the top of it has to be level with the ground. Fill it with beer—some-say stale beer, although it goes stale soon enough.

We think the brand does make a difference. In a moment of frugality we once bought the cheapest beer we could find (in a discount store) and succeeded in catching exactly one slug with the six pack. The yeast in the beer is what attracts the varmints, while the alcohol befuddles them and makes it harder for them to climb out. An entomologist at Colorado State University, Whitney Cranshaw, conducted a beer tasting for slugs in 1987, killing four thousand of them in eight weeks in the name of scientific inquiry. Kingsbury Malt Beverage (from Heilman Breweries) came away with the top honors by attracting the most snails.

We advise adding a bit of bakers' yeast to the beer to make it even more effective. Some people insist that the snails drink their beer and then go home to sleep it off. Adding a little dish soap or Basic H or even flour to the beer will make it harder for them to get out. You can strain the dead snails out of the liquid and reuse it, covering it during the day to keep it from evaporating, but it is going to be most effective in the first twenty-four hours. True teetotalers prefer to use grape juice.

Another beer trap uses plastic milk containers, coffee cans, or cottage cheese containers with a number of one-inch holes around the sides, several inches from the bottom. Sink the containers into the ground up to the holes. Pour in beer and wait for the creatures to crawl right in. These traps are much harder to escape from; also, if you cover the containers, the dog can't lap up the beer. Another way to keep the dog out of the beer is to use the beer bottle itself, laid on its side.

Here's another bait that takes advantage of their attraction to yeast—and it's cheaper than beer. Mix 2 tablespoons flour with ½ teaspoon baker's yeast and 1 teaspoon sugar in 2 cups warm water. Fill your containers with this mixture. One thing about these traps that is horrid but effective: slugs and snails are attracted to the dead bodies of their own kind.

Another way to deal with slugs and snails is to provide them with the hiding places they will seek out when morning comes. Then you can go and pick them off at your leisure. Eliminate hiding places and debris they like from the garden; then they will more likely go into your traps, especially those placed in the shade. Traps can be made from such things as shingles, small boards, or overturned clay pots propped up a little on one side. Two-gallon nursery pots can be stacked together and laid on their side, with a little space between the bottoms. The snails love to crawl into this trap. Another good trap is a plastic lawn and leaf bag, preferably a green one. It helps if you dampen the ground underneath it first.

Set out grapefruit or orange rinds, like little domes, propped up a with a small stone. Or use banana peels. Slugs will be attracted by the odor and crawl under. During the day you can go get the slugs. The rinds only last a few days, however, before they start decomposing. Other hiding places of doom include cabbage leaves, lettuce leaves, and potato slices. Some people dip the cabbage leaves in kitchen grease to make them more attractive. Slugs and snails are also drawn to raw bread dough and, believe it or not, dry dog food nuggets.

Long boards laid down between beds and propped up a little will provide ample hiding places for slugs and snails. Some people lay down two boards on top of each other, separating them with a couple of stones. In the morning, remove the stones and stomp on the boards. The dead snails can be left in place to attract more the next night.

You can easily build an effective snail trap by nailing one-inch wooden strips on two sides of a board (between twelve and fifteen inches square). Redwood makes a very durable trap. Crushing a few snails on the underside of the board will draw in others. This trap was devised by entomologists from the University of California at Riverside.

Many slugs hide in the soil, so rototilling is a good way to get rid of them.

POISON

Snail poisons and bait in the form of powders, pellets, and even gloppy gooey substances are dumped on yards and garden and public landscaping by the ton. The empty snail shells leave gloat-worthy proof that these poisons work. Furthermore, they're one of the few poisons you can spread around without inhaling some of it or getting it on yourself.

Using these poisons, however, leads to highly resistant snails. And what else are you killing when you kill snails in this way? Earthworms, for one, are very vulnerable to snail poisons. And earthworms are said to deter slugs and snails since their castings are inimical to them.

Birds are other victims of snail poisons. Starlings, for example, which eat garden snails, seem to avoid gardens where poison is used. You also run the risk of poisoning your own pets and even children, since the pellet baits are attractive to them. Furthermore, certain poisons are absorbed by plants that we eat and can thus poison us.

HANDPICKING

If you have a major snail or slug infestation, the best method of control is handpicking. Because these creatures are nocturnal, begin collecting them about two hours after sundown. Water the vegetation lightly late in the afternoon; this will make the snails more active. Get your family together and give everyone a good flashlight. Tell them the snails are running (just like the grunion), and organize a contest to see who can get the most. Children are quite easily motivated by a monetary reward in these matters.

For handpicking slugs use tweezers, kitchen prongs, or an iced-tea spoon. Equip family members and guests with buckets or jars with a layer of salt in the bottom, or else use soapy or salted water in the container. Dump the dead snails (with the exception of the salted ones) onto the compost heap. Or crush the snails and bury them. They will add nutrients to the soil.

At first go out several nights in a row. Not all the slugs and snails venture out to pillage every night. When the infestation has been controlled, you will only need to go out about once a week.

Some people hate slugs so much they use shish kebab skewers and spear them up. Others have had success with small vacuum cleaners or vacuums like D-Vac made specifically for pest control.

SALTING AND SQUIRTING

If slugs are your chief problem, and you don't feel up to handpicking them, tape closed all the holes of a saltshaker except one. When you see a slug, sprinkle it with a few grains of salt. This will cause the slug to crawl out of its own slime coat. Then apply a second time—this is the lethal one. Do this several nights in a row. If you are worried about adding salt to the soil, try sprinkling the offenders with ammonium sulfate. It kills them like salt does but fertilizes the soil, too.

A squirt bottle filled with a mixture of equal parts ammonia and water will finish them off in one squirt, and the ammonia won't hurt the soil either. Another solution consists of one part vinegar and one part water. Both these techniques can be used on snails extended out of their shells.

PLANT PROTECTORS

If you have just planted a lot of new seedlings and your snail control efforts have just begun, you can protect the seedlings by cutting the bottoms out of used cans and placing them around the plants. This will protect them from other pests, too. Styrofoam cups will also work.

Old window screens (or new screening) can be cut into snail barriers. Copper screen would be ideal. In a ten-inch square of screen make a slit from one corner and cut out an opening for the plant. This is even more effective if you shred the edges of the screen by removing a few wires from the perimeter.

PREDATORS

Many beetles prey on slugs and snails, including rove beetles, carrion beetles, soldier beetles, and a big impressive specimen called the devil's coachman. In a greenhouse, where slugs are a problem, the ground beetle can be brought in to do slug duty. This beetle hunts all night and hides during the day.

Outdoors, other natural predators of snails and slugs include chickens (they like snails better than slugs), ducks, and geese. But these are not always practical in a home garden, because they'll eat your plants, too. Toads (the best), frogs, skunks, shrews, opossums, rats, moles, box turtles, birds, snakes, and lizards will also eat slugs and snails. Certain flies will prey on them, too. Birds will be more likely to eat snails if you provide them with a big flat stone that they can use to crack the shell on.

The decollate snail, a somewhat smaller snail, whose shell looks like a seashell, is the most effective natural enemy of the brown garden snail. In Southern California, a number of gardeners and citrus growers have successfully imported these snails to control the brown garden snail. Check with the mail order snail suppliers to see if you can get them where you live.

Decollate snails have the same requirements for moisture and the same nocturnal habits as the snails they prey upon. They may eat an occasional tender leaf in contact with the ground or a fallen bruised fruit, and they can be hard on some low-growing plants. But this snail actually prefers decayed vegetation, and it will not eat the healthy leaves in your garden. It does not do well in dry places, so if you order these snails try to provide some sort of damp haven just as you would for a toad or frog. The decollate does its best job on smaller snails, so you will still need to handpick the biggest snail pests in your garden. And it may take them a few years to eradicate the brown snail, so use barriers but don't use poison!

RESISTANT PLANTS

Here is a list of some of the plants that snails and slugs don't seem to like: azalea, basil, bean, corn, daffodil, fuschia, freesia, grape, ginger, holly, hibiscus, parsley, poppy, rose of Sharon, sage, sunflower, and rhododendrum. A border planted with low, spreading rosemary is one they won't want to cross. They love the fallen blossoms of hibiscus, however; these can be used as bait in traps.

247

SQUASH BUGS AND HARLEQUIN BUGS

▼▼▼▼▼▼▼▼▼▼▼▼▼▼▼▼▼▼▼▼▼▼▼▼▼▼▼▼

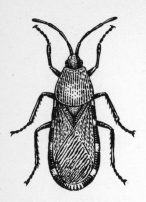

Squash Bug

Both squash bugs and harlequin bugs belong to a fairly small group of insects; they have the honor of being designated "true" bugs. Like other members of the true bug family, they have shield-shaped bodies sporting a pattern of triangular shapes on their backs. Both of these bugs are stinkers: when disturbed, they release foul-smelling chemicals.

Squash bugs are fairly large, three-eighths to one-half inch, blackish gray bugs, covered with fine black hairs like a horsehair sofa (although their close relatives may have no hairs). *Harlequin bugs*, as their name suggests, are much more colorful, black with red, orange, or yellow markings.

Squash bugs dine on squash, cantaloupe, cucumber, melons, and pumpkins. They suck leaves and stems, causing them to wilt, turn black, and die. They will also damage the fruit. Look for masses of their orange-yellow or bronze eggs in the early spring on the undersides of leaves, then destroy them. When young, the bugs are green with red appendages, later losing their color. These insects are prime candidates for handpicking.

Squash bugs are repelled by nasturtium plants and also by onion, marigold, and tansy. Some people place onion skins into newly planted cucumber hills. You can also set out boards at night around the plants. When they go into hiding after a hard night's sap sucking, they like to hide under flat surfaces. In the morning, go out and squash them.

The food that attracts squash bugs most—summer and winter squash plants—has a bitter odor. Try spraying the leaves with a solution of water and artificial vanilla flavoring. Be sure to get the undersides of the leaves. This disguises your plant from the marauders.

Also be sure to clean up all crops after harvest and rotate the planting of your crops each year.

Harlequin bugs go after members of the cabbage family, including broccoli, turnips, and kale, leaving yellow and white blotches on the leaves. They are one of the major pests of cabbage. Look for their striking white-and-black-ringed eggs under leaves.

As with squash bugs, the strongest, cleverest weapons you possess are your hands—for handpicking. But wear gloves, because these insects smell foul. Rather than crushing them, drop them into a can of soapy water or water laced with rubbing alcohol or ammonia. Planting a trap crop of mustard greens, which they love, will lure them away from your other plants and make them easier to find and pick off.

If you don't like the idea of handpicking these bugs, zap them with a squirt of soap spray or soap and alcohol spray. Sabadilla and pyrethrum can also be used in dust or spray form if you really get desperate.

Harlequin Bug

THRIPS

▼▼▼▼▼▼▼▼▼▼▼▼▼▼▼▼▼▼▼▼▼▼▼▼▼▼▼

This is another one of those what-in-the-world-could-be eating-my-plant? insects. Thrips are so tiny, they are almost invisible. About the width of a fine sewing needle endowed with feathery wings, they damage plants by scraping at the tissue and then sucking sap out of the wound. They get into tight places where sprays can't get to them. Often flowers and leaves fail to open and look twisted. Flower thrips are especially attracted to white flowers like roses. Other kinds attack onions, beans, and many other vegetables.

Sometimes the damage they cause looks like that done by mites, except that thrips do not make little webs. Instead they leave tiny dark specks of excrement and

249

whitish streaked areas on the leaves. The plant may also become susceptible to disease.

Like little daggers, thrips make a tiny slit in the plant and deposit their eggs inside it. The eggs hatch and the nymphs feed on the plant for a week or two. Some nymphs drop off the plant and spend time in the soil before climbing back up the stem.

An old remedy for thrips was to use tobacco water spray. New ones include ordering ladybugs, lacewings, and specific predatory mites and nematodes that will attack thrips. Insecticidal soap, rotenone, oil spray, or homemade garlic/hot pepper spray can be used, as well as a dusting with diatomaceous earth.

Thrips are attracted to the colors yellow and blue, so sticky traps of these colors can be used to trap the adults, or using a yellow container of soapy water. Some growers paint the plant stems with sticky substances to keep the young thrips from traveling up the plant. As with aphids, aluminum strips or mulches around the plants will confuse thrips and keep them from landing.

Remove all infested flowers and buds. Controlling weeds is also important when thrips are a problem because they thrive in them. They tend to be attracted to plants that are water stressed, so be sure to provide plenty of moisture. Put a good mulch around the plant stem, the more impermeable the better.

TOMATO HORNWORMS
▼▼▼▼▼▼▼▼▼▼▼▼▼▼▼▼▼▼▼▼▼▼▼▼▼▼▼▼

There is nothing subtle about this gargantuan caterpillar. With its impressive three-to-four-inch size, chlorophyll green color, delicate white stripes, and distinctive horn protruding from its rear end, it's hard to miss. All over the United States it goes to work stripping tomato, eggplant, pepper, and potato plants. A similar caterpillar, the tobacco hornworm, prefers tobacco but also eats tomato plants.

Handpicking the hornworm is a must. Check on the ground for little piles of caterpillar droppings, then look up straight from the evidence into the plant above. Don't worry about its horn—it seems to be little more than show. But take a good look at the caterpillar first. If it has little white cocoons stuck to its skin (they look like pearls of rice), leave it where it is; it will not live to reproduce. The cocoons are those of parasitic braconid wasps, and they will soon emerge and go find other hornworms to lay eggs on.

Planting borage, basil, and marigold around in the garden is said to keep them away.

If hornworms are a serious problem, consider using a light trap at night for the moths. (See *Tactics of Tiny Game Hunting.*) The moths, called hummingbird, sphinx, or hawk moths, are large, grayish brown and sport a five-inch wingspan. They appear soon after sunset and feed on nectar from blossoms. They then lay eggs on your favorite plants—unless they get caught in your trap.

Tomato Hornworm

Hornworms can be dissuaded from eating plants by spraying with hot pepper spray or limonoid spray. (See *Tactics of Tiny Game Hunting.*)

Infecting them with the *Bacillus thuringiensis* pathogen works very well, killing them rapidly after they take a bite of leaf sprayed with the pathogen.

Other predators include trichogramma wasps, ladybugs, and lacewings. A trap crop of dill, which they like, makes handpicking easier because they show up so well on this plant.

WHITEFLIES

▼▼▼▼▼▼▼▼▼▼▼▼▼▼▼▼▼▼▼▼▼▼▼▼▼▼

There is something very discouraging about a plant that's been infested with whiteflies. If you shake it, these tiny, mothlike creatures fly up from the undersides of the leaves in great flitty numbers. When they settle back down, they select an even fresher and more tender leaf than before.

Only about one-sixteenth of an inch long, covered with a powdery wax, and sometimes called "flying dandruff," they reproduce fast (generally in one month), can build up in great numbers, and are known for developing quick immunities to pesticides. Each whitefly lays about twenty to twenty-five practically invisible eggs in a circle around her. These hatch into scalelike larvae or nymphs, which move around for a few days before picking a spot and settling in for a suck feast.

An abundant whitefly infestation can cause a plant to wilt, fade, droop, and die. Along the road to destruction, the honeydew they secrete nourishes a sooty mold, which grows and further damages the plant.

Whitefly

CONTROL

Yellow sticky traps are quite effective with whiteflies, which are drawn to the color. Place traps on a stick or hang them slightly above the plant; the whiteflies' tendency to fly upward and to land on yellow will do them in.

You can buy sticky traps or make your own from yellow pieces of plastic, stiff paper, cans, or objects coated with a sticky substance. Besides commercial preparations for sticky traps, like Stikem Special or Tanglefoot, people have used mineral oil, STP, or molasses.

One gardener we know uses a two-by-three-foot sheet of stiff yellow paper nailed to a stake. She plants it in the ground behind the plant, then lightly sprays the plant with water from the opposite side, forcing the whiteflies off the plant and right onto the trap.

Sprays can reduce whitefly populations, but they have to be applied fairly frequently—every four or five days for several weeks. Effective sprays include homemade soap spray, insecticidal soap spray, horticultural oil, or alcohol/soap spray. Use pyrethrum as a last resort.

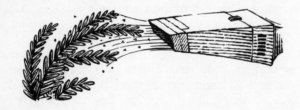

Vacuuming Whiteflies

You can also suck up these pests with a portable hand vacuum. To make the job even easier, wrap the end of the vacuum with bright yellow electrical tape. Shake the plant to disturb the whiteflies. They will fly toward the yellow end of the vacuum cleaner, and you can suck them right up. As with handpicking, this method works well on cool early mornings when the insects are sluggish. Put the vacuum cleaner bag in the freezer to kill the bugs. Do this once a day for several weeks.

There is a good chance that phosphorous or magnesium-deficient plants play host to these pests. Try to adjust the soil chemistry to include these nutrients.

Ladybird beetles and lacewings eat whitefly larvae, but the best control for this pest is the minute *Encarsia formosa*, a parasitic wasp also known as the whitefly

253

parasite. It lays an egg into the whitefly nymph, causing it to turn into a little speck of black. In greenhouses this wasp can control the population of whiteflies to the point where damage is negligible.

WIREWORMS (CLICK BEETLES)
▼▼▼▼▼▼▼▼▼▼▼▼▼▼▼▼▼▼▼▼▼▼▼▼▼▼▼

Wireworms (the larvae) get all the attention as bad bugs, while click beetles (the adults) have achieved fame with their odd acrobatic abilities. A click beetle can right itself when it is on its back by flipping in the air, accompanied with the sound of a click.

Wireworms, shiny, yellowish or brown, hard-shelled, segmented, wormy creatures, feed underground on seeds, roots, tubers or bulbs of potatoes, beets, beans, peas, onions, carrots, and cabbage, among others. They are quite destructive.

Although they look a little bit like millipedes, they have only three pairs of short legs up near their heads. Unlike most other insects, they live a long time, from two to five and sometimes even eight years. They were even excommunicated for their bad deeds by the Bishop of Lausanne in 1479. This did nothing to curb their appetite.

Make bug juice from the wireworms you have collected. Spray it on the plants and pour it into the soil around the base of the plants. (See *Tactics of Tiny Game Hunting* for how to make bug juice.)

You can use the wireworms' attraction to potatoes to trap them. Cut potatoes in two and bury them cut side down in the ground. The wireworms will burrow into the potatoes, and then you can dig them up, pull them out, and dispose of them. A carrot will also work. Place the traps about one foot apart, mark the spots with

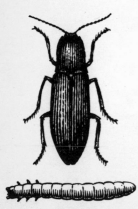

Click Beetle and Wireworm

stakes, and dig them up in the evening a couple times a week. Even better, stick the stakes right into the potatoes so you can pull them up easily.

Cultivating the soil after harvest allows predators, especially birds, to get to the wireworms. Because wireworms seem to like soggy ground, add humus to improve soil aeration. They do not do well in soil with a high organic content, either. Withholding water will kill many of them. Mexican marigolds are planted by many gardeners to eliminate wireworms.

Certain beneficial nematodes (*Neoaplectana carpocapsae*) kill wireworms.

NOT SO PESTIFEROUS

 The following insects and animals have often been classified as pests. We think they deserve a little more tolerance—even appreciation—as they can often be found doing more good than damage in your garden.

CENTIPEDES AND MILLIPEDES

Centipede

We all know the centipede was named because of its one hundred legs, but someone wasn't getting close enough to count. A centipede actually sports anywhere from 30 to 346 legs, depending on the species. A millipede is even more of a misnomer. It starts out with only three pairs of legs, growing new ones every time it sheds its skin. The most legs it can hope for are around four hundred—considerably short of a thousand, but still quite impressive.

Millipedes generally look like round, hard worms with lots of stubby legs. If disturbed, a millipede has a habit of rolling up in a coil and playing dead like a pillbug.

Both millipedes and centipedes live nocturnal lives, hiding out in dank, dark, and damp places—under rocks, bark, and leaf litter. As a rule, they need lots of moisture, for their bodies are vulnerable to dehydration. Millipedes feed instead on decaying plant material and are industrious recyclers. They also eat dead snails and insects. In times of drought, however, they will eat live plants for their moisture. Some species suck on plants and feed on roots whatever the weather happens to be.

Centipedes have certain advantages over millipedes, namely a pair of venomous claws with which they can pinch and paralyze their victims. They can also move quite a bit faster. Thus equipped, most centipedes are fine predators. In the garden they will eat snails, slugs, and many other pests. In the tropics, where centipedes can grow to a fearsome foot in length, their victims include mice, birds, and geckos.

In this country, house centipedes will come indoors, especially into basements, where they prey on insects like cockroaches, clothes moths, and flies—doing these good deeds at night and keeping out of sight during the day. Its "bite," though painful, has rarely been fatal to humans.

A destructive little creature called the garden centipede is not really a centipede, but rather a symphylan. Very tiny, only a quarter of an inch long, and looking quite like a white centipede, it does a lot of damage to plants in the warm states where it lives (and in greenhouses), and it gives centipedes a bad name. Symphylans can sometimes be destroyed by flooding the soil. Or make a tobacco tea by soaking a handful of tobacco in a gallon of water and adding a tablespoon of liquid soap to it. Drench the soil around the plant with this liquid. Or drench it with garlic spray. (See *Tactics of Tiny Game Hunting*.)

Millipede

If millipedes are doing obvious damage to the garden, and you may have to go out at night to see if they are the culprits, you can devise several traps around the yard. Dig a hole in the ground and fill it with compacted decaying vegetation from a neglected corner of the yard. Down at the bottom of this millipede habitat, place a little plastic fruit basket or cottage cheese container with holes cut in it, filled with sliced potatoes or potato peels. Keep the trap damp, and every few days uncover it, pull it out, and dunk the millipedes in soapy water.

You can also concoct the tobacco tea described above and pour it on the soil. When the millipedes come to the surface, they can be killed.

EARWIGS

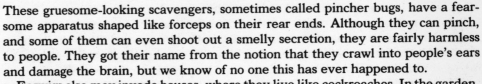

Earwig

These gruesome-looking scavengers, sometimes called pincher bugs, have a fearsome apparatus shaped like forceps on their rear ends. Although they can pinch, and some of them can even shoot out a smelly secretion, they are fairly harmless to people. They got their name from the notion that they crawl into people's ears and damage the brain, but we know of no one this has ever happened to.

Earwigs also may invade houses, where they live like cockroaches. In the garden, for the most part, they do very little harm. Many earwigs feed on decaying plant matter and dead insects and thus improve the soil and add to its fertility. They also eat aphids, grubs, and other insects.

Some people, however, insist that earwigs eat their dahlias and hollyhocks and other plants and cause huge problems in the gardens. It's probably the same as with dogs and their fleas—some gardens are bothered by them and some aren't. If you have too many of them, and you can see for sure that they are causing damage, they can easily be defeated by their own habits.

CONTROL

Trapping these insects, which love to hide in dark, narrow cracks and crevices, is fairly easy. One method is to roll up newspapers, dampen them, and leave them in a moist, shady location for a few days. The earwigs crawl in at night; in the morning, unroll the newspapers and shake the bugs into a bucket of hot or soapy water. Hollow bamboo stakes, rhubarb stalks, or short sections of cut-up garden hose, one to two feet in length, can also be used. Six or eight of these can be tied together for an earwig apartment. In the morning, shake them into a container of soapy water.

To make the traps more effective, remove as many of their usual hiding places as possible—like stones, boards, and garden debris.

English gardeners stuff a little flower pot with some moss and hang it upside down on a stick. This is a charming way to trap earwigs, as the pots look like little bells around the garden. If you don't have any moss, use moistened shredded newspaper.

In *The Bug Book*, the authors suggest hanging empty matchboxes, open just a slit, on stakes and fences around the garden. English gardening lore from the 1700s had a more ornamental flair and advised hanging "hoggshoofs and lobster tails" on sticks to capture them. Another English practice was to leave dampened rags around in the yard. In the morning they were stomped on to kill the earwigs.

Earwigs can also be caught in beer traps or even containers of water set around the garden or placed near the foundations of the house, where they like to congregate. See *Snails and Slugs* for more information about beer traps.

Chickens will eat earwigs happily if you have them—both chickens and earwigs that is.

Earwigs can also be caught in the act and eliminated as they munch on flowers at night. Simply go out with a flashlight and a spray bottle filled with soapy water and zap them in the act. We recommend this because it takes care of the earwigs actually doing the damage. Earwigs are often blamed for things they didn't do, proving once again that looks do matter.

MOLES

▼▼▼▼▼▼▼▼▼▼▼▼▼▼▼▼▼▼▼▼▼▼▼▼▼▼▼▼▼

We're pretty hard on moles, but actually they do a lot more good than harm. Most of their bad reputation is undeserved and comes from an unfortunate association with gophers and mice.

Moles have darker fur than gophers, much smaller eyes (they can hardly see at all), no visible ears, paws like flippers, and a pronounced pinkish snout. Like gophers, they spend most of their lives underground, coming up occasionally to shove a little dirt out. A molehill is round and shaped like a volcano, unlike the large (one-foot across) fan-shaped mound of a gopher.

The good that moles do comes mainly from their great appetites for insects. Night and day they travel, aerating the soil and eating all kinds of pests like grubs, beetles, slugs, snails, and caterpillars. In the past, in England, moles were even deliberately introduced into gardens infested with chafer grubs. Unfortunately, they also eat earthworms, but a healthy population of earthworms will not be eliminated by the moles.

On the down side, moles make unsightly ridges in perfect looking lawns, and their tunnels can injure roots, mainly because mice and shrews sometimes run around in mole tunnels, and they can be harmful to plants. When you discover these ridges, stomp the earth firmly back down to collapse the tunnels and water it well afterward.

CONTROL

If your lawn has moles, chances are it also has plenty of Japanese beetle grubs or other harmful pests for the moles to eat. You can thank the moles for pointing this out to you. Get rid of the grubs using an application of milky spore disease (*Bacillus popilliae*) and the moles will leave. (See *Tactics of Tiny Game Hunting*.) It will take some time for the disease to take effect, however. Other grubs in the lawn can be controlled with beneficial nematodes, microscopic roundworms that attack and kill them. These are also available through mail order sources.

Around evidence of mole activity, some gardeners bury soda pop bottles almost up to their tops in the ground. The sound created by wind passing over the tops of the bottles is very unpleasant to the moles, which have ultrasensitive hearing. Children's pinwheels can also be placed in the ground near tunnels.

Moles can be barred from your garden by digging a trench at least two feet deep all around and filling it with stones and hard, claylike soil, which, especially if you keep it dry, the moles will not be able to dig through.

Other ways to repel moles include putting peeled garlic cloves down in the tunnel. Folk wisdom of the sixteenth century said garlic would make moles leap right out of the ground. You can purchase porous stones (under the name Rodent Rocks, available from mail order catalogs) that have been impregnated with the odor of garlic and onions; these are supposed to last for months as an underground repellant.

Sprinkling hot pepper into the tunnel is another way to repel them. Some people have even used pet droppings. The heads of salted herring are an old remedy for moles, used in the 1800s. Another repellant was elder leaves, which have an odor the moles don't like.

A much newer method is to place pieces of rolled up Juicy Fruit gum into the mole tunnel. Be sure to wear gloves when unwrapping and placing the gum. If the animal can smell you, it won't touch it.

Castor beans or castor plants are often cited as a mole repellant or poison, but we do not recommend them because they are so poisonous and just too dangerous to have around children. Castor oil, however, is not poisonous, and some gardeners pour it on the ground around evidence of moles and claim it works quite well. Mix it in water using a little dish soap to get it to disperse. A plant called spurge, caper spurge, or the mole plant, is sometimes planted as a mole repellant.

Thorny twigs and branches from roses, raspberry bushes, mesquite, or any prickly plant can be shoved into the tunnel to make it inhospitable to moles. If they get cut, they bleed to death because their blood doesn't coagulate readily.

In warm weather, moles make foraging tunnels quite near the surface, while in the winter they go deep underground just like the earthworms do. In the summer, sometimes, you can actually see their movement as they "swim" through the ground near the surface. You can get a shovel and dig them out right on the spot. They can easily be dispatched with the shovel or put into a container and removed to another location.

Flooding can also be used to get moles to move. Stick a garden hose into the main tunnel, turn it on, and wait until water fills up all the tunnels, which can be extensive.

If you feel you must trap moles, use meat baits, because moles are carnivorous. Knowing the high volume of insects they eat, you wouldn't really want to trap them to death, however. A better method consists of a trap that allows you to capture the mole and move it to another location. Find the tunnel that is active by slightly depressing the earth where you see a ridge. If the mole is using this tunnel, it will soon be repaired. Wearing gloves, carefully open the tunnel and dig a hole into which a large (two quart) can or glass jar can be placed. The top of the container should be level with the bottom of the runway. Let a little dirt from the top of the tunnel fall on either side of the jar to hide it. Set a board over the top of the hole in the tunnel and cover it well with dirt so that no light gets in. Traveling through the tunnel, the mole will tumble into the container and be unable to get out. You can then relocate it. Don't leave it in the container too long, however, or it will starve.

Mole Trap

SOWBUGS AND PILLBUGS

▼▼▼▼▼▼▼▼▼▼▼▼▼▼▼▼▼▼▼▼▼▼▼▼▼▼

Are they insects? Are they bugs? Are they incorrigible pests? The answer is no to all three, although many people would answer yes. Sowbugs and pillbugs are terrestrial crustaceans, related to lobsters and crayfish. Both pillbugs and sowbugs possess seven pairs of legs and segmented bodies; the difference between them is that pillbugs are darker and roll up into tight little balls, whereas the gray sowbugs can't roll up as tightly and have to rely on running away when disturbed. Sometimes called woodlice or "roly-polies," they are actually quite useful, as they recycle decaying vegetation.

They will sometimes go after young plants, especially ground cover plants, eating the roots and stems or even munching on the skins of ripe melons, cucumbers, squash, and strawberries that happen to touch the ground. (When these vegetables and fruits come in contact with the ground, they can get too much moisture and start to rot, so the bugs move in.) They will also happily crawl into holes created in fruits and vegetables by other pests like slugs and then get blamed for the damage. If they seem to be a problem, try to keep the garden a little drier. Prop the plants up on tin cans, upside-down berry baskets, or improvised "lifts." Or make little mats for them out of squares of stiff paper.

Sowbugs and pillbugs are frequent tenants of greenhouses, where the dampness provides them with a comfortable habitat. Here, however, they wear out their welcome quite quickly by gnawing on the plants.

CONTROL

To repel pillbugs and sowbugs, sprinkle the ground with onion spray. (See *Tactics of Tiny Game Hunting*.) Or sprinkle lime around the young seedlings you want to

263

protect. Many garden advisers say to remove all dead leaves and in essence don't keep any organic mulch around. We would rather have the benefit of the mulch and wrestle with the bugs. Mulch provides a haven for many beneficial insects, too.

These insects are night feeders and find dark, damp places to spend their days. They can be trapped by turning a dampened clay pot upside down and propping up one edge. They are especially attracted to corncobs, which can be placed inside the pot. In the morning tap off the bugs into a bucket and move them to another place in the garden or use soapy or boiling water to kill them. But don't pour boiling water on the plants.

If you're having potatoes for dinner instead of corn, add a few potato peels to the clay pot. Or take a potato, slice it in half, scrape out a little of the inside and place it face down on the ground. In the morning, the bugs can be found having a pillbug potato conference. Half an orange peel makes another good habitat trap. You'll probably get some slugs, too. Rolled up, dampened cardboard or newspapers will also trap them, and frogs are quite fond of eating them.

Sowbugs and Plastic Bottle Trap

We have invented another trap that works quite well. Take a two-liter plastic soda pop bottle and cut it in two across the middle. Invert the top half as a funnel into the bottom half, leaving a gap between the bottom and the top. Seal the two halves together with masking tape. Drop the bait into the trap and lay it on its side near the infestation. Sowbugs and pillbugs will walk in through the "tunnel" and drop into the enclosed space in their eagerness to get to the food.

One reader of *Organic Gardening* magazine wrote to say she used dried dog food around her plants. The sowbugs liked it so much they left her plants alone.

In dry weather, we turn on a drip irrigation system; when the pillbugs and sowbugs gather around the moisture, we simply scoop them up and toss them into the compost heap. There's plenty of work for them to do there.

YELLOW JACKETS AND WASPS

▼▼▼▼▼▼▼▼▼▼▼▼▼▼▼▼▼▼▼▼▼▼▼▼▼

All yellow jackets are wasps, but not all wasps are yellow jackets. Many people also confuse wasps and honeybees. Yellow jackets get our attention, not only because their bright yellow and black raiment makes them more visible, but because they are highly attracted to our good-smelling food. Easily angered, they have nothing to lose by stinging us. Since they don't have barbed hooks on their stingers, as honeybees do, they can withdraw and sting over and over, which they will do. The venom of yellow jackets and wasps can cause severe allergic reactions in some people.

Yellow jackets like birthday parties, picnics, outdoor weddings, and barbecues. There's hardly a summer social occasion *al fresco* that they will not visit, provided, of course, refreshments are served. Sweets, fruit juice, soda pop, and fresh fruit appeal to them, as do meats and fish.

However, they're not just party animals. Yellow jackets are also excellent insect predators. They possess very strong jaws with which they tear apart insects and take them back to their nests to feed the grubs.

Yellow jackets present a potential danger to us; as social wasps, many species build their nests in the ground (often in abandoned animal burrows), in holes in logs, or on shrubbery near the ground. A nest can have as many as five thousand inhabitants, and wasps will protect it ferociously. Anyone who has the misfortune to step on one of these nests and then run for his or her life with an angry swarm of stinging, yellow jackets in pursuit is not likely to forget the sheer, unadulterated terror.

Yellow jackets and hornets are virtually the same, except that hornets build their nests higher than yellow jackets. *Polistes wasps* or paper wasps are other familiar species of social wasps. They build their nests under the eaves of buildings and in

NOT SO PESTIFEROUS

TINY GAME HUNT

Yellow Jacket

265

sheltered spots. Making their nests from chewed-up pieces of wood and plants mixed into a pulp with their saliva, these wasps may have first given people the idea how to make paper. They have also been used successfully in biological control; their nests have actually been moved and placed close to crops so that they can control pest caterpillars more effectively.

Other species of wasps much less dangerous to humans live and work alone, seeking out insects to paralyze and lay their eggs on, thus providing their young with a source of ever-fresh meat. These longer, more slender wasps are quite beneficial because of the insect mortality they cause, although some also kill spiders and other "good" predators. As adults, the wasps themselves feed on nectar and fruit juices, while busily hunting down insects and dragging them off to special burrows where they become fodder for their young. Entomologists often collect the nests of solitary wasps as a shortcut to finding and collecting insect specimens.

Two of the most common solitary wasps are the digger wasp and the mud dauber. *Digger wasps* are hardworking, good predators. Some *mud daubers* build their nests on sunny walls out of mud and stone, but others build in out-of-the-way places. They rarely sting, and their venom is not as powerful as that of other wasps. Many species of wasps have a preference for one type of insect over all others. Caterpillars rank high in popularity. One spider wasp actually specializes in hunting and capturing black widow spiders.

CONTROL

As a group, wasps are more friend than enemy. Wasps are very good at controlling noxious insect pests such as grasshoppers, gypsy moths, tomato hornworms, corn earworms, and cabbageworms. They also pollinate crops such as melons and spinach. Of the twenty-five hundred or so species, only about fifty will sting at all.

Sometimes it is difficult to decide what to do about a wasp nest that seems too close to the house. When one of us lived in Montana, years ago, a paper wasp nest appeared under the eaves of the house. The next-door neighbor came over and ordered us to get rid of it. We dutifully called an exterminator, and we will never forget the sight of the man walking around the side of the house with his pressure sprayer going full blast. We ran into the house, but were not even able to get the patio door closed before a good dose of whatever insecticide he was using splashed inside. (Those Montanans are really fearless when it comes to pesticides.) Montana summers are so short, we wish we'd known enough then just to wait for the cold weather to come and kill off the wasps.

The best thing to do to prevent a nest from getting established in the yard is to watch for wasps and yellow jackets in the early spring when the queen is just beginning the colony. You can usually try to discourage her then by knocking down the foundations of the nest as she begins her work. She may have made up her mind that this is the place, however. She can be easily killed by swatting her then. This is much easier than trying to kill several thousand wasps later. Some people hang sticky flypaper near a paper wasp nest to trap these insects.

If the nest is in the ground, you can place a clear glass bowl over the entrance. The hole is very small, but there may be more than one, so be sure to cover them all. This technique will starve the colony. Some people go out at night and pour gasoline or kerosene into the hole. We do not recommend this as it is not good for the soil. Soapsuds in a spray bottle do wonders, however. There are also pyrethrum sprays on the market. Any monkeying with the nest must be done at night when these wasps are quiescent, and it must be done in full protective regalia with absolutely no skin left uncovered.

According to *National Gardening* magazine, a naturalist working for the East Bay Regional Park System in Oakland, California, poured honey near the entrance holes to underground yellow jacket nests in a park at closing time. The next morning all the nests had been dug out by skunks or raccoons. These animals are known to prey on yellow jackets for their brood. For this to work for you, you'd have to have raccoons or skunks in the neighborhood.

As with flies, keeping waspy nuisance pests away means keeping garbage cans covered to keep yellow jackets from scavenging around the house. Do not leave drink cans around. If possible drink from cups with lids and straws. Don't leave ripe fruit lying around under the trees, and don't feed the pets outside. Be careful when picking up wet towels, because these wasps are highly attracted to moisture.

TRAPS

A number of wasp or yellow jacket traps are on the market. Many have very small holes for the wasps to crawl into. It is advisable to leave the bait outside of the trap, until the yellow jackets have picked up the scent and located it. Wait until they are going back and forth and taking the message to their brethren, then put the bait in the trap. When the trap is full, drop it in soapy water to kill the wasps.

Yellow jacket traps are also very easy to make. The good thing about traps is that they pick off the annoying individuals without destroying the colony. And we actually need yellow jackets because of all the insects they kill and the plants they pollinate.

One very simple trap consists of putting Kool-Aid or apple juice in the bottom of a glass or plastic jug and setting it out where the yellow jackets are a nuisance. They will enter and can't get out.

Always have a yellow jacket trap on hand at any outdoor party where these wasps are prevalent, because someone will always demand, "Can't you do something about these awful bugs?"

You can make an old standard trap by hanging a fish over a bucket of soapy water. The yellow jackets always pull off a big piece (not from greed, mind you, they are taking food back to the grubs in the nest). Dropping down before they can fly off, they land in the water. If there is soap in the water, they can't get out.

The only problem with this trap is that people don't always happen to have a fish on hand when the wasps arrive. However, a piece of raw meat will work just as well. You can hang the meat or spear it with a fork and lean the fork upright against the side of the bucket so that the meat is just above the soapy water. Another trap can be made by smearing a sticky substance on a board or paper plate and putting a little meat or fruit on it for bait. Or smear the inside of a jar with sticky substance (like Stikem Special) and put a lump of liverwurst inside. Punch one hole about five-sixteenths of an inch in diameter for the wasps to enter and also a couple of tiny air holes. When the trap is full, throw it away and make another.

These traps should be placed downwind from the picnic, because wasps come in from that direction. Stop them at the pass!

During the beginning of the summer up through August, wasps will be looking for protein, like meats and pet food. Later in the summer they are more attracted to sugar. Bait the traps accordingly. However, if sweet traps are attracting bees, switch to meat.

Yellow Jacket Trap

MAIL ORDER

▼▼▼▼▼▼▼▼▼▼▼▼▼▼▼▼▼▼▼▼▼▼▼▼▼▼

A-Gro-Elite Co.
265 South Federal, P.O. Box 308A
Deerfield Beach, FL 33441
(800) 822-5882
Manufactures Maestro-Gro products—plant food, fertilizer, soil builder, soil conditioner, compost builder, etc.

All Pest Control
6030 Grenville Lane
Lansing, MI 48911
(517) 646-0038
Traps, botanicals, bacterials, and miscellaneous garden supplies.

The Alsto Company
P.O. Box 1267
Galesburg, IL 61401
(800) 447-0048
Gardening supplies, birdhouses, some traps.

Audubon Workshop
1501 Paddock Drive
Northbrook, IL 60602
(800) 322-9464
All for the birds: feeders, food, baths, and houses.

Bat Conservation International
P.O. Box 162603
Austin, TX 78716-2603
Bat houses and more.

Beneficial Biosystems
Box 8461
Emeryville, CA 94662
Fly traps.

Beneficial Insectary
14751 Oak Run Road
Oak Run, CA 96069
(916) 472-3715
Predatory insects, mites, wasps, worms, and wheast.

Bio-Control Co.
Box 337
Berry Creek, CA 95916
(916) 589-5227
Beneficial insects and honeydew to attract them.

Biofac, Inc.
P.O. Box 87
Mathis, TX 78368
(512) 547-3259
Good supply of beneficial insects.

Bio-Pro Industries, Inc.
201 Standard Street
El Segundo, CA 90245
(213) 640-7648
Makers of the Zap-Trap, the trap that uses a combination of pheromones, electricity, and sticky glue to trap great numbers of roaches.

BIRC
The Bio-Integral Resource Center
P.O. Box 7414
Berkeley, CA 94707
(415) 524-2567
Excellent source of information on worldwide least-toxic pest contol methods. Publications, journal, and quarterly.

Bountiful Gardens
19550 Walker Road
Willits, CA 95490
(707) 459-3390
Untreated seeds, biological controls, supplies, and educational materials.

Bramen Company, Inc., of Cabot Farm
P.O. Box 70
Salem, MA 01970
(800) 234-7765
Horticultural supplies and tools, earthworm castings, guano, root maggot collars.

Bricko Bricker's Organic Farms, Inc.
824-K Sandbar Ferry Road
Augusta, GA 30901
(404) 722-0661
Organic gardening supplies.

Brody Enterprises
9 Arlington Place
Fair Lawn, NJ 07410
(800) GLU-TRAP or (201) 794-3616
Poison-free products for all kinds of pests—fleas, lice, and rodents. Traps, repellants, and exclusion products.

Bronwood Worm Farms
P.O. Box 28
Bronwood, GA 31726
(912) 995-5994
All kinds of worms.

Bug-Off
Route 3, Box 27A
Lexington, VA 24450
(703) 463-1760
A natural herbal bug repellant.

BUGS
Biological Urban Gardening Services
P.O. Box 76
Citrus Heights, CA 95611-0076
(916) 726-5377
Newsletter and catalog for BUGS members.

Cape Cod Worm Farm
30 Cedar Avenue
Buzzards Bay, MA 02532
(508) 759-5664
Breeders (bait-size) and bed run (mixed sizes).

Charlie's Greenhouse Supplies
1569 Memorial Highway
Mount Vernon, WA 98273
(206) 428-2626
*Beneficial insects, traps, barriers, and supplies
for the greenhouse.*

Connecticut Valley Biological Supply
P.O. Box 326
82 Valley Road
Southhampton, MA 01073
(800) 628-7748
*Huge catalog of science materials including
biological pest control supplies.*

Digger's Product Development Company
P.O.Box 1551
Soquel, CA 95073
(408) 462-6095
Sells wire baskets to protect plants from gophers.

Earlee, Inc.
2002 Highawy 62
Jeffersonville, IN 47130-3556
(812) 282-9134
*Organic soil conditioners, animal traps, and
botanical and microbial insecticides.*

Earthly Goods
P.O. Box 4164
Tulsa, OK 74159-1164
(918) 587-8958
*Nonpoisonous insect controls for the garden and
home, including pets.*

Eco Source
9051 Mill Station Road
Sebastopol, CA 95472
(707) 829-8345
*Environmentally friendly products, including
pet, lawn, and garden supplies.*

Erth-Rite, Inc.
R.D. #1, Box 243
Gap, PA 17527
(717) 442-4171
Diatomaceous earth.

Etex
916 South Casino Center
Las Vegas, NV 89101
(800) 543-5651
Electrogun for termites.

Foothill Agricultural Research (FAR)
510 1/2 West Chase Drive
Corona, CA 91720
(714) 371-0120
*Beneficial insects, parasites, and decollate snails.
Minimum $50 order.*

Gardener's Supply
128 Intervale Road
Burlington, VT 05401
(802) 863-1700
*Innovative catalog including live traps and animal
repellants, Rodent Rocks, birdhouses, and safe
pest controls.*

Gardens Alive!
National Gardening Research Center
P.O. Box 149
Sunman, IN 47041
(812) 623-3800
*Catalog filled with safe products for a healthy
garden. Plus lots of good tips.*

Great Lakes IPM
10220 Church Road NE
Vestaburg, MI 48891
(517) 268-5693
*Good selection of pheromone and many other
types of insect traps.*

Green Earth Organics
9422 144th Street E
Puyallup, WA 98373-6686
(206) 845-2321
*Informative catalog of organic fertilizers, mulches,
soil amendments, pest and disease controls, and
horticultural supplies.*

Growing Naturally
P.O. Box 54
149 Pine Lane
Pineville, PA 18946
(215) 598-7025
*Compost supplies, fertilizers, controls, traps, and
repellants.*

Harmony Farm Supply and Nursery
3244 Gravenstein Highway
Sebastopol, CA 95472
(707) 823-9125
Irrigation systems, ecological pest controls, tools, and supplies.

Hogil Corp.
P.O. Box 1590
Port Chester, NY 10573
(914) 937-0551
Lice combs and other products.

Hydro-Gardens, Inc.
P.O. Box 9707
Colorado Springs, CO 80932
(719) 495-2266
Commericial greenhouse supplies and hydroponic nutrients. Good selection of beneficial insects.

Insects Limited
10540 Jessup Boulevard
Indianapolis IN 46280-1451
(317) 846-5444
Pheromone traps and insect attractants, especially for stored-product pests.

IFM
Integrated Fertility Management
333 Ohme Gardens Road
Wenatchee, WA 98801
(800) 332-3179 or (509) 662-3179
Beneficial predators and parasites; products and services for natural growing.

Ken-Bar
24 Gould Street
Reading, MA 01867
(800) 336-8882 or (617) 944-0003
Fabric crop covers, tunnels, and mulches.

Kinsman Company
River Road
Point Pleasant, PA 18950
(215) 297-5613
Shredder, compost bin, birdhouses, good selection of garden tools and miscellaneous garden supplies.

Kunafin
Route 1, Box 39
Quemado, TX 78877
(800) 832-1113
Biological fly control parasites.

Ladd Research Industries, Inc.
P.O. Box 1005
Burlington, VT 05402
(802) 658-4961
Fruit tree pest insect kits (reusable).

M & R Durango, Inc.
Bio Logical Pest Control
6565 Highway 172
Ignacio, CO 81137
(800) 526-4075
Beneficial insects, nematodes, producers of Nolo Bait (biological control for grasshoppers).

Medina Agricultural Products Co., Inc.
P.O. Box 309, Highway 90
West Hondo, TX 78861
(512) 426-3011
Soil activator ("yogurt for the soil"), organic fertilizers, compost activators, water filters, drip hoses, etc.

Mother Nature's
P.O. Box 1055
Avon, CT 06001
Worm castings.

The Natural Gardening Company
217 San Anselmo Avenue
San Anselmo, CA 94960
(415) 456-5060
Garden supplies and natural pest controls.

Nature's Control
P.O. Box 35
Medford, OR 97501
(503) 899-8318
Beneficial insects, fly parasites, nematodes, traps, insecticidal soap, magnifier.

Necessary Trading Company
P.O. Box 305
New Castle, VA 24127
(800) 447-5354
Good selection of traps, beneficials, biological controls, organic lawn and pet care products, books.

Nitron Industries, Inc.
4605 Johnson Road
P.O. Box 1447
Fayetteville, AR 72702
(800) 835-0123
Organic soil conditioner, soil builders, kelp and fish products, pest control products, compost supplies, misccellaneous garden supplies.

North Country Organics
RR #1 Box 2232
Bradford, VT 05033
(802) 222-4277
All natural farm and garden supplies.

Rincon-Vitova Insectaries, Inc.
P.O. Box 95
Oak View, CA 93022
(805) 643-5407

Beneficial insects, predatory insects and mites, fly parasites, predator (decollate) snails. Minimum order $50.

Ringer
9959 Valley View Road
Eden Prairie, MN 55344-3585
(800) 564-1047
Composting materials, natural garden products.

Safe-N-Sound Live Traps
Morrison Manufacturing Corp.
P.O. Box 52
Morrison, IA 50657
(800) 648-CAGE or (319) 345-6406
Makers of live animal traps.

Sea Born
Lane, Inc.
P.O. Box 204
Charles City, IA 50616
(515) 228-2000
Many kinds of seaweed fertilizers.

Seabright Laboratories
4026 Harlan Street
Emeryville, CA 94608
(800) 284-7363 or (415) 655-3126
Makers of the well-known Stikem Special for traps and barriers. Yellow jacket trap, roach traps, and a humane mousetrap.

Solarcone, Inc.
P.O. Box 67
Seward, IL 61077
(815) 247-8454
Manufactures the GreenCone Composter, a food waste composting system.

Spaulding Laboratories
760 Printz Road
Arroyo Grande, CA 93420
(805) 489-5946
Fly traps and beneficial insects.

Trece
P.O. Box 5267
Salinas, CA 93915
(408) 758-0205
Insect monitoring kits and traps.

Unique Insect Control
5504 Sperry Drive
Citrus Heights, CA 95621
(916) 961-7945
Beneficial insects and nematodes, fly parasites, earthworms. Informative pamphlet.

Zook & Rank, Inc.
R.D. #1
Gap, PA 17527
(717) 442-4171
Erth-Rite composted soil builders and other fertilizers. Send in a soil sample to find out which formulation will improve your particular soil.

SELECTED BIBLIOGRAPHY

▼▼▼▼▼▼▼▼▼▼▼▼▼▼▼▼▼▼▼▼▼▼▼

Abraham, George and Katy. 1976. *Organic Gardening Under Glass*. Emmaus, PA: Rodale Press.

Andrews, Michael. 1977. *The Life That Lives on Man*. New York: Taplinger Publishing.

Ball, Jeff. 1988. *Rodale's Garden Problem Solver*. Emmaus, PA: Rodale Press.

Ballantine, Bill. 1967. *Nobody Loves a Cockroach*. Boston: Little, Brown and Company.

Barrett, Thomas J. 1976. *Harnessing the Earthworm*. Ontario, California: Bookworm Publishing Company.

Bem, Robyn. 1978. *Everyone's Guide to Composting*. New York: Van Nostrand Reinhold Company.

273

Berenbaum, May R. 1989. *Ninety-nine Gnats, Nits, and Nibblers.* Chicago: University of Illinois Press.

Blassingham, Wyatt. 1975. *The Little Killers.* New York: G. P. Putnam's Sons.

Boland, Maureen and Bridget. 1976. *Old Wives' Lore for Gardeners.* New York: Farrar, Straus and Giroux.

Bubel, Nancy Wilkes. 1979. *The Adventurous Gardener.* Boston: David R. Godine.

Coleman, Elliot. 1989. *The New Organic Grower.* Chelsea, VT: Chelsea Green.

Davidson, Ralph H., and William F. Lyon. 1987. *Insect Pests of Farm, Garden, and Orchard.* New York: John Wiley & Sons.

Debach, Paul. 1974. *Biological Control by Natural Enemies.* Great Britain: Cambridge University Press.

Dick, B. 1879. *Dick's Practical Encyclopedia of Receipts and Processes.* New York: Funk & Wagnalls.

Ebeling, Walter. 1978. *Urban Entomology.* Berkeley, CA: University of California.

Ernst, Ruth Shaw. 1987. *The Naturalist's Garden.* Emmaus, PA: Rodale Press.

Evans, Howard Ensign. 1966. *Life on a Little-Known Planet.* New York: E. P. Dutton.

Evans, Howard Ensign. 1985. *The Pleasures of Entomology.* Washington, DC: Smithsonian Institution Press.

Farallones Institute. 1979. *The Integral Urban House.* San Francisco: Sierra Club Books.

Flemer, William, III. 1988. *Nature's Guide to Successful Gardening and Landscaping.* Los Angeles: University of Southern California Press.

Foelix, Rainer F. 1982. *Biology of Spiders.* Cambridge, MA: Harvard University Press.

Foster, Catharine Osgood. 1972. *The Organic Gardner.* New York: Alfred A. Knopf.

Frazier, Claude. 1980. *Insects and Allergies.* Norman, OK: University of Oklahoma Press

Gibbons, Euell. 1966. *Stalking the Healthful Herbs.* New York: McKay.

Graham, Frank, Jr. 1984. *The Dragon Hunters.* New York: E. P. Dutton.

Grounds, Roger. 1976. *The Natural Garden.* New York: Stein and Day.

Hartnack, Hugo. 1939. *202 Common Household Pests of North America.* Chicago: Hartnack Publishing Co.

Hess, Lilo. 1979. *The Amazing Earthworm.* New York: Charles Scribner's Sons.

Hillman, Hal. 1978. *Deadly Bugs and Killer Insects.* New York: M. Evans and Company.

Hunter, Beatrice Trum. 1971. *Gardening Without Poisons.* Boston: Houghton Mifflin.

Kramer, Jack. 1972. *The Natural Way to Pest-Free Gardening.* New York: Charles Scribner's Sons.

Kress, Stephen, W. 1985. *The Audubon Society Guide to Attracting Birds.* New York: Charles Scribner's Sons.

Lehane, Brendan. 1969. *The Complete Flea.* New York: Viking.

Merilees, Bill. 1989. *Attracting Backyard Wildlife.* Stillwater, MN: Voyager Press.

Ordish, George. 1976. *The Constant Pest.* New York: Charles Scribner's Sons.

Our Insect Friends and Foes and Spiders. 1935. Washington, DC: The National Geographic Society, 1935.

Philbrick, Helen and John. 1974. *The Bug Book.* Pownal, VT: Garden Way Publishing.

Ritchie, Carson I. A. 1979. *Insects, the Creeping Conquerors.* New York: Elsevier/Nelson Books.

Schaeffer, Jack. 1978. *Conversations with a Pocket Gopher.* Santa Barbara, CA: Capra Press.

Stawell, Mrs. Rudolph. 1921. *Fabre's Book of Insects.* New York: Tudor Publishing Company.

Stout, Ruth. 1961. *Gardening Without Work.* Old Greenwich, CT: The Devin-Adair Company.

Teale, Edwin Way. 1962. *The Strange Lives of Familiar Insects.* New York: Dodd, Mead & Company.

Tuttle, Merlin. 1988. *America's Neighborhood Bats.* Austin, TX: University of Texas Press.

Wickenden, Leonard. 1954. *Gardening with Nature.* New York: The Devin-Adair Company.

INDEX

▼▼▼▼▼▼▼▼▼▼▼▼▼▼▼▼▼▼▼▼▼▼▼▼▼▼▼

ABOUT THE AUTHORS
▼▼▼▼▼▼▼▼▼▼▼▼▼▼▼▼▼▼▼▼▼▼▼▼▼

Hilary Dole Klein is an award-winning writer whose articles have appeared in the *Los Angeles Times*, the *Chicago Sun-Times*, and other major media. This is her seventh book.

Adrian M. Wenner holds a doctorate in zoology and is a professor of natural history at the University of California at Santa Barbara, where he has taught since 1960, and is also Provost of the College of Creative Studies. He is affiliated with the American Society of Zoologists, the American Association for the Advancement of Sciences, and the Crustacean Society, among others. Together with Patrick H. Wells, he published *Anatomy of a Controversy: The Question of a "Language" among Bees* (Columbia University Press). Both he and Ms. Klein have practiced tiny game hunting for more than twenty years and have devised and tested many of these methods themselves.